C000225214

CONFLICT AND CLASS

CONFLICT AND CLASS

SCOTTISH WORKERS 1700–1838

W. HAMISH FRASER
Department of History
University of Strathclyde

JOHN DONALD PUBLISHERS LTD
EDINBURGH

To Helen

ISBN 0 85976 207 6

Distributed in the United States of America and Canada by Humanities Press Inc., Atlantic Highlands, NJ 07716, USA.

The Publisher acknowledges subsidy from the Scottish Arts Council towards the publication of this volume.

Phototypeset by Quorn Selective Repro, Loughborough.
Printed in Great Britain by Bell & Bain Ltd., Glasgow.

Acknowledgements

As with any book produced over a long period of time, this one would not have been possible without the tolerance and assistance of many. But for the congenial atmosphere created by colleagues and students at the University of Strathclyde, who remained positive and enthusiastic despite all the pressures on universities that the last few years have brought, it would have been difficult to retain the motivation to complete the work. Without the happiness provided by my wife and daughter — and their forbearance — it would have been difficult to use evenings and weekends to get the book written. To these my main thanks must go.

The atmosphere and helpfulness of libraries varies greatly, but generally the ones with which I had to deal proved ever ready to make an effort to assist. My thanks are due to the librarians and staff of the British Library, the National Library of Scotland, the British Library of Political and Economic Science, the Goldsmiths' Library of the University of London, the Mitchell Library, Glasgow (particularly the Glasgow Room), Edinburgh Central Library, Aberdeen Reference Library, Dundee Central Library, Motherwell Public Library, the libraries of the Universities of Glasgow and Strathclyde and of the Co-operative Union in Manchester. Special thanks are due to the staff of the Scottish Record Office at Register House and at West Register House, and to the staff of the beautiful Signet Library in Edinburgh, for so willingly allowing me to search through the voluminous Court of Session Papers. The Strathclyde Regional Archives, as always, went out of their way to be helpful.

Professor R. M. Mitchison and my colleague Dr. J. H. Treble read a draft of the work and made many constructive and corrective comments. I am most grateful for their help and advice, which allowed me to eradicate many foolish errors. No doubt some still remain. For these the responsibility is entirely mine. Others who have helped with specific queries or by drawing my attention to sources are John Butt, Ian MacDougall, Chris Whatley, Charles Munn and John Robertson. Finally, my thanks are due to Mrs. Irene Scouller, who typed and retyped a manuscript which, it must have seemed, would never go away.

W. Hamish Fraser

A Note on Money

Scots money was one twelfth of the value of sterling: £1 Scots = 1s.8d.; a merk = 13s.4d. Scots = 1s.1d. sterling. When using sterling I have retained predecimalisation money throughout.

Contents

		page
	Acknowledgements	v
	Introduction	1
1.	The Economy Transformed	11
2.	The World of the Eighteenth-Century Tradesman	17
3.	The Emergence of Organisation	39
4.	Conflict and Conciliation	57
5.	The Attack	81
6.	The Years of Distress	100
7.	Conflicts over Control	114
8.	The Search for Alternatives	131
9.	Of Shootings and Sheriffs	151
10.	Conclusion	163
	Notes	171
	Select Bibliography	193
	Index	198

Introduction

This whole volume was originally intended to be a single chapter introducing a history of Scottish trade unionism in the nineteenth century. It seemed, at first glance, a small task to pull together a few scattered references to eighteenth-century workers as an introduction to a history of Scottish labour that would effectively start around the 1790s, perhaps jump to 1812 and the weavers' strike, then on to the post-war unrest and to the cotton spinners. All the signs were that such an introduction would be brief.

A look at Thomas Johnston's *History of the Working Classes in Scotland*, first published in 1920, showed that there was remarkably little activity. Although nearly half the book is devoted to the period before 1800, it wanders far and wide in a selective social history of Scotland, in which the author never entirely makes up his mind about who precisely are 'the people' or 'the working classes'. In his section on trade unions there is the odd reference to organisation before the 1790s. The Glasgow weavers 1787 are there, though in Johnston's work they become factory workers, and the Edinburgh masons in 1764 get a mention. There are references also to Edinburgh tailors in 1748 though the conclusion is that, 'It is nearly a century before the Edinburgh tailors again appear as attempting Trade Union activity'.

W. H. Marwick's *Short History of Labour in Scotland* (1967) provided a little more. He had noticed more activity among Edinburgh tailors in legal cases, and cited some examples of what he regarded primarily as friendly societies rather than trade unions. T. C. Smout's *History of the Scottish People* largely accepted these conclusions and in it a picture emerges of a remarkably docile people, accepting the rapid transformations of the eighteenth century with little protest. Even the obvious tensions of the 1790s and the more violent unrest of the 1816–1820 period are presented almost as aberrations in a society remarkably free from overt class conflict.

Smout's interpretation has been challenged, largely by assertion by J. D. Young and more carefully by Tony Clarke and Tony Dickson, but mainly with a focus on working-class *political* activities.[1] Ken Logue and others have revealed the extent of rioting and other popular disorder.[2] None of these adds much to the evidence of industrial organisation pre-1790. The assumption remains that trade unionism was substantially a product of the transformation of the textile industry at the turn of the century, and all concentrate on the handloom weaver and the factory spinner. Only Alan Campbell, in his pathbreaking study of the Lanarkshire miners, pointed towards some quite extensive early miners' organisation.[3]

The picture of apparent docility and the emphasis on textile workers and colliers for the origins of the labour movement are clearly out of line with recent work on other countries. The writings of R. J. Bezucha, William Reddy, Joan Wallach Scott and William Sewell on France have shown the extent of formal organisations among journeymen artisans[4] and Sewell's work, in particular, has brought out the continuity of language and assumptions that persisted from the eighteenth century well through the nineteenth. As he argues, 'The nineteenth century labour movement was born in the craft workshops, not in the dark, satanic mill'.[5]

Such work has influenced British historians, particularly the writings of John Rule and Ion Prothero, both of whom effectively rescue the experience of the artisan.[6] It is clear that in England too it is among the artisans that the first recognisable trade societies appear and it is among the artisans that the first steps at mutual support beyond the craft emerge. It is among the artisans that the first signs of a new political awareness that went towards the creating of a sense of class and of a working-class movement make their appearance. And the experience, language and attitudes of the eighteenth-century artisans feed directly into the nineteenth-century movements.

It would be surprising, therefore, if Scotland were different. The sense of a whole undiscovered world of Scottish labour was further strengthened by the publication of C. R. Dobson's *Masters and Journeymen*.[7] He listed some 350 disputes that he had identified between 1717 and 1790: only eighteen of them were in Scotland. Once again, either there was something remarkably odd about the Scottish experience or there was much that we did not know.

The route into this largely uncharted territory of the eighteenth-century Scottish tradesman, to use the more typical Scottish word for a skilled craftsman, proved to be through the Scottish legal records, both the printed submissions in the Court of Session papers and in the unextracted processes. Following up references to cases involving journeymen that had made their way to the law books, one discovered an extent of organisation and of disputes hitherto unrecognised. Far from being cowed and docile, the tradesmen in Scottish towns were organised effectively, boldy pushing their claims, facing prison sentences and challenging the action of their employers. Because of the basis of the Scottish legal system in Roman law, which recognised associations, there was almost an encouragement to journeymen to organise to present their cases to the courts. The legal way to change wages or conditions was through the courts, appealing to burgh magistrates and JPs and, if necessary, to the Court of Session.

There are, of course, difficulties in relying on legal records. Those cases that reached the courts and those organisations that used them regularly were perhaps not representative. Also, while in the unextracted processes there is often material, including minute books and letters, seized from the unions, in the printed submissions to the Court of Session the unions' views are mediated through the advocates. However, in the written presentations one has details of organisation and other aspects of crafts that could be challenged by the other side. The arguments used by the advocates are important in themselves in reflecting the perceptions of crucial issues within the dominant class of which the advocates were a part. The Court of Session accepted pleadings based on perceptions of what was for the good of society[8] and, again and again, in the Court submissions the terms of the debate which was going on about the way an industrial society was developing come out. The debate becomes particularly sharp in the twenty years between 1790 and 1813, when crucial aspects about the nature of industrial relations were thrashed out.

What emerges is evidence of well-organised craft unions from at least the 1720s onwards and, in some cases, possibly earlier. Journeymen organised for mutual support through their charity boxes, but these could quickly and easily become centres for industrial pressure. By the second half of the eighteenth century, such organisations were frequently about resisting the changes that capitalist modernisation was bringing. The changes, in one way, were many and complex: a widening social gap between prospering employers and their men; an influx of new workers, with limited skills; deteriorating working conditions; a loss of independence as employers sought to impose more controls, more regulation, more discipline, with scant reference to the traditions of the craft. It would be quite wrong to suggest that the experience was uniform. Industrialisation meant different things to different trades: the timing of change varied greatly. For this reason one has to look at the differing experiences and responses of different groups of workers. Nonetheless, some common features do emerge.

The struggles are often about authority, about the extent of 'independence' and the extent of 'subordination'. The law in the eighteenth century was the means by which journeymen were to be kept in subordination. The law laid down that journeymen had to work for specified hours at specified wages in a manner that the masters wished, just as the law laid down that all able-bodied had to work. But, there was a paradox, since the law was also the means by which the master craftsmen were kept in subordination to the wider community, with regulation of prices, markets, apprenticeship and wage rates. The law was not yet in the hands of the capitalists and, therefore, journeymen found it possible to use the courts to fight out some of the issues over authority. Tailors battled over control of their free time, in a decade of struggle over the breakfast hour. Other struggles focused on control of evening leisure time and break times during the day. Yet others, like the home-working shoemakers, concentrated on the central issue of the right of independent craftsmen to choose their own master. The courts were also the site of the struggle over control of the process of division of labour, which was essential to the expansion of crafts on the scale that some of the employers envisaged. Issues of apprenticeship, of control of entry through houses of call, of control over the labour market were all debated in the courts.

As the issues became more sharp, as the demands for change by employers became stronger, the courts initially strengthened their role. From 1790 to 1813 there was an extension of interventionism by the courts as they battled with a crisis that combined short-term depression, long-term secular change and political debate in dangerous mix. The courts tried to maintain an older pattern of a moral adjustment of wages that bore a relationship to need and to comparability and to fairness of distribution of profits. In the end, it required the intervention of the British state to destroy this, with the removal of the rights of the courts to intervene between master and employee on issues of wages and apprentices.

The law had, of course, been concerned with labour long before the eighteenth century. Regulation and control of the population were features of Scottish society at least since the sixteenth century. Not surprisingly, it was rural labour which first came under legal restriction.

Serfdom faded out in Scotland during the fourteenth century. In its aftermath, and aggravated by the chaos of war and plague, a major problem was vagrancy, landless labourers wandering the country and seen as posing a threat to individuals and to property. The earliest legislation on labour sought to deal with this development. An act of 1425 ordered sheriffs to arrest 'ydil men' and force them to work within forty days.[9] How effective such a law was we just do not know. The chances are that it was not much used. Whatever central government, such as it was in the fifteenth and sixteenth century, might seek to impose on a turbulent Scotland, it depended upon local initiatives to ensure that it was carried out and, generally, such initiatives were lacking. In addition, then as at later periods, there was probably a wariness about employing vagrants. Those forced to work were not the most reliable.

By the seventeenth century, the main labour problem seems to have been shortage of labour, made critical by a massive outflow of population as something like one in ten of the population left, some to settle in Ireland, others to earn their living as soliders of fortune throughout Europe.[10] To overcome this and to prevent the poor taking advantage of a strengthened bargaining position, there was a tightening of legislative compulsion by a reassertion of earlier laws. In 1605 the Privy Council allowed anyone in need of labour to seize beggars and if, before a sheriff, they were found to be able-bodied, they could be branded as serfs and forced to work.[11] Again, this legislation was probably not much utilised and, significantly, the 1605 Act had to be re-enacted in 1621 and in 1649 and further consolidated in a measure of William & Mary in 1692, to try to make it effective. By the principle of 'desuetude' in Scots law, statutes that were not put into practice ceased to have any legal force and, therefore, had to be re-enacted. Even with the 1692 re-enactment, there were still frequent complaints at the end of the century about the large number of vagrants.[12] To retain an adequate supply of labour for mining, an Act of 1606 was passed which deprived salters, colliers and coal bearers of the right to leave their employment without permission of their employer. It was intended to deter one employer from poaching labour from another at times of shortage, but, in practice, this measure came to form the basis of a system of serfdom for Scottish colliers for the next 170 years. In 1607 this was extended to cover metal miners and, to all intents, miners were now tied to their owner, to be bought and sold with the mine. The children of miners too were, in practice, bound to the coalmaster, with a symbolic payment of arles to the father by the employer at the time of the baptism, an act which by custom bound the colliers to place their children in the mine. A 1641 Act also extended this legislation to labourers around the collieries. Sir John Hope's leadminers at Leadhills were included in the legislation in 1649, but that was abandoned in 1695 because of the need to attract skilled labour from England.[13] Similar legislation covered fishermen in the North-East, but they were saved from bondage by a Court of

Session ruling in 1696 that they could not be restricted to the district where they were born.[14]

Valiant efforts were made in the seventeenth century, by both public and private enterprise, to attract and develop new industry in Scotland, and this added to the problem of ensuring adequate supplies of labour. There were loud complaints that skilled labour in Scotland was very expensive. In many cases the most highly skilled would be immigrant workers, and in order to attract them to Scotland in the first place they probably had to be paid twice the going rate. There was frequent tension between manufacturers over the poaching of skilled labour. The statute of 1641, which appointed commissioners to erect manufactories, contained clauses that allowed factory hands to be bound to the factories.[15] In 1661 this was extended to make it an offence 'to intyce, reset or intertaine any of the servants or apprentices of the manufactories without the consent of their masters', manufactories being defined as 'the workshops of any of the greater industries'.[16] In yet another attempt to deal with the problem of reluctant labour, the Earl of Eglinton in 1662 was given the monopoly of any vagrants in Galloway, Ayr and Renfrew to work in his new, and short-lived, woollen factory in Ayr. In the following year, the privilege was extended to all manufacturers, though Eglinton retained his monopoly in Ayr.[17] A linen factory in Leith, erected in 1693, had workmen bound for twenty-one years.[18]

Clearly, getting labour was also becoming a major problem in rural areas. There was much concern about farm servants 'going lowse, leaving their maisteris service' and refusing to be hired 'without great and extraordinary wages promised unto them'. Yet others, apparently, were freeing themselves from long ties and taking work 'at daylie or weeklie wages'.[19] Fletcher of Saltoun, at the end of the century, was complaining of 'that unspeakable vexation which we suffer by our hired servants, who though we bestow the greatest pains or cost to educate them, at the least cross leave us'.[20] Restrictions were imposed on the rights of farm servants to move at Whitsun unless they could prove that they had been hired by another master. They were not to be allowed to wander, even temporarily, in search of labour or to use the threat of leaving to exert pressure on their employer.[21]

Such restrictions on freedom of movement of workers were justified on the grounds that certain groups were 'necessary' servants, necessary for the public good, and in Scottish law there was an assumption that the individual had to be subordinated to some communal good. There was no tradition, such as existed in English common law, of the rights of the individual over the community. Before Adam Smith in the 1770s there was hardly any questioning of the right of the State to restrict the freedom of action of individuals for the public good. Rather, the emphasis was on the good of society, and the happiness of the individual had always to be subordinated to the needs of the nation. Viscount Stair in his *Institutions* of 1681 defended collier serfdom on the ground that 'the feual of coal is in most parts necessary at home and very profitable abroad'. Even in the middle of the eighteenth century, Erskine was prepared to defend the system as a free contract of perpetual service, different from slavery:

> There appears to be nothing repugnant either to reason or to the peculier doctrines of Christianity, in a contract by which one binds oneself to perpetual service under a master, who, on his part, is obliged to maintain the other in all the necessaries of life.[22]

It was a concept far removed from that which regarded labour as a commodity to be bought and sold like any other.

There were compensations in such a position, of course: it was not all exploitation. As Professor Duckham has argued, the system of servitude did provide some security for miners at times of sickness and even in old age: 'It guaranteed regularity of employment, subsistence at least, freedom from military service, half daily wages in old age, sustenance during sickness and a coffin at the final departure'. It meant free or cheap housing for the miner and for his children.[23] It generally meant work for the man's wife. Similarly on the land, the six-month or year's feeing meant that the farm servant was entitled to his wages even if he were ill for some of the time.

Nor did legal servitude necessarily produce a workforce that was servile in mentality. In the case of the colliers, far from it. They were noted for their unruliness and for their lack of deference to authority. The absence of the possible sanction of unemployment allowed an independence that few other workers could risk.[24] Their very exclusion from free society pushed them into 'brotherhoods' in the seventeenth century, through which they could fairly effectively control work practices in the mine.[25] There are numerous examples of the tricky job it was to keep groups of colliers in line and of how difficult it was to change their ways. In 1674 Glasgow coalmasters were claiming that hewers, as well as demanding 'exorbitant wages', were refusing to work more than four days in six and were demanding payment during seedtime and harvest when, presumably, they were not at the mine.[26] Perhaps because of such signs of defiance among colliers and others, doubts about both the morality and the economic practicality of servile labour were being expressed by the end of the seventeenth century. It never seems to have worked successfully in factories though it persisted in the coal industry. Colliers, for example, were expressly excluded from the provisions of the 1701 equivalent of Habeas Corpus Act in Scotland, and when heritable jurisdictions were abolished in 1747, the juridicial rights of the coalmaster and saltmaster over their colliers were retained.[27]

Another area of intervention was that of wages. By the seventeenth century there was concern about prices and wages in rural areas. An Act of 1617 gave JPs power, similar to that of burgh magistrates, to try to curb the independence of rural labour. The 1617 Act instructed JPs 'to appoint at their quarter sessions to be kept in August and February, the ordinary hyre and wages of labourers, workmen, and servants, and who shall refuse to serve upon the price set down by them, shall be imprisoned and further punished at their discretion'.[28] An Act of 1661 decreed that they should 'by mutual and conjunct advice, make and ratify ordinances for the fees of servants, shearers in harvest, and other labouring men, appoint prices for all handicrafts . . .'[29]

As always, it is difficult to know how extensively such wage-fixing legislation was being applied. In England it had fallen into disuse in the second half of the seventeenth century, apparently because JPs found it futile to try to impose legal rules that were increasingly out of line with market rates.[30] Where assessments were made by English Quarter Sessions, they tended to be done mechanically without change to take account of altered circumstances.[31] On the other hand, the fact that in some counties such assessments continued to be issued until the 1760s would seem to indicate that they were intended to have some role as a benchmark.

There are few records of Scottish Justices from the seventeenth century. Their role was a much more minor one than that of their English counterparts. However, during the strict period of the Protectorate in August 1656, a full assessment was made by Ayrshire JPs and printed for distribution to all parishes.[32] They fixed day rates that could be charged by masons, wrights, barrowmen, thatchers, tailors, shoemakers and labourers. A decision about smiths and weavers was postponed until the next session and in February 1657 it was ruled

> The no Smith take any more for working each pound weight of Plow Irons, or of any other rough work whereupon the File Cometh not, but ten penies Scots, and no more.

And

> That weavers are to have for weaving each Ell or Hardern or other Linin, under ten Lears in the pound, (being sufficiently woven) but twelve penies Scots and no more without bountieth.

The Lanarkshire JPs read the Acts on servants' fees and on craftsmen's wages in 1707 and decided to contact other counties to see what the pattern of assessing wages was in these. In March 1708 they made a new assessment, very little different from the Ayrshire one of 1656, though thatchers' rates had risen to 10s. without food and 6s. with food from the previous 6s.8d. and 3s.4d. The same rates were reaffirmed in 1716 and again in 1721.[34]

Generally, the payments laid down were for the day and covered the year from 1st March to the end of September. From October to February, wages were reduced by a sixth 'except such as work by Candle-light'. In a few cases, the payments were by the piece: 'biggers of fold dikes' were to be paid 20 pence Scots per rod; a shoemaker, 'for every Inch of measure of single soal'd Shoes, from Eight Inches to twelve Inches in length, is to have Eighteen Penies Scots; and for every Inch under Eight Inches, he is to have Sixteen Penies Scots. Item. For every Inch of measure of double soal'd shoes, sufficient Leather and work, from Eight to Twelve Inches, is to have Thirty Penies Scots; and for every Inch under eight Inches he is to have Two Shillings Scots'.[35]

The Dumbartonshire JPs were applying the 1661 legislation in the mid-eighteenth century. The farmers were facing labour shortages and had the constables compile a list of men and women who were unemployed, 'louse and out of service'. They had earlier, in 1744, publicised the regulations about rates. In 1759, 'it being represent ... that by the cheapness of Meall at this time and other reasons the Servants thro' this County are turned insolent and made demands for exhorbitant fees and bountays', the JPs declared that they would take action, 'upon application of any private party', against those who refused to serve 'at the customarie fees and prices'.[36]

The JPs, responsible for the rural areas, were concerned with the wages they themselves might be asked to pay their workers and servants and with the price that itinerant craftsmen might charge them for their services. No distinction was made in the legislation or in justices' rulings between prices and wages; the latter were the price a man could charge for his services.

A substantial part of any payments for the principal farm servants would be in kind. The Edinburgh JPs in 1656 laid down that

> A whole Hind is to have from his Master, a convenient Dwelling-house (commonly called a Coat-house) and a Kail-yard; And for a whole Year's Service, he is to have fifteen Bolls sufficient Oats [c.140lbs] at the usual Terms of Payment, six Furlets Pease in Summer [1-furlot = .998 bushel] Ground to sow Six Furlets of Oats and one Furlet of Beer [i.e. barley] (the Seed being his own), and if he live in the lower parts of the shire, two Soumes [i.e. pasture that will need two cows] grasse, or pasture for two cowes, but if in the higher part of the shire, three Soumes grasse.[37]

With others the pattern of payment in kind was declining in the seventeenth century and both the Edinburgh and the Ayrshire JPs generally laid down two rates, one with meat and drink and the other without. So a wright could expect 12s Scots per day in 1656 or 6s if he had meat and drink, a barrowman 6s or 3s. 'A Taylor, getting [Meat] in the House where he W[orks]s is to have Four Penies Scots, for a dayes Wages, and no more.' The manner in which the minutes note that 'The prices of the Task-Work mentioned ... are understood to be in full satisfaction therefore, and without any Bounteth, Morning or Four Hours Drinks' would seem to indicate that the abandonment of these was a fairly recent innovation.[38] On the other hand this may have been no more than a traditional legal formula, since the Lanarkshire JPs half a century later were noting that 'it is ordained that the respective pryces aforesaid both for craftsmen and servants shall be in full satisfactione of all bounties, rewards morning and four hour drinks, sowing of corns, bear, lintseed or of any other thing which formerly hath been given to servants or craftsmen'.[39] As Donald Woodward has argued for England, 'the mere provision of such rates on paper proves neither that they were paid nor that workers were presented with a choice'.[40] On the other hand, the timing of the eradication of non-cash payments may have varied. In 1719 the Lanarkshire JPs were decreeing that farmers need no longer provide their servants with ground for sowing linseed, 'understanding the great and many inconveniences arising'.[41] It may also be that the use made of them changed. Rab Houston has shown how the Lasswade colliers received a coal allowance, which they used partly for their own needs and partly to augment their wages by selling to neighbours. To them it was a customary part of their earnings. In 1703 Sir John Clerk of Penicuik was seeking to have the coal allowance regarded as an incentive to regular work, a bonus, not a customary part of wages.[42]

The Justices were laying down maximum rates of payment and it was an offence punishable by imprisonment for 'any Labourer, Work-man or servant' to refuse to serve at the prices laid down. Masters, on the other hand, were bound 'from time to time [to] sa [tis] fie and Pay their Servants fees, and Wages, as the same shall become due'. If they failed to do so 'upon complaint thereof', the 'saids Masters shall be compelled to pay the saids fees, by and attour the Damages (to be moderated by any two of the Justices of Peace) sustained by the said Servants for the want of their Fees and wages, and that summarily without any tedious or long process of law'.[43]

The problem in the burghs was sustantially different from that in the countryside. In these there was less of a shortage of labour. As at any period, towns pulled in people from the surrounding areas: the larger the burgh, the greater the pull. There was no great tradition of craft skills in the Scottish burghs. Goods produced tended, on the whole, to be crude imitations of imports or functional home products showing little sign of high levels of skills or of aesthetic awareness. One can perhaps counter such a generalisation with reference to fine silverwork in the seventeenth century in church ware and sword hilts and ornamental pistols. But there is little doubt that such work was limited and exceptional. No nobleman accompanying the restored monarch to the Court in 1660 would depend on Scottish cloth or on Scottish tailors or shoemakers for his dress, any more than he would depend on Scottish furniture or pewterware for his furnishings. For at least two centuries, the refrain of any interested in stimulating the Scottish economy was that quality had to be improved. Most manufactured goods of any worthwhile standards were imported, largely from England or from the Netherlands, with imports paid for by the export of primary products like livestock, fish, skins, wool, coal and salt. What manufacturing there was aimed at the poorer end of the domestic market and essentially for a local market. Coarse woollen cloth and linen cloth were produced in most parts of the country, both in town and country, using local materials and relatively limited local skills. Weavers, for example, according to Lindesay, were held 'in no Esteem and their business little understood or regarded'. There were tailors who could produce clothes to order and wrights who would undertake any task in wood, but outside the main burghs there were relatively few specialist craftsmen.

However, in the towns too, the burgh magistrates were performing a regulatory role, laying down wage rates and hours for craftsmen under an Act of 1426. So in Aberdeen in 1668 a dispute between master shoemakers and their journeymen was ended with the magistrates fixing rates of 5s. for a pair of best men's shoes, 4s. 6d for seconds and 3s. 6d. for best women's shoes. They also regulated hours from 6 a.m. to 6 p.m. and, eventually, after complaints over many years, banned journeymen undertaking new work in their own homes, 'but only in his maister's schope, excep he have ane relevant excuse'.[44] What did not exist in Scotland was any equivalent of the English Statute of Artificers by which statutory apprenticeship was laid down in a range of crafts. In Scotland the system of apprenticeship and its duration was informal and varied according to custom in different trades.

From the fifteenth into the eighteenth century Scotland was a society where control and regulation was exercised over craftsmen, whether free or unfree, and over rural workers. It was a society where JPs and magistrates were expected to act for some greater public good and to ensure that individuals were subordinated to community need. There had, undoubtedly, been a concept of the fair price and the just wage in early centuries. How much of that still persisted in the seventeenth century is hard to say. Clearly there were sound financial reasons for controlling wage rates or the price that craftsmen could pay. The system survived because it was in the interest of those who exercised power. But the belief that the state could and should intervene had important repercussions in developing relations between masters and men.

Scotland at the end of the seventeenth century was a poor, predominantly peasant society afflicted by the poverty and dearth that is generally the lot of the underdeveloped. Industries were few and only in the infancy of their development. There were towns: the great burgh of Edinburgh, with probably more than 30,000 inhabitants, crowded into the squalor of the High Street and its extensions, could match any English city but London in size. There were the lesser burghs of Aberdeen, Dundee and Glasgow, the last growing, but still with only 12–14,000 'in-dwellers'. But most of the seventy royal burghs and, even more so, the two hundred or so burghs of barony that existed, were tiny and hardly deserving of the adjective 'urban'. They were little more than features of an agricultural society, with the burgesses in many cases still much involved in the agriculture of the surrounding countryside. Nine out of ten of Scotland's population depended upon agriculture for subsistence. Over the next century much was to change.

1
The Economy Transformed

The eighteenth century was the time when Scotland made the crucial transformation from an underdeveloped to a developing industrial society. While signs of potential areas of change were apparent before 1707, there is little doubt that the opening of access to English markets and especially to English overseas trade did much to stimulate growth. Glasgow, now with the advantages of the English Navigation Acts, began its rapid development as the great entrepôt of the West. Edinburgh, although deprived of its status as the seat of Parliament, nonetheless retained its significance as the meeting place of the main courts of law and church and continued to grow at an even faster rate.

However, the gains of access to wider markets were slow to come and there was no sudden unleashing of growth. There were immediate setbacks to the textile industry of wool and linen, already in some difficulties before 1707, and now facing the full brunt of English competition. There was none of that sudden expansion so glibly predicted by the advocates of the Union. Linen suffered particularly as a result of a duty on exports imposed in 1711 and not lifted until 1717.[1] Fortunately, a decade of good harvests kept prices down and helped maintain a reasonable home market. That came to an end in 1724 with the start of a number of bad harvests contributing to a year or two of crises at the end of the 1720s. War with Spain did not help the situation. Food prices doubled and there was comment on 'the universal poverty of the country ... and the languishing condition of our manufactorys'.[2] 1727 was a year of general depression as linen and cattle prices tumbled. A slight upturn in 1728, when peace was restored, proved to be short-lived and the economy was back in difficulties and in growing depression.

An improvement in trade in the 1730s was gradual, but exports did begin to expand slowly, and with this came a rise in domestic prosperity. Generally, the effect of this was to pull in imports, since home-manufactured products were of such atrocious quality that any rise in income would lead customers to abandon crude Scottish products in favour of the finer cloth or furnishings that could be got from England or the continent. Even the porter of Edinburgh's breweries was 'the most stupefying stuff ever was contrived' according to Cockburn of Ormiston, and imported London porter was what anyone who could afford it drank.[3] A new awareness of the basic problems was apparent in the 1730s, with growing calls for improvement in agriculture and in industry. There was a sense of the possibilities of betterment as the farming community began to raise their levels of comfort, extending farmhouses and generally looking for better-quality furnishings and fittings for their homes.

Changes came only in brief spurts, however, since it was still an economy that was very vulnerable to fluctuations in demand inside and outside its borders and to financial crises. The early 1740s were bad years. Failed harvests, war and a bitter winter in 1740 brought shortages of grain and coal in 1740 and 1741, though it was an indication of a new strength in the economy that the balance of payments was such as to allow the importation of grain in sufficient quantities to stave off famine. There was probably a fairly general recovery in 1743, helped by a subsidy on linen exports under the Bounty Act, but the Jacobite rebellion of 1745 confirmed many of the doubts that English investors had about trusting their money in Scotland, and recovery was slow. Defeat, however, eventually brought a new stability and renewed growth. The debts of the forfeited estates were paid off in 1747 and the land was probably better cultivated than it had been under the previous owners. Large numbers of troops brought state money into the country and 'gave new life to industry and enterprise of every kind', and compensation of £164,233 for the loss of heritable jurisdictions brought ready money to spend.[4] These helped catapult economic change. The Scottish economy, over the next thirty years, began a rapid expansion on all fronts that brought the kind of economic development that had taken two centuries to achieve in England. Glasgow, which had been growing rapidly with the American trade, began to show off its new wealth in better houses and furniture and public entertainments. The 'Tobacco Lords' learned to spend with a notorious conspicuousness.

The linen industry, encouraged by state and private investment, was in the vanguard and production doubled in the decade after 1742, after years of little growth. It was still, however, an easy victim to fluctuations in demand. The temporary withdrawal of the bounty on exported coarse linens in 1753 threw the industry into severe depression in the next two years.[5] 1756 was a year of 'great scarcity', according to Adam Smith.[6] It was saved by English wars, cutting off imports from Holland between 1756 and 1760. In these years output of linen rose by almost fifty per cent. Fortunes could be made, according to Ramsay of Ochtertyre, as money flowed. That symbol of a new economy, the Carron Iron Works, opened its doors in 1759. London manufacturers from Spitalfields hired Paisley linen weavers to work on silk gauze that same year, and within six years there were over 700 silk looms.[7] Farming, too, experienced good harvests, and all levels of society seem to have improved their standard of living at this time.

Natural and manmade uncertainties were never far away to remind people of the precariousness of their new-found prosperity. A renewed financial crisis came in the 1760s, perhaps reflecting English political hostility to the Scots, apparent in the Wilkesite attacks on Lord Bute and his fellow countrymen. English money began to be withdrawn in 1761 and the persistent cash shortages, which had always been a problem in Scotland in the past, reappeared. Banks had to pull in their loans and expansion ground to a halt. A bad harvest in 1762 did not help and a period of recession continued through to 1766. These years from 1763 to 1765 were ones of substantial social unrest, on a level not experienced since at least the 1720s. There were meal riots and strikes in Edinburgh and Glasgow, and worries among the authorities at the large number of the unemployed who were tramping the countryside in search of work.[8]

A new confidence appeared at the end of the decade. Improvement was now all the rage in agriculture, and wages were rising faster than grain prices. Demand for labour was extraordinary high. The commitment to the New Town of Edinburgh was made in 1767, to the Forth and Clyde Canal in 1768. Such enterprises put an immense strain on the resources of capital and of labour. Once again the linen industry was a barometer of the economy as output rose. However, as before, neither domestic demand nor domestic credit facilities were adequate to sustain a long period of growth. In addition, foreign competition and trouble in the American markets produced a glutted English market. Linen prices began to fall and the Ayr Bank, which had been established in 1769 to help encourage expansion of the linen industry, crashed in 1772. Doubts about the financial stability of Amsterdam at this time were causing a general tightening of credit, other houses followed Douglas, Heron & Co. into oblivion, and the economy went into recession again. There were comparisons with the disaster of the Darien Co. of eighty years before as the linen trade seemed laid in ruins, as building work came to a halt everywhere and as the Carron Company tottered.[9] Again riot and disorder and widespread discontent followed in the wake of economic crisis, while weavers and other tradesmen searched for work. There was widespread emigration.

Impending war and war itself in America proved a much-needed boost to the economy, although, as it dragged on, it brought trouble for some. Already by the end of 1777 there was talk of unusual stagnation in the linen trade. When France, Spain and Holland joined the war, trade became even more difficult and the last year of the 1770s saw a number of West of Scotland trading houses going down. Bad harvests in the early 1780s could still cause great distress and produce conditions of near famine in some parts in 1783. But now a new level of economic development was being reached, as the cotton industry began its great expansion in the West, attracted by the now high level of skills available among the fine linen weavers. Unfinished building work of the 1770s was resumed and a surge of progress was once again apparent at the end of the 1780s. As the *Glasgow Mercury* noted in 1787, everywhere there was ‘a spirit of industry’, improvements were taking place in cities and countryside, and products such as gauzes, stoneware and crystal glass were reaching new levels of quality.[10] Cotton was the catalyst of change. It had started gradually with the mixing of West Indian cotton with linen and silk from the 1750s. By the 1790s imports of raw cotton were approaching 2 million pounds. The expansion was made possible by the development of water-powered spinning mills at places like Catrine in Ayrshire, Deanston in Perthshire and New Lanark on the Clyde. These, together with continuing domestic spinning, supplied a growing labour force of some 39,000 handloom weavers. By the end of the decade, cotton had taken over from linen as the leading manufacturing industry, though linen, now increasingly concentrated in the East in Angus, Fife and Perthshire, remained important.

With these developments had come new economic fluctuations, not just the result of harvest failures or of war, but shaped by the investment patterns in the fixed capital of the industrialising society. Now boom and slump in demand for labour came with predictable frequency. They also tended to affect all sectors of the economy. Earlier in the eighteenth century fluctuations in the different parts of the economy did not always coincide, but, as the size of markets grew, then more people were affected at the same time and for longer periods. Few engaged in productive activity could escape the effects of periodic depression. This had major implications for the workforce. No longer did distress just take the form of rising bread prices, it now tended to mean lengthy unemployment and wage cuts.

The boom conditions continued into the 'nineties, as coalmines and ironworks joined cotton in advancing the economic fortunes of Glasgow and its neighbourhood. Nearly fifty new streets and squares were built in the city between 1788 and 1791, according to the *Scots Magazine*.[11] In Edinburgh the building of the New Town continued apace. Movement between East and West was facilitated by the opening of the Forth and Clyde Canal in 1790. Money wages were rising, though so too were prices. It was too good to last. In December 1792, as the revolutionary armies of France made spectacular advances in Europe, there was a dramatic loss of financial confidence. The great cotton firm of James and Archibald Buchanan went down and took several others with it. James Dunlop, one of the wealthiest of merchants, with substantial coalmines around Glasgow, also failed. By the Autumn of 1793 there was unemployment and distress on a great scale, with Scottish spokesmen warning Pitt that levels of unemployment in Paisley and Glasgow would reach 160,000.[12] Prices were being pushed up by wartime inflation and emergency relief measures were having to be taken to assist the poor. Other areas were much less badly affected, however, and the economy as a whole continued to expand. Demand for linen continued high in Fife and the war brought new profitable demands for Carron and other ironworks. Despite a bad harvest in 1795, which did cause some discontent, generally the demand for labour remained high and the cotton industry quickly recovered from the setback of 1793. Fears of a French invasion caused a temporary panic in 1797 and it was generally a period of growing uncertainty. Bad harvests did not help and food prices rose much faster than wages in 1799, 1800 and 1801, resulting in severe shortages of basic food and in serious meal riots in the spring of 1800.

The striking underlying trend, however, was the continuing growth of the economy. Coal, linen and cotton were all expanding. The population grew to over two million. The cities mushroomed. Edinburgh's population almost doubled in size in the first quarter of the century. But the greatest transformation was in the West around the expanding cotton industry. Glasgow's population passed 100,000 in the 1811 census and reached over 150,000 in the early 1820s. Initially a dependence on water power had made Paisley and Renfrewshire the most important areas; only as the new century progressed and steam power was gradually applied did mills move into Glasgow. In 1787 there had been nineteen cotton spinning mills throughout the country. By 1812 there were 120 and, increasingly, these were in Glasgow and Lanarkshire. Trades, services, farming all expanded to meet a growing domestic demand. Demand for labour too was high and many new jobs were created so that for many with scarce skills there were gains to be made. Changes in technology and in patterns of production, however, threatened the jobs of many others.

Although the long war with revolutionary France kept up a demand for military supplies, and barrack and fortification building brought an exceptional demand for the services of building workers, it also created sharp fluctuations and serious disruptions to trade. The short-lived peace of 1802, for example, while helping exports, meant unemployment for shipwrights and builders and tailors dependent on war demand. For those in work, however, the signs are of improved living standards in that first decade of the new century. Valiant efforts were made by merchants to get round the barriers to trade, whether Napoleon's decrees or the British Orders in Council, by means of blockade running and smuggling.[13] But there were undoubtedly serious disruptions and the laying off of workers. 1809 was particularly bad with the blocking of raw cotton supplies from the United States by the Embargo Act and of continental markets by Napoleon and his allies. Mills were closed and looms stood idle. A short speculative boom as new markets were discovered in South America ended in bankruptcies for a few and disastrous unemployment for many in 1812. From then until 1814–15, when Napoleon's domination was broken, uncertainty continued. Weavers suffered particularly badly in these last years of war from the erratic fluctuations in the demands for their services and, for them, there was never again to be a significant improvement.

Peacetime brought its own painful readjustments. Initial demand for consumer goods that had suffered from the high levels of wartime taxation boosted employment in some sectors. But in others wartime demand had created over-capacity for peacetime needs. Farming, too, was in difficulty as prices and rents moved downwards. The burden of cost-cutting fell upon the rural poor, who began to make their way into towns in increasing numbers. The Corn Laws offered some protection to the rural community, but they aggravated price fluctuations and the consequent distress. In Scotland, as in England, the postwar years from 1816 to 1819 were bleak ones for many. There were signs of the beginning of long-term problems. Soldiers demobilised from the army, migrants from the Highlands, Ireland and the rural areas were moving into the cities and creating a permanent surplus of labour.[14] The effect was to undermine drastically the position of urban workers and to push down their levels of wages. The winter of 1816–17 saw widespread unemployment among both craftsmen and labourers, just as prices began to rise sharply as a result of a poor harvest. Distress among cotton workers in Glasgow reached unparalleled depths. The struggle by workers to protest at deteriorating conditions reached a new level of intensity. Labour shortages in most sectors were no longer a serious problem for employers or a protection against wage cuts for workers.

An upturn in demand in the 1820s helped restore a measure of social peace. The building industry, in particular, flourished and in Edinburgh it reached mania proportions in 1823–24. Speculative building in the New Town and in the Southside produced new streets and squares with unprecedented rapidity and workmen with a modicum of building skills flocked into the city from all corners of the country. Elsewhere there was substantial expansion in cotton, linen and coal.

It came to an end with the financial crisis and subsequent slump of 1825–26. As debts were called in in the Autumn of 1825, the building bubble burst and streets and houses were left unfinished — some for nearly a quarter of a century. A disastrous year in farming in 1826, the 'dry year' or 'the year of the short corn', when potatoes and turnips failed too, added to the difficulties.[15] Recession persisted for the rest of the decade.

Symbolic of a turn of fortunes and of new directions was the founding of the Gartsherrie Iron Works by William Baird in 1828. Using Neilson's hot blast, Gartsherrie and the other furnaces that appeared in the 1830s were able to exploit the rich blackband iron-ore seams of Lanarkshire. Scotland entered its era of heavy industry. Textiles retained their importance for decades to come, and for cotton there was a remarkably buoyant market through until 1836–37, but the signs of future trends were already apparent even before then. Linen, now largely concentrated in Tayside and in Fife, faced with Irish and continental competition, had been struggling for some time. A very large number of linen firms were wiped out in the crisis of 1825. Cotton too was having its difficulties in finding markets for its fine-quality cloth and even the home market was being penetrated by foreign cloth. French-made Indian pattern shawls could undercut the Paisley equivalent. At the cheaper end, Lancashire had long been able to rival Scottish products and was now challenging in finer quality. A major crisis hit the Scottish cotton industry in the mid-'thirties, necessitating structural changes that were bound to lead to conflict with the workforce.

For the workers, the period from 1831 to 1836 was generally one of marked improvement. In most trades demand for labour was high and workers were able to reorganise and to push for improvements. Those in industries exporting to the United States were the real gainers, but they were aso, of course, the most vulnerable to hiccups in the American economy. When financial crisis hit in 1836 they were the ones who suffered most.

In the 1830s the Scottish economy was entering a new phase. The rate of industrialisation from now on was to be very rapid. Concentration on textiles gave way to an economy geared to heavy industry and its specialist needs. The transformation from an under-developed, predominantly agricultural society to an industrial society had been completed, though many remnants of the old lingered on. It is easy to be dazzled by the new and fail to detect the persistence of much that remained only slightly changed. Even the textile factory with its high technology was dependent upon domestic workers. James Cleland estimated that of the 36,000 people in Glasgow engaged in textiles in 1831, less than a third were factory operatives; the rest were artisans and mechanics or domestic weavers.[16] The consumer trades remained largely untouched by technology. These, as Richard Price points out, are not residues of a past world but an integral part of a developing economy.[17] Nonetheless a transformation had taken place that had major implications for all aspects of the life of the people of that society. How the workers responded to the changes that had taken place is what this book is about.

2
The World of the Eighteenth-Century Tradesman

The skilled craftsmen in the early Scottish burghs, supplying their neighbours with shoes, clothes and furnishings, were regarded as a group that needed to be controlled by the 'lieges' of the town. In practice this meant by the powerful merchant guilds that dominated the town councils. As early as 1426, the magistrates in royal burghs were given the right to fix the prices that craftsmen could charge, and this is a law that *does* seem to have been utilised. It was reaffirmed in 1551 and gradually extended from royal burghs to other burghs. In the seventeenth century it was again reaffirmed.[1]

Much later than in England and in most other European countries, it was not until the fifteenth and sixteenth centuries that craftsmen in Scotland effectively organised to challenge this merchant domination. As part of this struggle craftsmen formed their own protective organisations or 'incorporations', and these were well estblished in most large Scottish burghs in the sixteenth century. Gradually these incorporations achieved a measure of representation on the burgh councils, but they never seem to have achieved that dominance which craftsmen's guilds won in many European towns. Merchants, naturally, sought to retain some control over the prices and the quality of the goods produced, and it was this that led to numerous riots and disturbances throughout the sixteenth and seventeenth centuries. In Edinburgh especially, assemblies of craftsmen were prone to raise the symbolic blue blanket and, on more than one occasion, stormed the Council Chamber when the Town Council sought to impose prices of which they disapproved. James VI, now safely out of the place and transmuted into James I, wrote in his *Basilikon Doron*, 'The craftsmen think that we should be content with their work, how bad and dear soever it be, and if they in anything be controlled, up goeth the blew blanket'.[2]

Where perhaps the craftsmen were less strong the sanction of the law could be brought against them. Indeed, in all burghs the magistrates and the council could regulate prices, administer the markets and control the craftsmen, irrespective of the incorporations. Thus in 1628 seven Cupar shoemakers were imprisoned for refusing to produce boots and shoes at prices approved by the Council.[3] The law could also be used to maintain quality, which was, of course, something that also concerned the merchants, and this persisted into the eighteenth century. In Glasgow, the magistrates and town council in 1726, 'being informed that there are a great many abuses committed by several of the weivers and other manufacturers of cotton and linnen hand kercheiffs', imposed fines and imprisonment on those who used 'logwood or false colours' instead of indigo, 'quhich will not stand in the washing, whereby the lieges are imposed upon and the credit of that manufacture abused'. They also dealt with those who did not produce square and evenly worked handkerchiefs.[4] In Edinburgh, in 1736, the Court of Session ordered the magistrates to take action to regulate the price of candles, after this rose to the extent that 'inhabitants were having to purchase candles from other burghs'. The magistrates specified the precise profit margins that candlemakers were to be allowed.[5]

While resenting burgh council interference on prices, craftsmen did generally welcome a measure of control over the craft when it involved the maintenance of a trading monopoly. They had their incorporations approved by seal of cause by the burgh councils in the fifteenth and sixteenth centuries, as a means of ensuring that their exclusive privileges would be sustained by the local authorities. They controlled who could work at the craft and ensured that goods from outside the burgh could only be sold on certain days and at certain places and only in regulated markets. Through their own courts under the Deacon and, if necessary, through the burgh courts they imposed rules and regulations on their craft. The incorporations had an obligation to supervise the quality of goods produced and the 1726 case against the weavers, initiated by the weavers' incorporation, indicates that here, at least, the issue was being taken seriously. Supervision could mean not just the work of members, but any aspects of their life that might impinge on the reputation of the craft. It meant overseeing also the journeymen and apprentices and their lifestyles. All came under the jurisdiction of the deacons and their courts. They sought the sanction of law to ensure that only those who had served a full apprenticeship, passed their essay work and had paid the entry fee and been accepted as burgesses of the town would be allowed to work at the craft. Entry was not cheap. The Banff Hammermen in 1700 enacted that 'any that hath served their prentiship within the toune and intends to make them self freman shall be oblidged to make ane sufficient sye [essay] piece of work, and after pay in twelf punds Scots, together with twentie s. Scots. with ther bill and 20s. Sc. with the sye, and ane denner or a feue hairs to the traid, to the walve of any competent thing that the said traid shall think them able for'.[6] For a time-served apprentice in the Edinburgh Canongate to become a freeman hammerman in 1669 cost £89.11.6 Scots; for a freeman's son, it was £42.18s Scots.[7] For tailors in 1746, the entrance rate was £6 Scots, for the son of a member £20 Scots, and for the man who had been apprenticed to a member £30 Scots. Only those who had paid and been accepted into the incorporation would be allowed to employ others.[8]

Craftsmen welcomed the restriction on numbers that such rules implied. On such matters, burgh councils generally went with the wishes of the incorporation. So in 1630 the Edinburgh printer, John Hart, bringing out a new edition of the Bible, had to receive special permission from the Council to take on a new apprentice 'notwithstanding the time of three years be not passed since he replaced an apprentice last'; but he was not allowed to take on another apprentice until after six years. Most incorporations laid down that their members could only have one beginner apprentice at a time.[9] James VI contrasted the monopolistic situation that prevailed in Scotland with the more open system he found in England, advising his son:

> But for their part take example of England how it hath flourished both in wealth and policie since the strangers craftsmen came in among them. Therefore, not only permit but allure strangers to come here also; taking as straite order for repressing the mutining of ours at them, as was done in England at their first in-bringing there.[10]

Yet, more than a century later, Sir Patrick Lindesay, in his *Interest of Scotland* (1733), was still inveighing against the power of the craft incorporations 'which these many ages have served no other purpose than to render themselves idle, poor, and miserable, and to keep the Towns to which they belong, from increasing either in Wealth or Inhabitants'. He was particularly concerned about the inability of many country-bred children with craft skills to find work in Scotland, and he singled out tailors, gardeners and joiners as three groups, in particular, who had to seek work abroad in the plantations because they could not set up in business in the burghs.[11] It was the kind of attack on guild privileges which had been underway in England since at least the end of the seventeenth century and which had led to the decline of the influence of English guilds. In Scotland the incorporations retained legal support for their restrictions into the second half of the eighteenth century.

Membership of an incorporation could bring with it a number of additional advantages. Money (6d a quarter in the case of the Canongate tailors) was collected to assist aged and indigent members of the craft and to maintain their widows and orphans, though in many this function seems to have been in decline by the eighteenth century. There were almshouses and the certainty of a mortcloth to cover the coffin to ensure that there was no indignity in death. By the eighteenth century many of the incorporations had built up substantial reserves of funds and were able to lend money to members. The sudden bankruptcy of the Edinburgh Canongate Incorporation of Tailors and Shoemakers in 1741 caused a major crisis in the city, since it undermined confidence in all the Edinburgh incorporations.[12] Debts had to be called in quickly and many craftsmen found themselves in difficulties. Membership could also give the privilege of cheap food since an incorporation could get involved in bulk buying and storage of food, a useful perquisite in a country afflicted by periods of scarcity.[13]

With the rise in the population of some burghs, it was often difficult to restrict the numbers coming into the craft as much as many would have wanted, though all newcomers were expected to register with the relevant incorporation when they came into town. Even in the sixteenth century in Edinburgh, however, it was proving difficult to maintain accurate records of men with craft skills coming into the burgh from the country.[14] In Glasgow there were complaints about the large numbers of wrights and masons that had been brought into the city after the great fire of 1652. Journeymen and apprentice wrights took direct action in the winter of 1653 to drive out these 'straingers', and the magistrates succumbed to pressure by prohibiting any further importation of strangers without the consent of the bailies. Apparently many of these strangers were journeymen, with no intention of becoming masters and no intention of seeking to become freemen of the burgh.[15]

Most incorporations tried to insist that all journeymen being employed were 'booked' with the deacon of the trade. They could work on trial for eight days — later fourteen days — and then their names and details of the agreement between master and journeyman were supposed to be 'booked' with the incorporation. From 1713, at least in the case of the Glasgow Hammermen, the agreements were supposed to be in writing and the Deacon could act as mediator in the case of dispute. There was, however, a booking fee, which was probably passed on to the journeyman, and it is likely that booking was frequently ignored. In the 1760s it was being actively resisted by the journeymen tailors in Queensferry, when their bargaining position was strengthened by wartime demand, 'looking upon themselves as of so much greater consequence'.[16] But it was not until the 1790s that it was formally abandoned by some of the Glasgow trades.[17]

When trade was expanding, when there were opportunities for increasing output as there were in the eighteenth century, then incorporation rules tended to get ignored. The rules of the weavers' incorporation in Glasgow, for example, laid down that 'no freeman should take a stranger from the country but for serving his master two years space for half his winning except those that come from royal burghs'. In 1732, when all was for expansion, the Trades House of Glasgow thought it 'reasonable that any freeman weaver take what journeymen he thinks fit without distinction of town or country for what wages the master and he can agree'.[18] Sir Patrick Lindesay, writing about the same time, reported that in Edinburgh the weavers 'are indeed exceeding easy upon this head, they are in use to admit any good tradesman to the Freedom of their Incorporation upon terms that are easy and reasonable'.[19] Soon after, in Dundee, the magistrates were allowing that 'all the free masters of the Weaver Trade of Dundee to employ as many unfree weavers as they please to work in their own houses', but they were still trying to stop their employment outside their master's house.[20] It was not a time either for being too concerned about the quality of skills. Essay works began to be dropped as a test of skill.

In other cases, newcomers could avoid the controls of the incorporation by moving beyond the burgh boundaries, where the remit of the incorporation could not run. But when these developments became a real threat to the burgh craftsmen they could get agreements to extend control. The cordiners and the weavers in Glasgow both came to agreements with fellow tradesmen, first in the Gorbals and then in Calton in 1725, that no one should be allowed to set up without the approval of the crafts,

> And that it shall not be leisum or lawfull to the said weavers of Calton and Blackfaulds to take ane apprentice for less time than five years, or to take ane apprentice but house apprentice to be maintained in their own family, and that they shall not give more wages or hyre to servants or journeymen than the weavers of Glasgow are or shall be allowed to do by acts and statutes of their incorporation.

Similar agreements were worked out between the tailors in Glasgow and the

Gorbals and Port Glasgow, where they were 'to be a pendicle of the taylors of Glasgow'.[21]

One group over whom the craft incorporations had little control were the King's freemen, discharged soldiers who were free to enter any craft without the sanction of the Incorporation. This was a source of pressure on the crafts that increased during the eighteenth century and caused tensions. The numerous wars of the eighteenth century made this a major factor in eroding exclusive privilege. The practice had been used before, but it was re-enacted at the end of the Seven Years' War in 1762. It became worse during the Revolutionary and Napoleonic wars, when even three years in the militia was recognised by the courts as sufficient qualification for a King's freeman. The Act was also extended to widows and children of sailors and soldiers and the incorporations could regulate neither the hours, nor the quality nor the charges of such people.[22] The development of new skills also allowed groups to break free from control. Examples of these were the staymakers and the hose makers, both of whom were able to separate themselves from the tailors, and the cabinetmakers who separated themselves from the wrights. Wigmakers and hairdressers were able to set up in business in Edinburgh, without entering the Incorporation of Barbers. But even within the burghs it was difficult to control the activities of those skilled craftsmen who could not or would not pay the high burgess fees. None the less, there were enough cases of legal action being taken against unfreemen, by which their work could be seized, for them to have some deterrent effect. Much work remains to be done on the role of the courts in eighteenth-century Scotland, but one has the impression that they were prepared to uphold exclusive privilege much later than they were in England. The Incorporation of Bakers in Glasgow, for example, was able to get a new seal of cause from the Town Council in 1791 reasserting its rights against 'outentowners' and to get Court of Session backing in 1803 against John Wotherspoon, who was selling bread that had been baked outside the Royalty.[23]

The assumption behind craft incorporations was that demand would be largely static or growing only slowly and, therefore, it would be possible to adjust the supply of authorised skilled men to meet needs. The theory was that, given a restriction on apprenticeship, all qualified craftsmen would be able, in time, to find a place in the incorporation. The period of journeymanship was to be a limited one, when the qualified man would polish and extend his skills by tramping for a number of years — in some cases a minimum of five was prescribed — but in time, he could expect to return to his own burgh and enter his mastership. At least by the eighteenth century this was becoming quite unrealistic. Many skilled craftsmen were to remain journeymen throughout their lives. In some crafts, the cost of setting up in business on one's own behalf was too high for many. In others, the incorporations pursued a policy of high burgess fees which effectively excluded the majority.

No doubt many incorporations deliberately put a limit on numbers. The Edinburgh tailors' incorporation pushed up its entrance fees in the seventeenth century to exclude the majority of workmen from the freedom of the burgh.[24] The skilled journeyman wishing to set up in business on his own, but lacking admission to the incorporation, could choose to ignore the regulations and press ahead illegally, risking a fine, or he could move just beyond the burgh boundary and beyond the jurisdiction of the incorporation. In other cases incorporations, while strictly limiting numbers of freemen, tolerated non-incorporated tradesmen on payment of an annual sum, 'stallinger money'. The majority of journeymen would have to accept that they would remain wage-earners for the rest of their working lives. For yet others, there was a world between independence and dependence, between master and journeyman. Many would work on their own with perhaps an apprentice or a journeyman, certainly aided by wife and family, regarding themselves as independent, but ready, or forced by necessity, to take work from larger masters. It was not uncommon for a man to work as a journeyman in a burgh in the winter and then to tramp, as his own man, in rural areas in the summer months.[25] Many others had to be prepared to take on jobs other than their own trade. For long into the nineteenth century, the division between master and journeyman was a blurred one. This very ambiguity caused tensions: there was uncertainty about status and standing. The journeyman was expected to be subordinate to the master and to work as instructed, but piece-working journeymen in particular regarded themselves as independent tradesmen free to regulate their own patterns of work. A recurring issue, from the end of the seventeenth century, was the attempt by craft incorporations to ensure that journeymen did not work on their own behalf at home in the evenings. It led to pressure for regular and longer hours.[26] In a variety of ways the relationship of the journeymen to the incorporation was becoming increasingly problematic.

In the eighteenth century, traditional patterns were beginning to disappear. In some trades the apprentice would be formally indentured to the master and would live in the master's home. He would be under the authority of the master, who would take responsibility for all aspects of his conduct in his personal life. But in many cases this aspect was disappearing, especially where there was a widening social division between employer and worker. An expanding trade meant that there could be less selectivity of apprentices. One did not, after all, want one's daughters associating with apprentices of unsuitable background, especially if one had hopes of their advancing socially through marriage. Change came gradually, but even in 1658 there were complaints in Glasgow that among the cordiners there 'be prentises workin on thair awin meit' (i.e. providing their own food).[27] More than a century later, the First Statistical Account reported that there had been great changes in the twenty years since the 1760s. Few masters now took apprentices into their houses and paternal supervision of them was abandoned. They no longer interested themselves in their personal lives outside work: 'If they attended hours of business, masters took no further charge'. The training of apprentices was left to the journeymen.[28] This whole process was speeded up by the imposition of stamp duty on formal indentures, which encouraged an already well-established tendency for these to be dropped, with the result that apprentices lost any legal protection. In other cases employers, in expanding trades, would be happy to employ workers from the country, who had not necessarily served a formal apprenticeship, but would have acquired some of the skills in woodwork or stonework or tailoring which could be refined in the city. This was cheaper and certainly more convenient than having to train a young man and keep him for five or seven years. But it did mean that many masters saw themselves less as tradesmen, part of the same craft as their journeymen and apprentices and with responsibility for the development of their craft, than as employers concerned with the profitability of their own firm first and foremost. Their concern was much more with their own business and there was a widening social gap between employer and worker. The development of payment only in cash added to this gulf.

The traditional relationship between master and man was not a simple contractual one based on wages. The apprentice, having lived for five years in the master's house and worked alongside the master, would undoubtedly have developed a complex relationship with the master and his family. For the journeyman, the fact that some payment was in kind involved an assumption that the master had a responsibility for his man's basic needs. There was no uniform pattern, but in many cases food would be provided, breakfast, drink and dinner. Some journeymen, in addition to their wages, could expect to receive a pair of shoes, others two pairs, yet others a new shirt and a pair of shoes or a suit of their master's old clothes each year. It implied a responsibility for the man's appearance. This, of course, was for the worker who stayed with the same employer for a year. When that began to change and when some employers began to take on more journeymen, the older patterns gave way to a more strictly cash relationship, and with that came a different personal relationship. For craftsmen the change seems to have come gradually throughout the eighteenth century. Among Glasgow bakers, for example, payment in kind still persisted in 1753 when one reads of 'The ordinary ffial which is Ten punds Scots and a pair of shoes at the expiration of the year'.[29] In the parish of St. Ninians, near Stirling, tailors were still paid 10d. 'with victuals' in 1796, and bakers still lived in with £11 per year 'with board'.[30] By 1811, however, it was reported that 'they are allowed no beer but what they pay for themselves in Scotland in any trade'.[31]

Although there are common trends in relations between workers and masters, it is important to bear in mind that the rate of developments and the patterns of work did vary considerably between different crafts. Some retained traditional forms into the nineteenth century, others changed rapidly during the eighteenth.

The tailoring trade was the one in which the greatest changes took place in the early eighteenth century. The traditional pattern for the well-to-do was to buy or have produced some cloth to their specifications and then to have the tailor visit and make up the cloth. In 1584 the members of the Edinburgh tailors' incorporation had bound themselves to send men at twenty-four hours' notice 'perfectly competent to cut and to sew to the houses of the leidgis, who were to gang in at five o'clock in the mornin, ungang and out till aught o'clock at een, and to get, theairfor, thair meit and twalve penies ilk day for ilk man'.[32] By the late seventeenth and early eighteenth centuries, however, merchant tailors had appeared who were catering for the quality trade among visitors to Edinburgh and for the town's growing population of professional men. Ministers and their families coming to the city for the annual General Assembly of the Church of Scotland would order a new broadcloth; the meeting of the Scottish Parliament until 1707 and, after that, the meeting of the peers to elect their representatives to the House of Lords would take the gentry to town. The large masters would employ the journeymen in workshops, cutting and making up the cloth that the customer would have purchased from the draper.[33] By the 1730s there were anything from three hundred to four hundred journeymen tailors in Edinburgh, a substantial rise in numbers over the previous forty years.[34] The Poll Tax returns for the Old Kirk Parish in 1694 had listed only fifty-two tailors, half of whom were journeymen.[35]

It was not a trade that required a great deal of skill and was, therefore, easily expanded, particularly since it was open to women. Numbers were erratic, because work depended upon the season and upon extraneous events. Seasonal demand was at its highest in the months of May to July and at its lowest in August through to October. Coronations, court mournings and elections were always times of high demand. At other times, Edinburgh tailors would travel out of town and tramp in search of work. This made it almost impossible for the Incorporation actually to control the numbers in the trade.

Tailoring was a trade that depended almost entirely upon individual customer demand. A ready-made clothing industry producing low-quality goods for the plantations was around from the 1780s. Such 'slop shops' for the export trade had the distinct advantage for journeymen tailors of creating a regularity of employment for many. Goods could be produced for this trade at low points of seasonal demand, and by 1801 it was asserted that export tailors could earn 2s. 6d. a day. However, it is likely that those employed in such firms were not time-served tailors, but new, poorly skilled, 'dishonourable workers'. Such firms were also starting to penetrate the domestic market. There is a report of a case in 1808 in Glasgow involving 'a slop shop, or man mercer's hop' where ready-made clothes were being made or where a customer could select his cloth and have his suit made up at the same place, with cloth and making all included in the price.[36]

The tailors' working day was extraordinarily long. In the seventeenth century in Edinburgh the typical day was 5 a.m. until 9 p.m. at a rate of 6d. a day. Just before the Union they achieved a reduction to 8 p.m. closure, and in 1734 a 6 a.m. start was agreed. These hours included an hour for breakfast and a dinner hour at twelve noon. There had also traditionally been a morning drink provided, but by the 1730s this had disappeared and been commuted to an extra 1d. on pay. The hours actually worked clearly could fluctuate with demand and, at rush time, it was not unknown for tailors to have to work throughout the night to finish an order, though for this they would receive extra payment.[37]

At some stage, breakfast had been provided by the master, but this was being eroded during the eighteenth century. By the 1770s, some master tailors were being accused of operating what amounted to a truck system by obliging men to buy their bread and ale for breakfast at above price (2d. for a mutchkin of ale and a roll); but most journeymen had their breakfast ('ale, milk and even tea') brought in. The workplace was most likely a garret, often badly overcrowded, where tailors were liable to be 'smoored with heat in summer, and starved with cold in winter'. Some workplaces were so low that it was not possible to stand upright in them. The tailors, in their loose jackets and trousers, which they kept in the shop, sat cross-legged on tables and platforms. But they had 'their bottle and the news brought to them for their amusement'. Their day could also be broken by being sent out with deliveries, from which they could expect to get a tip, 'drink money'. It is impossible to tell how general such conditions were, but in the 1770s the journeymen gave an example of a workshop where there was so little air that the candles would not stay alight. When the men complained, holes were cut in the roof.[38]

Payment was on a daily basis, but there was no guarantee of regular work, and tailors complained that they could be dismissed after an hour's work. They were among the first trades to find themselves fully exposed to the vagaries of market forces. Because of this it is very difficult to know what the earnings of tailors were actually like at any particular period. We have the daily rates laid down by the incorporation or by the magistrates, 6d. a day in 1703, 8d. won in 1734, 1s. in 1767; and this, despite numerous struggles, remained the rate until 1787 when 1s. 3d. and then 1s. 6d. was granted. In 1793 it became 1s. 8d. These rates were maximum rates and the Incorporation on many occasions took action to ensure that employers did not pay more than these rates. There were fines, though relatively small ones, for those who broke the rules.[39] Yet it is clear that some skilled men did get more. How many got less is unknowable. Regular piecework seems to have come in in the 1770s and 1780s, for certain articles, but it was probably into the next century before it was general. Attempts by journeymen to get agreed piece rates in 1780 failed. Under either system, the constant surplus of tailors meant that there was a great deal of waiting around for work. This would be done at various eating and drinking shops and it was a system that lent itself to accusations of corruption. A journeyman tailor, looking for work, had to tip the cookshop or tavern owner to ensure that work was put his way when available. It was to try to eradicate this that journeymen set up their own club house in the 1740s.[40] But it was always a trade that was relatively easy to enter.

The pattern in shoemaking was rather different. Up until the middle of the eighteenth century, journeymen shoemakers or cordiners in Edinburgh seem to have worked at their masters' houses. By the 1780s and 1790s, however, most shoemakers were working in their own homes, a development that apparently came about as a result of pressure from the journeymen. Certainly the men resisted any attempts to change this, boycotting work from shops where a master took men 'on the premises'.[41] While such men had a nominal independence, they were dependent on a merchant manufacturer to supply them with the raw materials and to sell their product. They were what John Rule has called a 'dependent artisanry'.[42] But these were men with considerable skills which gave them a strong bargaining position and, despite their dependence, they were proud of their independence, with a 'hereditary and deeply-rooted dislike to be called a servant'.[43]

The cut-out leather would be provided by the master manufacturer, and the journeyman was expected to furnish thread and silk. For some years a separate allowance of 1d. a pair was paid for what was called 'finishing' and was understood to be for candle wax, gum and other requirements. By the 1790s, however, this had gone and it was just a fixed price for a pair of shoes. Payment was by the piece, and the shoemaker was likely to be assisted by his wife and family and, perhaps, by an apprentice.[44] It was journeymen who took on apprentices or gave training in higher skills to the 'half-bred' from the country. One attraction of home working was that masters were not allowed to have apprentices, so that it was the journeymen who retained control of entry into the trade. How much could be produced by a skilled shoemaker was always debatable. In 1790 masters claimed that if a man started at 5 a.m. he could complete a pair of boots by 8 p.m., allowing two hours for meals, and that a man of moderate skill could produce three pairs of boots and three pairs of shoes a week. On the other hand, the journeymen argued that it would take three days to make a pair of boots and a full day to make a pair of shoes. Five pairs of shoes were regarded as a good week's work. In the 1790s, payment were 4s. for boots, 1s. 4d. for men's shoes and 1s. 6d. for women's shoes. We have some information about employers' costs and prices at the same time. In 1798 a pair of men's boots would sell at £1. 10s. The costs to an employer were 14s. 2½d. on materials and 7s. 6d. on labour. On men's shoes, wages and materials were claimed to be 6s. 8½d. on shoes sold at 9s. 6d.[45]

More than in tailoring, because of the piecework pattern, there was a far from clear distinction between masters and journeymen. There were some large employers, such as Alexander Stewart in Edinburgh, who had twenty-five to thirty men in the early 1790s, but most had only one or two, and most journeymen did some jobbing work on their own account. In Glasgow, eighty master shoemakers employed 600 journeymen in 1798, though it is not known how these were distributed.[46] The work structure gave the shoemakers a relatively strong bargaining position, since they were free to move to another master to get better rates. There had been a steady improvement in the quality of work towards the end of the eighteenth century, with some journeymen going to London to learn higher skills. As yet, at the top end of the trade at any rate, there seems to have been little division of labour. But, at the same time, a cheap, ready-made trade was developing. As early in 1738 offal leather was being sent from London to Scotland to be made up into shoes to be sold to the colonies. In 1756 James Dunlop in Glasgow, making shoes to export to the plantations, had won a case brought against him by the Cordiners' Incorporation on the ground 'that the monopoly which craftsmen enjoy is singly that of vending their manufactures within the town'. By the 1790s Dunlop's shoes were selling in the domestic market.[47] Elsewhere there were concentrations of shoemakers. The parish of Duns in Berwickshire sent 300 pairs of shoes weekly to the Edinburgh and Glasgow markets in 1778. Perth too had a large shoe manufactory. In Hamilton there was a manufactory employing 120 in 1792.[48] There was much adverse comment on the quality of goods in such 'sale shops', where, it was asserted, a pair of sheepskin shoes could be passed off as finest Morocco. The pressure, however, must have been great for even quality workmen to take on work for the sale shops.[49] Three cheap shoes could be made as quickly as two bespoke ones. The advantage also of the sale shop and the export trade was that it gave the journeyman shoemaker a reasonable regularity of work since bulk orders could be made up when the quality trade was slack.

It was among the shoemakers that the Monday off-day (not Saint-Monday in Calvinist Scotland) was kept, with some taking Tuesday morning also. While this could be taken by employers as a sign of idleness, it was defended by the journeyman on the grounds that Monday was a rush day at the masters' cutting-out workshop and he might, therefore, have to stand around for a whole day before he received his supply of leather. A five-day week seems to have been quite common among shoemakers, but his might mean the occasional all-night session on a Friday to complete orders before the Saturday night deadline.[50] Like other independent workers, leisure was important to them. Certainly the accepted orthodoxy among eighteenth-century Scottish commentators was that 'necessity alone forces people to labour and every hour over and above what is absolutely necessary for gaining a livelihood will be spent in idleness'.[51] In the 1790s, when earnings rose, it was suggested that the journeymen were becoming less industrious and had reduced the length of their working week. Whether some of this was accounted for by the fact that workers were jobbing for themselves is not clear. Perhaps it was an assertion of a control over his working time that the skilled artisan felt to be essential to his status.

A third group of workers, in the building trades, were perhaps the worst victims of fluctuations caused by demand and by the weather. Slaters and masons, in particular, worked for only part of the year, though wrights had more opportunity for inside work. On the other hand, it was the workers in the building trades who were most in demand as the burghs began a rapid expansion in the second half of the eighteenth century. To build Edinburgh New Town many thousands of workers were required: an observer in 1800 calculated as many as 10,000 immigrant workers.[52] This was at a time when Glasgow, Paisley and other towns were also growing, all of whom required the skills of building workers.

It is difficult to know how far these men ought to be regarded as dependent wage earners and how far as independent craftsmen. Their position was an ambiguous one. It was an industry dominated by small craftsmen, and many master building craftsmen both employed journeymen and, themselves, took employment from architects. There clearly were some building employers by the 1760s for journeymen masons to strike against, but we know little of the scale of their enterprises.

The mason was the worker in stone and the craft consisted of two main tasks. There were the hewers who, working in narrow wooden sheds, chipped and cut the stone into shape and pattern. Secondly, there were the builders who set the stones in place. Some would have the skill to undertake both tasks, but there was a growing tendency towards specialisation. Hewing the stone was an unhealthy and unpleasant task. The sheds were unventilated and the air was filled with a fine dust. The Craigleith stone with which much of Edinburgh's New Town was built was particularly bad for its dust and few masons escaped lung disease, 'mason's trouble'. 'An old Craigleith man was done at thirty, and died at thirty-five.'[53]

There was, early in the century, no distinction between the joiner and the cabinetmaker, both going by the name of wright — further evidence of the lack of advanced craft skills. As late as 1778, in Edinburgh, carpenters, joiners and carvers were in the same trade society and involved both in housebuilding and in cabinet- and chairmaking. By the 1780s specialisation had come about and separate crafts of cabinet- and chairmakers and upholsterers had emerged, distinct from the wrights, who did joinery work. Joiners tended to be less well-paid than masons. On the other hand, demand for their services was less liable to fluctuations. There was a social division between joiner and mason: 'The latter may serve fifty masters in the course of his life-time; the former may live fifty years and only serve with one'. Joiners rarely had to tramp in search of work because of the range of tasks they undertook. It was they who built sheds for the masons and fitted the joists; it was they who set up the laths for the plasterer and formed the gutters for the plumber; it was they who put the roof 'serking' for the slaters. Joiners developed a wide knowledge of the various processes of building and, therefore, many joiners eventually set up as architects, while others became foremen, responsible for calculating costs as well as for general supervision. The joiners had to supply their own tools, costing anything from £10 to £25, which meant that they had to develop an early pattern of thrift to afford them. They were the group most attracted to self-education and improvement, recognised as 'beyond comparison the best educated, most intelligent, and most temperate of men connected with building'.

Also employed by the master joiners were the sawyers who sawed the logs of wood into planks. They worked in pairs, one below in the pit, the other balancing precariously on the wood and walking backwards. To set the different saws and to cut straight required considerable skill, but there was no regular apprenticeship. It tended to be a 'fraternity of relations', with the skill passed from father to son and only the occasional country-bred lad brought in and taught by the sawyers at a price of £5 or £6.

Plastering began to develop as a trade distinct from the wrights during the mid-eighteenth century when more skilled specialists were required for the ever more elaborate moulded ceilings coming into fashion. It was relatively well-paid, with wages of 16s. to 18s. per week in 1800 and probably substantially more for those with the necessary mixing, coating, finishing and ornamenting skills. Up until the end of the eighteenth century, the joiner provided the laths for the plasterers, but in the 1790s a new process of lathsplitting by means of large knives, rather than sawing as formerly, came in and with it the well-paid trade of lathsplitting. Wages were initially as high as 25s. to 30s.

Among the most dangerous of the building tasks were those of the slater, fitting the heavy Easdale or Ballachulish slate. Their rate was 1s. per day during most of the century, rising to 2s. only in 1800. However, the wartime boom in building pushed their earnings up to as high as 20s. or 25s. a week. Less obviously dangerous, but none the less in the long term extremely hazardous, were the trades that made use of lead. The plumbers cast ornamental cisterns and pipes in lead.

Great muscular exertion was required as well as skill to ensure that the pipes were cast without pores. Although the dangers of lead were known there was apparently considerable resistance from masters and men to the use of zinc as a substitute. For the painter, the hazard was 'painter's cholic', lead poisoning from the white lead that formed the base of paints. Then, as now, it was a seasonal demand, since the fashion was for painting, even inside, to be done in the summer months. This meant a great influx of temporary workers — 'In the busy season the trade was flooded by all the idle vagabonds in the country. Country weavers deserted their looms for three months to become painters in Edinburgh. Tobacco spinners deserted their trade to take up the brush'. Only for a very few was there work for part of the winter, grounding white lead and colours. Probably there were as few as eighty journeymen who got such work in Edinburgh c.1800, with numbers rising to 400 or 500 in the summer.

Some wrights turned to cabinetmaking and chairmaking, and some improvement in the quality of Scottish cabinetwork came in mid-century, due to the efforts of the Edinburgh firm of Trotter. Workshops were not large: a few Edinburgh cabinetmakers employed from six to ten men, with only one, Mr. Lamb, employing up to thirty. Most master cabinetmakers, however, were 'little better than journeymen themselves', employing perhaps one man and subcontracting on piecework for one of the larger employers.[54]

In 1734, Edinburgh rates were 10d. for a cabinetmaker, for a day running from six in the morning until six at night, compared with 20d. a day for a slater (these were clearly in short supply) and a merk for a mason. At this time, the Glasgow day was from 6 a.m. until 8 p.m. for wrights, and it was not until 1745 that Glasgow men succeeded in reducing it to a 6 p.m. stoppage. In 1754 cabinetmakers in Edinburgh were paid 1s. per day with apprentices on 2s. a week, and official rates remained at that level for the rest of the century. However, in part of the trade, chairmaking, piecework came in in the later decades of the century.

With urban expansion at the end of the eighteenth century and a high demand for the services of skilled workers in stone and wood, wrights and cabinetmakers made substantial gains in earnings. Edinburgh wrights in 1795 were on wages of some 12s. a week and, by 1800, it was claimed that Glasgow cabinetmakers averaged 17s. a week and with 'overwork' could reach 35s. to 2 gns., with the 'lowest journeyman' on 14s. On the other hand, the men, from the early eighteenth century, had had to invest in a chest of tools, which in the 1780s could cost as much as £30, and these tools had to be maintained and sharpened at a cost calculated at 2 gns. a year. But independent jobbing work certainly went on and one of the complaints of employers was that tools were blunted by evening work.[55]

Examples of new trades developing in the eighteenth century were printing and bookbinding. In 1740 Edinburgh had only four printing houses and bookbinding hardly existed; by the 1770s there were twenty-seven printing houses in the city, and what was to develop into one of Edinburgh's most important industries was well-established. Payment to printers seems to have been always by the piece, but, with earlier books, the rate of wages was by the dimensions of the page and a rough calculation of the number of sheets. At a later stage work was estimated by the number of inches, but by the 1760s the new generally adopted system was counting the 'ens'. This brought a substantial improvement in journeymen's earnings — some suggested a doubling of earnings from the former 10–12s. a week — and a shorter working day. A 6 a.m. to 8 or 9 p.m. day had not been uncommon before the new system came in. Afterwards their working day tended to start at 9 a.m., and still they made substantially higher earnings. However, those printers involved in printing papers for the Court of Session, among the most extensive parts of the business, could find themselves called out for night work to produce documents for the following day. Attempts to get an advance in 1785 resulted in arbitration in favour of the employers. In 1792, however, an advance was made for bookwork, and during the decade wages rose by about a sixth. By the beginning of the nineteenth century some, it was claimed, were on 25s. a week. In 1803 it was asserted by the employers that the minimum was 25s. a week and it was shown to the Court of Sessions that of a sample of twenty-three compositors (a third of those in Edinburgh) the average earnings over the previous twelve months had been £53.8.1¼d. Samples of earnings of journeymen employed by different employers were provided to the court. In 1773 the average earnings had been 14s.6d. per week, in 1791 the average was 19s.8d. and, in 1802, 18s.5d. In 1803 the Court granted the men's request for an additional 1d. per 1000.[56]

By the end of the century, printing was undoubtedly one of the best paid of crafts and the printing trade was flourishing. Fast smacks sailing daily to and from London allowed the London booksellers to use Scottish printers, making Edinburgh the most important printing centre after London. The Edinburgh compositors began pressing to be placed on the same rates as those in London. Because it was expanding so rapidly there seems to have been little restriction of entry into the trade. The need for a reasonable level of literacy imposed some limit but there was no incorporation to control the trade. Printers had to pay no apprenticeship fee and the most junior could start on 3s. a week.

The trade of bookbinding in Edinburgh was very much a product of the decades after 1780. Before then the bookbinders were few in number and engaged only in the roughest work. Wages ranged from 8s. to 10s. 6d. a week, but the work was not regular. However, presumably because of a shortage of skills, some skilled men were kept on regular wages, with the proviso that they work overtime when required, without payment.[57] With a dramatic growth in demand and a new elegance in bindings in the 1790s the journeymen now found a new pressure of work. New work patterns began to emerge as boys and girls were brought in to the lightest parts of the work, while the heavy work of beating the leather and the pages with great 16lb. hammers was left to the men. This division of labour led to an intensification of hard work for the men, and new technology led to a deterioration in work conditions. The leather work had to be undertaken in damp cellars, to keep the hides flexible; the gilding work necessitated that there should be no dust flying around, so windows and doors had to be kept closed. To get the blue mottled lining pages, indigo and sulphuric acid had to be used, which could result in men getting sprinkled or burned with a fine shower of acid. To give a gloss to the leather, serum of blood and egg glaze was used, which if kept too long went putrid. Information on wage rates is sparse; but, in 1811, Edinburgh journeymen claimed that the average wage rate was 16s to 17s. 6d. a week, compared with the London rate of 30s. At the same time, however, the president of the master bookbinders claimed that, since 1805, wages had risen from 18s. to 23s. a week, with some on 25s. and 26s.[58]

By far the largest group of tradesmen were in the textile industry, first in coarse wool and linen and then, at the end of the century, in cotton. The Scottish woollen industry had fought a nearly hopeless battle against English competition, but a coarse woollen industry did survive. By 1733 Kilmarnock, Stirling, Aberdeen, Edinburgh, Musselburgh and Galashiels were all significant centres for coarse woollen goods, at least some of which were being exported. By the 1760s Stirling was reported to have 'many hundreds' of looms.[59] But linen was the main cloth from the 1730s until the 1790s, with almost every parish in the country involved in its production. After the industry had been badly undermined by English competition in the aftermath of the Union, the state set out to encourage linen production through the Board of Manufacturers from 1727. Foreign workers with skills in weaving and spinning were encouraged to come to Scotland. Spinning schools were set up in Edinburgh, Perth and Glasgow and Dutch weavers gave instruction in the operation of Dutch looms.

The preparatory process of the flax from steeping and drying through to heckling required sophisticated processes in a lint mill. these were owned by merchants or manufacturers who either imported or bought home-produced flax for dressing. The spinners and weavers were in the farms, villages and towns throughout Scotland. In rural areas the manufacture of linen was a by-employment of country work, with the whole family involved in the spinning and weaving processes. In the towns and villages it was generally a full-time occupation, though sometimes carried out alongside other crafts. The finishing processes of bleaching, printing and dyeing again required substantial capital and were in the hands of merchant capitalists. Capitalist manufacturers, therefore, dominated both ends of the process and soon moved to organise the spinning and weaving parts. Merchants provided the yarn and bought back the finished cloth. Spinning came under their control when during the 1730s and 1740s manufacturers' agents, keen to expand output for both home and export markets, began to tie spinners in the rural areas to themselves. How far this brought a challenge to the domination of the occupation by women is difficult to assess, but undoubtedly spinners lost an earlier independence, when they got caught up in debt to a particular dealer who would give them credit.[60] However, demand for their services was high since five spinners were needed to supply the yarn for a single handloom weaver. Not surprisingly, it was in spinning that pressure for the invention of labour-saving machinery was felt. By the 1780s, the spinning jenny was in widespread use.

Handloom weaving was a male task, with the weaver sitting at the loom, thumping the treadles with his foot to separate the warp threads and throwing the shuttle through. The work patterns of weavers altered during the century from being a communal occupation to being that of a man working on his own. To produce a broad cloth early in the century, two weavers were necessary, sitting side by side throwing the shuttle through the web from one to the other. A third person was necessary as cord-drawer. Gradually, as a result of technical improvements, especially the arrival of the flying shuttle from mid-century, the second weaver was no longer necessary and, except when patterns were difficult, the cord-drawer too could be eliminated.

The work of the handloom weaver was probably a tedious rather than a physically exhausting task, but it was never a healthy one. Not only did it involve long hours on a narrow wooden bench, but, to prevent threads breaking, the workroom had to be kept cool and damp with an earth floor. There was always a strong, distinctive odour about the place, the 'waugh' from the oil in the flax and from the oatmeal or potato flour coating put on the threads. A great deal of the weaver's time would be taken up with tasks other than weaving, such as beaming the warps of new webs and dressing them with paste to keep them moist.

Weaving as a craft had long existed in the Scottish burghs, regulated by incorporations which imposed an apprenticeship structure of five years followed by two years as a journeyman before a weaver could set up on his own. Its eighteenth-century expansion was in the Lowland counties, from Angus and Fife in the East through Perthshire to Lanarkshire, Renfrewshire and Ayrshire in the West. In 1726 it was claimed that there were 2000 looms covered by the Incorporation in Glasgow alone. From the 1740s growth was spectacular and by the 1770s Glasgow, the largest linen centre, had over 4,000 working looms, Dundee 2,800, Paisley 1,360, and Perth, Dunfermline and Montrose over 300 each. By the 1780s there were something like 25,000 handloom weavers in Scotland and nearly 60,000 by the end of the century. They worked in wool, from the stocking makers of the North-East to the blanket, flannel and serge makers of the Borders to the carpet weavers of the Lothians; they worked in linen almost everywhere, but towards the end of the century becoming concentrated especially in Dundee and Fife in the East. From the 1750s Paisley, which had developed as an important fine linen centre, began to specialise in silk gauze manufacturing, with about 5000 weavers involved in it at its peak in 1784. By 1776 it was claimed that over 12,000 people were employed in Paisley in linen and silk manufacture. Much was to change, however, from the 1780s with the coming of cotton. Within a decade it took over as the main Scottish textile. Of the 60,000 handloom weavers at the beginning of the nineteenth century, 50,000 were in cotton, six times more than eight years before. There were new workers, some formerly part-time country workers, many others the unemployed or the displaced from other trades. Plain weaving involved very little skill. It could be picked up in about three weeks, so there was potentially almost no limit to the expansion of the labour force. As a result, the weaver had very little bargaining leverage against an employer.[61]

There were various kinds of working relationships. There were master weavers with their own loom in their own cottage buying their own yarn and selling either to their own customers or in the local marketplace. There were journeymen weavers working alongside a small master in his workshop, renting their looms and getting the work from the master, who could get a third or even a half of the journeyman's earnings. There were others who would rent a loom from a large manufacturer, would receive his yarn and sell back to him. Yet others might work in weaving factories of anything from twenty to seventy looms. These had begun to develop in the 1740s in linen. Most, however, by the second half of the century were part of a putting-out system centred on a growing number of merchant/manufacturers based in Glasgow or Paisley, who would supply the yarn to weavers owning their own looms and working at home. They would receive back the finished cloth at an agreed date. The price would have been agreed in advance on the basis of individual bargains between the weaver and the merchant/manufacturer's agent and an advance payment would be given. There was always room for dispute, when the finished cloth was returned, over the quality of work or the amount of material used. The nature of the process of production made it impossible to calculate or to account for all the raw material. It was very difficult to check that all the yarn had been used and accusations of embezzlement were widespread.[62]

With new mixtures of material coming in, merchants were concerned to ensure regularity of supplies and, therefore, to have their own known and reliable weavers. On the other side, independent weavers could not afford the risks involved in experimenting with the ranges of new mixtures now available, and, therefore, they were pushed into dependence upon a specific agent. All these pressures led to a loss of independence for many weavers. The more that weaving became a full-time occupation, the more the weaver was likely to be concerned with maintaining good relations with the manufacturer's agent. Even the customer weavers, clinging to their independence (and these were still around in the 1790s), might become tied to particular merchants, and it was easy to get caught in a circle of debt which brought growing dependency. A. J. Durie, in his study of *The Scottish Linen Industry*, quotes a comment from 1747:

> The people who deal this way keep the poorer Sort very Dependent on them. They get or give them Credite for Meal Butter Cheese Hardfish Coals Lint Lintseed and such like things And take their payment in Small Sums of every Web or small parcell of Yarn they bring them. By this means the poorer Sort are Thirled perhaps for Life to the Richer Sort And dare Dispose of nothing they have to Sell but to them only. The Richer Sort Run risque and sometimes must lose by this Credite they give But then I suppose the profite they have on the things they furnish will do no more than Satisfies them for the Interest of that part of their Stock so laid out and make up that Loss too. Besides the advantage they have in point of Trade which is the main thing they have in view in trusting these poor people.[63]

As Stephen Marglin has provocatively argued, advance payments 'were to the capitalist what free samples of heroin are to the pusher'.[64]

These who clung to a kind of independence were often among the poorest, dependent upon demand and often unable to buy yarn in the open market, particularly in the Spring and Summer when yarn was in short supply and expensive because of other demands on the time of the spinners (like the harvest). Not until Autumn and Winter was there a steadier demand for the weavers' services.

The desire to increase output further led to the removal of the remaining restrictive powers of weavers' incorporations in 1751 when 'every Weaver or Manufacturer of Linen, Flaxen or Hempen cloth. [was free] . . . to exercise the said respective Trades within any City, Town, Corporation or Burgh in Scotland without any let or hindrance . . . and without being chargeable or charged with payment of any Entry-Money'. This had the desired effect of bringing many new peoples into weaving. By 1778 there were 4000 looms in Glasgow and its immediate neighbourhood, with 500 of them in Anderston alone. Paisley, which had about 100 looms at the Union, had 1,360 in linen by 1778.[65] The coming of cotton and with it the movement of spinning into factories brought a great demand for handloom weavers' services in the late 1780s and in the 1790s. This was the so-called 'Golden Age' of the handloom weavers when, it was reputed, they could earn 25s. or 30s. a week. As Norman Murray has warned, such claims need to be treated with some caution. By no means all could attain such levels, and anything near that was likely to be for a very short period. It was a trade bedevilled by seasonal fluctuations and by cyclical fluctuations. An increasingly idealised 'Golden Age' grew in the telling as it faded into the past in the second and third decades of the nineteenth century. It was useful to be able to paint the contrasts from comfort to penury, but the reality of the late eighteenth century seems likely to have been less 'golden' for most. None the less, weavers at this time were clearly amongst the best-paid groups and attracting increasing numbers.[66]

Details of the work patterns of other craftsmen are harder to come by. In the seventeenth century hours of 5 a.m. to 9 p.m. seem to have been not uncommon among most. By the 1730s, 6 a.m. was a usual starting point, and although tailors were still working through until 8 p.m., and from 7 till 10 in Aberdeen, other trades were moving towards a 6 p.m. or 7 p.m. finish. By the end of the century, the official tailors' day was 6 till 8, but this was recognised as exceptionally long. An enquiry in Edinburgh in 1812 found that a ten-hour day, exclusive of two hours for meal breaks, was common among blacksmiths, coppersmiths, ironfounders, brass founders, marble cutters, carpenters, coachmakers, joiners, cabinetmakers, coopers, turners, millwrights, lathsplitters, plumbers, tanners, plasterers, printers, cutlers, silversmiths, jewellers, carvers and gilders, clock-makers and musical instrument makers. An eleven-hour day was typical among tinsmiths, japanners, gunsmiths, saddlers, wireworkers and confectioners. The long twelve-hour day of 6 till 8 was confined to brushmakers, trunkmakers, dyers and tailors. Such hours were those normally performed in periods of regular work, but most trades were subject to underemployment or unemployment at different times.[67] Holidays as something separate from work were hardly known, though it was common for most to take a day or two at the old New Year or at a fair day.

Shorter hours in themselves must have meant some improvement in the quality of life for tradesmen, though greater insecurity, greater fluctuations in earnings, loss of status, and heavier work patterns, for some at least, countered improvements. For what they are worth, some scattered data on money wages are brought together in Table 1, though how to interpret the available figures is not very clear. In some cases these are declared averages, in others they are legally imposed maxima, in yet others they are random statements by one group of what they believe another is earning. How typical these were of earnings is impossible to say. There was hardly any change in rates in the first half of the century, at a time when the prices of oatmeal and bere, the basic cereals, remained fairly constant, although there were rising prices in wheat and, as a result of taxation, in beer and salt.[68] The tailors and the wrights were two groups that made gains in the 1760s and 1770s and the tailors had some rise in earnings in the 1780s, again a time when meal prices rose sharply. It is only with the more extensive figures available for the 1790s that one can see clear rises in earnings. From the 1790s to 1812 for most craftsmen there were increases, although money wage increases probably did not exceed price rises. For all of the century, wages in Scotland were substantially lower than those in England. They were perhaps only half the London rates: in 1751, when Scottish tailors were on a fixed 1s. a day, those in London were on a fixed 2s. for half the year and 2s.6d. for the other half, with the Scots working an extra hour.[69] Dorothy George suggests that the 'common wages of a journeyman' in the less well-paid trades up to about 1765 were 12s. to 14s.[70] Even printers in Edinburgh barely made the lower of these figures. Compared with Lancashire too, Scottish wages were clearly lower. Towards the end of the century and at the beginning of the nineteenth that gap was probably narrowing, but they were still a long way behind the 25s. a week that London saddlers — amongst the lowest paid of artisans — could earn in 1811 or the 48s. of a London compositor in 1805.[71] Some, at any rate, made gains even if only short-term ones. The development of urban trades gave opportunities for those who drifted from the rural areas in Scotland, being 'pulled' by opportunity much more than being 'pushed' by necessity into towns.

The eighteenth century brought a massive transformation in the life of the urban craftsmen. It brought the transformation of numbers, as trades expanded and as control of entry weakened. The case of the weavers is the most spectacular and best known, but transformation too was found in most other skilled crafts. To give one further example, take the case of those covered by the term 'hammermen'. In the last twenty-five years of the seventeenth century, the average number of new journeymen being registered by the Glasgow Incorporation each year was five; in the next twenty-five years the average was ten; in the next it was twenty; and in the last quarter of the eighteenth century it was twenty-six per year.[72] Even that is an underestimation, since increasingly large numbers were probably not registered. Such figures, repeated over other trades, meant a transformation of the workplace and the community within which the tradesman operated.

There was a transformation too, in status and security. To be a tradesman in 1700 meant something clear and understandable to those around. At the end of the century it could mean anything from the most skilled of mechanics to the most

TABLE 1. WAGE RATES*

	1703	1716	1720	1734	1750	1757	1760	1767	1770
Tailors	3s. 6d.[2]	1s. 9d. +	2s.[2]	4s.[1]		4s.[1]	4s.[2] –6s.[1]	6s.[1]–9s.[3]	6s.–7s. 6d.[1]
Masons	6s. 6d.[1]	6s. 6d.[1]		6s. 6d.[1]			5s.–6s. 6d.[1]		
Wrights	6s.	6s.		5s.[1]					
Slaters				10s.[2]					
Printers					10s.–12s.[1]				
Weavers				8s.[1]			10s.[3]		
Labourers		3s.[6]		6s. 6d.		3s. 6d.[5]	4s. 6d.–5s.[5]		

	1776	1778	1782	1787	1790	1792	1793	1796	1797
Tailors	7s.[3]	6s.[1]		7s 6d.[3]–9s.			10s.[1]	6s.–8s.[7]	7s. 6d.[2]
Shoemakers	9s.–12s.[1]			9s.–12s.[1]			9s.–12s.[3]	5s.–10s.[7]	
Masons				10s.–12s.			10s.–12d.[3]	9s.–10s. 6d.[7]	8s.–11s.[3]
Wrights	6s.–9s.[1]						8s.–12s.[1,3]	9s.–10s. 6d.[7]	
Printers						25s.[1]	10s. 6d.–18s.[3]		
Bookbinders						7s.–10s. 6d.[3]	8s.–10s. 6d.[1]		
Weavers					13s.–14s.		12s.–14s.		
Labourers	5s.	4s.–5s.	5s.		6s. 6d.–7s. 6d.[3]		6s.[4]		6s.–7s.[7]
Colliers	12s.								

	1798	1799	1801	1804	1810	1812	1820	1825	1838
Tailors			15s.[1]	30s.[1]		16s.[3]	20s.[3]		20s.
Shoemakers		12s.–18s.[1]		21s.–30s.[1]		18s.[3]			11s. 6d.
Slaters						20s.[3]		18s.[3]	19s.[3]
Masons					22s.[3]	15s.[3]	18s.[3]	18s.[3]	19s.[3]
Cabinetmakers						16s.–18s.[3]		18s.[3]	18s.–20s.[3]
Printers				15s.–18s.[1]		16s.–17s. 6d.[1]			
Bookbinders				15s.–18s.[1]	16s.–17s. 6d.[1]			18s.–20s.[1]	
Weavers	16s.–18s.					8s.	4s.–5s.[3]		
Shipwrights	14s.–16s.								
Labourers			9s.–12s.[1]			12s.[3]	7s. 6d.[3]		12s.
Colliers		24s.[6]		9s.–12s.			21s.[6]	20s.–25s.[6]	20s.–25s.[6]
Cottonspinners					21s.–27s.[3]		21s.–27s.[3]	20s. 2d.	28s. 10d.

1. Edinburgh 2. Aberdeen 3. Glasgow 4. Dundee 5. Midlothian 6. Lanarkshire 7. Kirkcaldy

*To allow for some means of comparison, day rates have been converted to weekly rates, assuming six days' full work. Average wages were likely to have been substantially less. No account is taken of winter reductions which were general in the building trades.

unskilled of weavers. At the beginning of the century, for most, the road from apprentice to master was reasonably clearly defined. At the end of it it was an overgrown path, barely visible to most. Only a tiny minority could expect to make the switch from journeyman to master. Workshops were becoming larger; the capital needed to set up in business was becoming greater; the divisions between the employer and the worker were becoming clearly marked. The journeyman craftsman was not, then, someone who could be expected to move up the social hierarchy, someone who could reasonably expect to end up in the Incorporation and even in the town council. Most, by the end of the century, were stuck as wage earners. This must have had major implications for how the tradesman perceived himself and was perceived by his contemporaries. Professor Smout, summing up the role of the craftsmen, in their tightly regulated world of incorporations in the seventeenth century, writes, 'You could not rise very high as a hammerman or a cordiner, but neither could you fall too low'.[73] A century later, the kind of security that craftsmanship bestowed no longer applied to most tradesmen.

How much of a transformation there was in life away from the workplace probably depended upon the particular trade. The world of the poetry-writing, book-reading, disputatious handloom weaver may well have been largely mythical and, certainly, whenever it was, it was short-lived and confined to an exceptional few. The rate of growth of the craft was rapid and the years of prosperity were very brief. However, in the small weavers' village there was probably a lively fellowship, based on long acquaintance and an established community. But in the rapidly growing towns like Glasgow, Paisley or Edinburgh, filling with new people, fellowship was likely to have been markedly absent in a struggle for survival and in competition for jobs and accommodation. To compensate, however, journeymen's hours were shorter. The extraordinary fifteen or sixteen-hour days which were acceptable in the seventeenth century grew shorter in the eighteenth, except for the self-employed or the piecework home worker. For many there was more time in the evenings for self-improvement or for conviviality, depending on taste. There were more opportunities for both. Also, the new conditions brought new responses, in particular new organisations, by which tradesmen sought to control and regulate their changing world.

3
The Emergence of Organisation

There is no definite date when journeymen came to see themselves as a group distinct from their employers. Conflict between employer and employed had, after all, always existed; there was no way that the tensions of the workplace and of work relationships could always be avoided. But the formalisation of this tension in organisational form comes in the eighteenth century with a widening of the gap between master and man. The process of separation was a gradual one, over many decades, and *when* it took place varied from craft to craft. Possibly the initiative came from masters, rather than from journeymen. Those masters who had pretensions to upward social mobility were likely to separate themselves from their journeymen and begin to abandon the traditional meeting places of the craft for their social activities, and to move away to new areas for their residence. On the other hand, many other small masters, who continued to work alongside their journeymen and were in that indefinite social world between master and journeymen, continued to live near their journeymen and to associate with them in their clubs.

Informal, spontaneous action, bursting forth to express some grievance, was there from earliest times, whenever a group of workers had a common employer. One finds in the seventeenth century complaints that farm servants were refusing to be hired 'without great and extraordinary wages'.[1] The workers at the Newmills manufactory in the seventeenth century were notoriously unruly.[2] Colliers and salters were a group who had to be handled with great care if there were not to be disputes, and there were complaints in 1674 that they were not just demanding 'exhorbitant wages' but were having 'the intolerable impudence to refuse to work more than four days in every six'.[3] Attempts to alter customary work patterns (of which the issue of the working week was a central part) could bring concerted resistance, generally by passive resistance, a stubborn refusal to obey new rules, or by community pressure on the overseer or manager. Occasionally a strike would be resorted to.[4] Such activities for industrial purposes were probably short-lived and spontaneous, often formalised, traditional protests against the breakdown of reciprocal arrangements, though natural leaders were likely to emerge, and there is a very fine line between organisation and spontaneity which is not always easy to recognise. Also, as William Reddy has argued, employers and authorities tended to look for leaders and, perhaps, tended to exaggerate the extent of organisation among their discontented workers. They disliked spontaneous outbursts of agitation. These could suggest that the men had some 'just' grievance. It was easier to see such disputes as the work of a few malcontents.[5]

It is doubtful if town workers learned much from the earlier experiences of either colliers or factory workers. Colliers, after all, who had perhaps most industrial experience to offer, were an outcast group whose pattern of life would have been regarded as hardly relevant to that of the artisan. It was in the eighteenth century that trade societies appeared among urban craft journeymen in Scotland, or, at any rate, that the records of such activities appear. But it is important to bear in mind H. A. Turner's point that

> people of the same occupation, who are regularly brought together in the same workplace or town, may acknowledge regular leaders, develop customs of workplace regulation and systematic 'trade practices', and can produce a disciplined observance of the latter without embedding these procedures in formal records.

There seems a possibility that unwritten, but none the less well-known customs, regulations and trade practices could have existed among groups of journeymen in certain trades before the eighteenth century. Dundee journeymen wrights, for example, in 1695 were breaking from the traditional contracts and insisting on being employed on a weekly or at most twenty-day basis. Such concerted action required organisation.[6] But given the fact that the numbers of journeymen were very small, even in Edinburgh, before the eighteenth century, it is likely to have been rare.

By the early eighteenth century, however, the towns, and particularly Edinburgh, the fastest-growing of them, were drawing in people in ever-increasing numbers from the rural areas. This brought challenges to the position of both masters and journeymen. Masters were faced with newcomers who were prepared to operate outside the Incorporation and to ignore regulations on the workforce, while journeymen faced the threat of a crowded labour market. Tailors were particularly badly hit. According to Patrick Lindesay, 'Our ordinary people have been long in use to breed their children to be tailors because they did it all at small expense'.[7] It is not surprising, therefore, to find the first signs of journeymen's organisation among the tailors.

There was trouble among the Edinburgh tailors in 1702 at the time of the death of William III, when troops had to be used to clear the streets and to force them back to work. The men were, however, successful in getting two hours cut off their working day and a rise in their wages of 2d. at day, from 5d. to 7d. 'with drink'.[8] In 1704 the Incorporation of Edinburgh Tailors, together with the separate Incorporations for the Canongate, Portsburgh and Potterow, petitioned the Town Council about the 'caballs and combinationes' among the journeymen tailors who had used the occasion of the sitting of Parliament and of public mournings, when there was a high and rushed demand for new clothes, to strike work to push up their wages. They were also concerned at incomers setting up in business on their own. The Town Council ruled that all tailors coming into the town had to produce a certificate of their honesty and their landlords had to register their names with the deacon of the trade.[9]

Just as the merchant guilds over the centuries had used their legislative powers in the Town Council to control and regulate generations of independent craftsmen, so now craftsmen used the influence of their incorporations on the Town Council to curb and control the activities of their journeymen. What were resented particularly were the attempts by journeymen to organise and assert a common identity, separate from that of their masters' incorporation.

One of the traditional roles of a craft guild was to look after the poor and the destitute among its members. The sums paid on taking up apprenticeships went for this purpose. What this actually meant in practice in the eighteenth century was not always apparent. Presumably the aid went to employers who got into difficulties or to the widows of masters rather than to a journeyman who had fallen on hard times. Indeed it may have been the failure of the Incorporations to carry out their charitable tasks that forced journeymen to look to their own devices. One assertion of independence, one sign that an attempt was being made to break free from a position of subordination to the masters was the emergence of charity boxes organised by the journeymen themselves. Among the tailors of the Canongate in Edinburgh, a journeymen's aid society was formed in 1714, again a year in which the death of Queen Anne and the new accession brought a high demand for new clothes and accompanying opportunities for journeymen. Initially, the decision to establish a journeymen's charity box received some encouragement from master tailors and an agreement was drawn up by which journeymen contributed three pence per quarter. It soon went beyond the Canongate and was opened to any journeyman tailor 'in and about Edinburgh'. Calling itself 'the Charitable Concert of Journeymen Taylors', it received the necessary approval of the Town Council. Although some master tailors were involved in administering the organisation's funds, by no means all of the Incorporation's members approved of the new body. A complaint was made, by some, to the magistrates, but these ruled that 'there was no law against charity' and that the 'Concert' was quite legal.[10]

Charitable 'boxes' are to be found elsewhere before this time. The Burgh of Queensferry had had one among the tailors from 1663, whereby all journeymen had to pay 30s. Scots to the 'Box' when they were hired, after having given eight days' trial to their employer.[11] The payment would be made by the master, but was deducted from the journeymen's wages. Something similar was devised in Saltcoats in Ayrshire in 1725 when some thirty-three tradesmen from different crafts devised what was called a 'constitutional bond', by which all journeymen and apprentices coming into the town from the rural areas had to pay a sum into the fund. Masters seem to have agreed not to employ anyone who did not subscribe.[12] But these were probably little more than extensions of the incorporation. The 'Charitable Concert' from the start was more independent.

In Edinburgh itself, the journeymen shoemakers followed the example of the tailors almost immediately, and in the years of depression in 1725–1727 the journeymen skinners and a number of other crafts set up charity boxes.[13] All such 'boxes' required sanction from the Town Council, and the usual stipulation before this would be given was that the meetings should be supervised by two 'proper persons', in other words by members of the relevant incorporation. What many masters feared, with justification, was that journeymen's charitable organisations could easily become the focus of industrial organisations and centres of discontent.

Clearly there were always masters who suspected any attempts of journeymen to break from what they saw as the correct position of subordination.

The death of George I in June 1727 once again gave the Edinburgh tailors an opportunity to press for wage increases, and it was this move that determined the Incorporation to take action. With trade generally depressed, apart from the short-lived boom created by the mourning, the masters were in the mood to resist. The charity box, it was claimed, now amounting to £1400–£1500 Scots, was a fund 'out of which refractory persons might be maintained, till their masters should be compelled to yield to their demands, however extravagant they might be'. At the request of the Incorporation, the magistrates seized some thirty striking tailors and had them incarcerated in the Tolbooth and in the House of Correction, charged with sedition.[14] They were ordered to be whipped through the streets. Such treatment of respectable craftsmen was unprecedented and reflects a new view of journeymen as a dangerous group that had to be controlled, not as future equals. It stirred deep resentment among the journeymen that they should be treated no differently from common criminals. In fact the whipping was not carried out and, instead, they were fined 100 merks and ordered back to work.[15] The Incorporation wanted to get control of the Charitable Concert, which they regarded as the heart of the journeymen's organisation, and they proposed a new Council of Managers, made up of six journeymen and six masters, plus the Deacon. The proposal was to be sweetened with a gift of at least 100 merks to the fund which would be formalised by being sanctioned by an Act of the Town Council.[16]

At least a section of the existing managing committee does seem to have been attracted by the proposal, but when it was presented to the wider membership for approval, it was rejected. The means of rejection was an extraordinary *Protestation*, in which the opponents of the new scheme warned that the new structure would allow the masters and the Town Council to control the journeymen's organisation. This would prevent journeymen tailors raising their wages 'when Scotland shall be restored to its Liberty'.[17] It appealed 'to the first lawful, free and independent Convention of Estates, or Parliament of Scotland; and in the mean Time, while such cannot be had, we appeal to all the unbyassed, unprejudged and rational part of Mankind, of Justice in this matter'. It is not necessary to see such language as indicating a deep nationalism; but one should bear in mind that the Union was never popular in Edinburgh. After all, the City lost more than most: not just the dignity of a real capital city, but the trade that went with it. Tailors must have been a craft that was particularly badly hit as the nation's legislators *and* their wives *and* their servants found their new fashions in London. Clearly in the memory of the tailors, 1707 and its associations were bad. The objectors went on to argue that the presence of a member of the Town Council would 'Threaten, Hinder, or Overaw the free members of the Concert'. With the Incorporation's proposals rejected, the masters now took more drastic action when, on 9 January 1728, 'under cloud of night', the Deacon of the Tailors' Incorporation, together with other masters, and a number of town officers, forcibly entered the house of Patrick MacDuff, the overseer of the Concert, and seized the box and arrested MacDuff. MacDuff was held for a time and then released, but he took the issue to the Court of Session, charging the Deacon with having been accessory to a riot. He seems to have been at least partially successful since the Deacon was held responsible for the costs of the case.[18]

Among the Edinburgh Tailors, combination for trade purposes probably existed before the mutual-aid organisations, but this was unusual. In most other crafts mutual aid came first. An Association of Journeymen Shoemakers of Edinburgh dated from 1727, open to anyone who was under the age of 36, 'brought up to the said trade' and a Protestant. The entry fee was 7s.6d. and the subscription was 1s.3d. per quarter.[19] The shipwrights of Leith had a society for relief of those 'who are sick or infirm' dating from 1731.[20] A similar body was formed by the journeymen tailors, staymakers and upholsterers in Glasgow in November 1732 to raise a fund by voluntary subscription 'to be applied for the relief for such of them and their widows, as should happen to be reduced to indigent circumstances'. It provided 3s. per week to a 'bedfast member' and 2s. a week to one ill, but not 'bedfast'. A widow could get no more than 5d. per quarter and a superannuated member 1s. weekly. Like other groups, the Glasgow tailors went out of their way to assert their organisation's independence of the masters, through modelling themselves on them. Elections for president or 'praeses' were held 'upon the day of the annual election of the Deacons of the Incorporated Trades of Glasgow', but 'no Freeman Taylor, of whatever denomination, shall be praeses'. Two freemen were, however, on the board of management.[21] All of these bodies reveal a search for security that neither the employer and his incorporation nor the state was providing. They indicate the sense of mutual dependence that journeymen were developing. Most important of all, however, they were also vital training grounds in organisation and procedures and in the disciplines of self-rule that were to be important for the future.

Signs of activity were to be found in 1732 among the wrights and coopers in Glasgow and in Aberdeen where hours were longer and wages lower than in Edinburgh. There were complaints to the Aberdeen Incorporation about journeymen 'entering into signed associations among themselves whereby they become bound to one another under penalty not to continue in their master's service or to work after seven o'clock at night contrary to the usual practice'. The Incorporation got the Town Council to approve an act banning journeymen's meetings, reaffirming hours of work from six in the morning until eight at night and agreeing that no master should employ journeymen who had been dismissed for breach of the ordinance.[22]

As Dobson found, in his study of several hundred eighteenth-century strikes, the most common cause of dispute was wages. In 1734, 'at the time of the last election of peers', most of the three hundred or so Edinburgh tailors went on strike for an increase. In other words, the journeymen's actions were not purely defensive, they were seizing the opportunity of moments of high demand to improve their rates. They had first collected money and petitioned the Incorporation. Having been rebuffed, they then applied to the magistrates. The journeymen were seeking 13d. a day, while the masters had agreed among themselves not to pay more than 8d. 'on pain of [a fine of] £20 Scots'.[23] The journeymen compared their wages with those of slaters at 20d. a day, weavers at 16d., masons a merk and wrights 10d. The tailors, it was claimed, worked fourteen hours a day, 6 a.m. to 8 p.m., while the others worked for only twelve hours. The magistrates rejected this comparison, on the grounds that building workers worked for only part of the year, though the tailors themselves could argue that for much of the year they too had little work. The tailors' advocate also put the case for comparison with London, where there had been legal regulation of tailors' wages since 1720. Wages there were 2s. per day for a quarter of the year and 20d. for the rest of it. In Edinburgh, he argued, where prices were about half those in London, tailors ought to get at least 1s. per day for a quarter and 10d. for the rest of the year, plus breakfast.[24]

While this was being debated, the Incorporation of Tailors made complaint to the Justices of the Peace against some forty tailors for combination. Six were eventually brought to trial, John Vert, James Edward, Hugh Paterson, John Gray, James Hay and John Pirie, and they were sent to the House of Correction until they found caution money and agreed to work at the usual rates, which the magistrates found to be 'adequate to the prices which the masters exercise at present'. Others apprehended were fined 100 merks. The six imprisoned applied to the Court of Session for a Bill of Suspension, that is a rebuttal of the magistrates' ruling. They argued that the higher court should set the wages at a merk a day, though the magistrates argued that this was a function only for the JPs. The Lord Ordinary, Lord Coupar, allowed a debate on the issue of (a) whether the Court was competent to give redress, (b) whether confinement in the House of Correction was lawful and just and (c) whether the magistrates' finding that the wages were adequate 'was equal and just', or if it ought to be overruled and higher wages granted. On the last it was claimed that 'in other trades the master is content with 40 pennies Scots [3⅓d.] above what the journeymen earns', but in tailoring a master could get £6 Scots (10s.) for a suit that a journeyman could make in a week, that is, more than twice what a journeyman could hope to earn. Lord Coupar advised that the journeymen return to the JPs and agree a rule with them for future guidance of the relationship between wages and profits. The journeymen did not feel that this gave adequate redress for their time in prison and they petitioned the inner court against the judgement. They asserted their right to leave work:

> The petitioners are free subjects who gained a narrow subsistence by working to such masters as they did agree for certain wages per diem so long as they should continue to serve them. But that we should remain and abide in their service for life, or for any determinate time to come, we were under no obligation either by law or by practice and therefore we were at liberty to leave their service as soon as we found by experience that the wages we formerly wrought for, were not sufficient to support us.

This was especially so, it was argued, since, until then, the JPs had not fixed tailors' wages and, therefore, customary wages could not be retrospectively applied.[25] The outcome of this petition is not known.

The problem of all crafts, but perhaps especially of the tailors, was the pressure of numbers coming into a rapidly expanding town. The elementary skills of tailoring could be picked up in any rural community, and it was a trade to which any young migrant to the city could readily turn his — or her — hand. To remedy this state of affairs the Edinburgh journeymen tailors set up a house of call in 1742, when, after two or three years of bad harvests, the exodus from rural areas was probably particularly bad. Up until then the tailors were dependent upon landlords 'in cook shops and ale houses' to provide information about available work. Clubs were associated with these ale houses in some cases and they could be subsidised by the masters, though 5s. might be charged for registration. The idea was that the club landlord would actually go in search of journeymen when work was available, but the belief was that the journeymen who spent the most money had the best chance of getting news of a job even if they were the 'greatest bunglers just from the country'. It was intended that the new house of call, under the control of journeymen, would put some restriction on who should actually register for work, by having a test that the applicant could make a suit of clothes properly.[26] If this were ever achieved, it soon broke down.

The house was run by an old member of the craft, in 1742 a man named Reat. He received payment of 1d. per week from the journeymen, and there were also payments from all new entrants (1s.6d. by 1777) which would cover the cost of candles, books and paying the clerk to keep the minutes. A friendly-society side also developed through the house of call, with new entrants having to pay 5d. into the charity box from which a sick member could get 4s. a week, plus his funeral costs and 20s. for his widow. After Reat's death a split developed in the organisation, with one group continuing to associate with Reat's widow, while a group of seceders set up a separate house under one William Urquhart. When Urquhart gave up in 1757, a single house was again established under Robert Williamson, who remained as call master until 1773. On his death there were again two competing candidates, James Ross and James Tait, and two houses were again established. Ross's house soon gave up and Tait's was the sole house until 1793 when he retired. James Liston was appointed his successor, but rival call houses were in operation between 1793 and 1796 before a single house was again established under William Hossack in Blackfriars' Wynd.[27]

The Edinburgh tailors remained an active group. Twenty-one were indicted in 1748 for striking for an advance. They were sentenced to forty-eight hours in the Tolbooth and to remain there until £6.6s. in damages and expenses had been paid and they 'severally enact themselves not to be guilty of such practices in time coming, on pain of being confined to the house of correction for three months, and afterwards banished from the city for ever'.[28] According to F. W. Galton, 'this action resulted in the collapse of the journeymen's organisation', but, in fact, this was far from the case.[29] If it deterred the tailors at all, it was only briefly.

By the middle of the century other towns in Scotland and the crafts in them were feeling the impact of population pressure. But alongside this phenomenon there was, as the economy began to expand, a growing demand for skilled labour which greatly strengthened the bargaining position of workers with mechanised skills. In

1748 John Calhoun and some thirty Glasgow hammermen were petitioning the Incorporation and the Trades House for a 7 p.m. stoppage of work on the grounds that their working day was too long and hard, particularly since they were only allowed time during the day to eat their food and no more, and that it deprived them of the opportunity of self-improvement by going to school in the evening. The employers asserted that the time would be used for 'vaguing on the Streets or in Tippling and Drinking' and denounced the men for having 'most illegally dared and taken upon them to erect themselves into a sort of society and elect a deacon and masters and make laws and rules to themselves repugnant to the laws and acts of the trade and to exact and levy fines and contributions from themselves'. The petition was rejected and the Incorporation made it an offence against the laws of the trade to reduce hours except where a workman was going to evening school.[30]

One of the arguments used against the demand for shortening the working day was that it would lead to the extension of evening work by journeymen. There were numerous complaints from members of the incorporations about this. The Glasgow Incorporation of Wrights got the town council to approve a ban in 1750,

> That no journeyman wright be allowed to have bench or loom or keep timber and materials for wright work or sale in their houses, or in any house, garratt, loft, howff, cellar or yeard within the libertys of this burgh, which does not belong or is not hired for the use and behoove of a freeman wright.

Perhaps it indicates a half-heartedness on the part of the councillors that the fine for a breach of the ordinance was reduced to a mere £4 Scots. The same battle was fought with similar results among the wrights in Dundee in 1752.[31] The Glasgow barbers tried for an 8 p.m. stopping time, but were refused on the grounds that they would use their time 'in tippling or drinking'. They could, however, be permitted an hour for improvement by means of 'useful learning'.[32]

A key industry affected by expansion in these mid-century years was the textile industry, both linen and wool; but the former in particular was subject to sharp fluctuations. A severe depression followed the removal of linen export bounties in 1754 and meetings of linen weavers, who in Paisley in August 1754 voted against accepting a reduction in rates. Here was a classic case of 'industrial relations by riot', in Hobsbawm's phrase, with 'their resentment ... chiefly vented against their masters' windows'.[33] The same decade saw an expansion of the woollen and linen industries in Aberdeenshire and an improvement in methods. Coarse woollens, particularly hand-knitted stockings, had been exported from this area since the seventeenth century, but it was not until 1743 that a finer finish was brought in. In that year, woolcombing was introduced by Alexander Dingwall, one of the leading stocking manufacturers, who had learned the trade in England. As with their counterparts in England, those with woolcombing skills were in great demand and they were able to command wages of 10s. per week. These were full-time workers, based in Aberdeen, preparing the raw wool yarn for the spinners in the rural areas of Aberdeenshire and Kincardine. Also, as with their English colleagues, they were quick to appreciate the value of organisation, particularly since there was obviously a pressure to expand the workforce as rapidly as possible. Numerous apprentices were brought in and by 1760, it was claimed, there were no fewer than six apprentices to each journeyman.

A Woolcombers' Society was founded by a dozen journeymen in November 1755. In return for a 5d. entry and a monthly fee of 7½d., the member would receive 2s. to 3s. per week in old age, 40s. to pay funeral costs, 10s.6d. if he were going on the tramp in search of work, and the Society would stand guarantor for burial charges should he end up in the town's infirmary.[34] Within three months another twenty-eight had joined, though five had been expelled. In addition to the mutual-aid side, however, the new society was concerned with restricting entry into the craft and it drafted a series of rules with this in mind: no ex-soldiers should get work as woolcombers, if any members of the Society were unemployed; nobody should work for less than the standard rate; nobody from other crafts should be instructed in the trade of woolcombing and any instruction had to be by time-served craftsmen. They sought also to impose what was called 'pad money', drinking money paid by every new apprentice or journeyman. The employer was to pay this sum and, presumably, deduct it from the man's wages.[35] It was reported in 1756 that the last rule, together with others restricting entry, was contrary to the law and, therefore, had been dropped, but there was probably little change in the actual aims of the Woolcombers' Society to keep a tight hold on entry. Initially, the journeymen seem to have been encouraged in their mutual-aid activities by the employers, and £30 of the Society's funds were deposited with Alexander Dingwall at 4.5% interest, in return for a promissory note payable in twelve months. A number of developments altered this cosy relationship. Firstly, one of the Society was sent to England, 'in order to establish a correspondence and intercourse with the clubs there'. The decision caused dissension in the Society and Leslie, the clerk, resigned in protest. Secondly, presumably as a result of the trip to England, cards or 'blanks' were introduced which enabled members to tramp in England and to seek work there, a development which the Aberdeen employers regarded as producing 'a factious and mutinous spirit'. Thirdly, apprentices had 'sometime since entered into a Society', which probably meant that they were organised along with the journeymen. At a time when employers were keen to expand the workforce, the woolcombers were tightening their grip on the labour supply, strengthening their bargaining position and learning from their more experienced Southern colleagues.

Matters came to a head in 1759 when the woolcombers struck against the employing of one Joseph Reid to teach apprentices, when he himself had not served a regular apprenticeship, but had bought out his indenture. They demonstrated on the town links, demanding a reduction in the number of apprentices to two per master, until the authorities threatened to use the military against them. The Woolcombers' Society now faced the prospect of legal action against its members, and, in anticipation of this, sought to withdraw its money held by Alexander Dingwall. Dingwall, however, refused to hand it over and, instead, brought a process before the sheriff, claiming that the Society had deviated from the primary purpose of the fund. It was at this stage that the Procurator Fiscal summoned two of the leading members of the Society before the burgh court (Dingwall, it should be said, was a baillie) on the charge of 'caballing, clubing and other lawless practices', contrary to several laws, but especially 12 George I, which was specifically against woolcombers and weavers combining. The magistrates found that 'presuming to enter and form themselves into any pretended society making by laws and contributing money is illegal and unwarranted'.

The men now appealed to the Court of Session against Dingwall and against the Procurator Fiscal. In July 1762, the Lord Ordinary, Lord Alemere, ordered Dingwall and the Fiscal to hand over the money, plus interest, to the Woolcombers' Society, but, at the same time, he instituted an examination of the rules of the Society. The men sought to be allowed to retain their charity box, while the masters argued that if this association survived, then every other trade in Scotland would follow suit in organising. The masters' argument was that they would only tolerate a charity if so many merchants and master manufacturers were allowed to administer it,

> but they never will allow, unless your Lordships force them to it, a number of servants and apprentices to meet, and to dispose of a common stock of money, without control or inspection, not only of the magistrates but of the graver and better sort of people.[36]

Otherwise, 'that just and necessary subordination which ought to subsist betwixt masters and journeymen, and more especially between masters and their apprentices' would be destroyed. Also, if the woolcombers got away with it 'they will found a precedent for the working hands and servants of all denominations to follow their example'. The Court now found against the men, ruling

> That such combinations of artificers, whereby they collect money for a common box, inflict penalties, impose oaths, and make other by-laws are of a dangerous tendency, subversive to peace and order, and against law.[37]

A few days before this decision, the Court of Session had delivered judgement in yet another case involving the Edinburgh Tailors. This one dated back to 1757 when the journeymen, once again united round one house of call, tried to obtain a rise of two pence, from 8d. to 10d. in their day's pay. They also wanted to take control of who could be employed by insisting that employers had to take journeymen in strict order of rotation from the list of those available for work held at the house of call. Masters would now have no choice. Finally, they also claimed the right to leave their masters' houses at the breakfast hour, between 9 a.m. and 10 a.m. Presumably because of strike action, the Procurator Fiscal took some of them to court and in July 1757 they were ordered back to work at the old hours and six of them were imprisoned until they found caution money for this.[38] None the less, disputes clearly still continued and, in 1758, the master tailors agreed to contribute 4s. for every journeyman in their employment to assist one another 'to exercise their utmost efforts against the present mutiny and rebellion of the unreasonable journeymen'.[39]

A revived spirit of militancy came in May 1760 when there was a rush of orders for military uniforms for troops going to Europe, coupled with the regular annual demand from the General Assembly of the Kirk. The tailors now sought 1s. a day and began taking their breakfast hour out of the workshops. The JPs ruled, in September 1760, that the tailors were not entitled to the hour of recess for breakfast, but they agreed to the new rate of 1s. a day. They added, however, that any unemployed tailor had to work for any employer, if he were required. Backed by this ruling, the masters were in a strong position to resist the usual troubles at the time of the mourning for the departed George II in October 1760. On that occasion they were able to import new workers from the country and to break the strike threat by organising them in a club that was quite separate from the men's house of call. But trouble persisted and a case reached the Court of Session in 1761. On this occasion, Lord Coallston agreed to hear arguments about conditions. He was impressed by the tailors' arguments about the unhealthy conditions in which they were expected to work and he granted them the right to a breakfast-hour recess. On appeal to the full court, however, the decision was reversed. The Court accepted that regulating working hours might well be an infringement of the liberty of the individual, but it was, they argued, a necessary one:

> Arts and manufactures are of two kinds. Those for luxury and for amusement are subject to no rules, because a society may subsist without them. But those which are necessary to the well-being of society must be subjected to rules, otherwise it may be in the power of a few to do much mischief. If the bakers should refuse to make bread or the brewers to make ale, or the coalliers to provide coal, without being subject to any control, they would be masters of the lives of the inhabitants.

Since it was accepted that wages could be fixed by law, then other regulations followed, 'for it is no purpose to fix wages, without also fixing the number of working hours; and it is no purpose to fix either, if the defenders have the privilege to work or not at their pleasure'.[40]

There was no unanimity among the employers on the issue of the breakfast hour. The staymakers, for example, who formed part of the Tailors' Incorporation, were favourable to it, arguing that bringing in ale and food for breakfast would dirty the stays.[41] It is clear, also, that a number of master tailors were allowing it, perhaps under duress; many journeymen apparently left Edinburgh rather than accept the new ruling. But, in 1763, after further wage demands, the Incorporation tried to eradicate this trend with a ruling.

> that no members should keep any journeyman or journeymen tailors to work for him for wages, except such as shall engage to serve him from six in the morning till twelve noon, without an hour's recess from nine to ten, such journeymen being at liberty to take his breakfast at his master's house.

Infringement would bring a fine of 40s.[42]

Tailoring was probably the trade that was developing most rapidly along capitalist lines. The gap between employer and journeyman was widening. In the country, it was claimed, masters were 'contented with moderate gain', but in the cities 'where Luxury prevails and where the Master Taylors sett up to live like gentlemen their voice prompts them to prey upon the poor Journeymen and enhance their own profits'.[43]

The summer of 1764 brought a series of disputes among the building workers in Edinburgh. Bad harvests and credit difficulties in 1761 and 1762 had produced general depression. On top of that, 1764 was a very wet year, and, presumably, work and earnings were erratic, while food prices were rising. Despite the unfavourable conditions, the masons, after a mass meeting, struck for a rise from a merk a day in the summer and 10d. in winter to 15d. in the summer and 12d. in winter. After a week, they advertised their services at the new rates to the public in the newspapers.[44] In addition twenty-six of them petitioned the Town Council for a rise, claiming that their wages had not been increased for a hundred years. The case was argued before the town magistrates. Significantly, the journeymen were prepared to have these new rates paid only to the skilful and experienced and were willing that these should be certified by two master masons. The employers warned of the 'ill tendency' spreading to other workers, while the journeymen argued that the masters had combined against them and claimed that wages ought to be ruled by 'the rate of viveris', the cost of living.[45]

It did not help the masons' case that the wrights went on strike at the same time (presumably for much the same reasons),[46] and, in August, the judgement was delivered against the journeymen masons, for having used 'illegal, tumultuous and unwarrantable' methods. The ruling was that they 'are bound to work to the freemen master masons for such wages as the said master masons shall think reasonable, agreeable to use and wont'.[47] The journeymen intended to appeal against the interlocutor and, in September, they were still advertising their services to the public, with the *cri de coeur* that 'the journeymen masons are resolved, one and all, to show the world that they are free men and not bond slaves'.[48]

The Edinburgh tailors remained by far the most active group in these years, perhaps because they were the most vulnerable to an expanding labour force. In 1767 there were again complaints that they had succeeded in pushing up their wages and in shortening hours. The aftermath of war had brought new people into the trade, who were not attached to the Incorporation and who were, in some cases, ready to pay 1s.3d. instead of the regulated 1s. a day. To block such a trend, the Incorporation persuaded the magistrates and the Town Council once again to reaffirm the prohibition on anyone paying more than the 1s. and on allowing the hour's recess. The Sheriff, in a separate ruling, extended this prohibition to the whole county. Strikes ensued, probably influenced by the tailors' disputes in London at that time, which were well reported in the Edinburgh newspapers.[49]

The arguments of the Edinburgh dispute were themselves publicised in a series of advertisements which both sides took in the press, evidence that it was felt important to influence public opinion and, therefore, presumably, the Town Council, on these matters. The masters claimed that they were seeking to resist an unjustified imposition on the public, while the journeymen were arguing that they had had no rise since 1748, in spite of a considerable increase in the cost of food and rent, and that their wages were now little better than those of a 'common barrowman', who worked at least two hours a day less.[50]

The advertisements revealed further the widening social gap that had developed between employers and journeymen. In 1762, the tailors had complained that the masters had enhanced their profits at the expense of their journeymen. Echoes of these same sentiments were to be found in 1767:

> The assertion made by the master-taylors, that their trade cannot bear an addition of three pence per day to each journeymen's wages, can easily be refuted. And the country villas, built of late by some of these gentlemen put a negative upon this hardy allegation; whilst the poor journeymen, the effects of whose labour these country seats are, are denied 15 pence per day.[51]

After a fortnight's dispute ten of the journeymen tailors were arrested and imprisoned until they found bail.[52] Three days later the strike widened, with wrights, masons and slaters all out on strike.[53]

The problem of tailoring was not confined to Edinburgh. There was also trouble in Aberdeen in 1764, when wages were 8d. a day and the men were pressing for 2d. a day rise. In 1768, they struck work and blocked any country lads being brought in. The employers, operating through the Incorporation, stood out against it and reaffirmed rules restricting the rate to 8d. a day, on pain of a fine.[54]

There was also a renewal of activity among the woolcombers of Aberdeen, when the journeymen refused to take on apprentices to learn the trade. The manufacturers imported new labour from England and, at the Autumn Circuit Court in 1769, seven woolcombers were fined and imprisoned for assaulting one of the English immigrants who was teaching apprentices. Despite this, the organisation and the disputes continued. When, in 1771, one Alex Frost broke away from the men's organisation and began to teach apprentices, he had his wool and tools destroyed. When he persisted, his shop was set alight and, when that failed to deter him, there was an attempt to stab him to death. Seven were apprehended and charged and five of them were found guilty of conspiracy. As we shall see in later cases of assault, however, there were often factors involved that had little to do with the particular issue of the dispute. Frost seems to have been an aggressive figure, who was soon afterwards brought to trial himself for assaulting a stocking merchant.[55] Industrial disputes could be an occasion for settling personal scores.

Towards the end of 1768, the Edinburgh shoemakers were campaigning for a rise. These were home workers on piece rates and their complaint was of hours wasted in having to carry the finished work to their employer's house and having to wait to receive the cut-out leather. This, they argued, could push a working day up to fifteen hours, although their earnings were sometimes only 4s. or 5s. a week. The masters rejected this assertion and claimed that it was possible for journeymen to earn from 7s. to as much as 12s. a week.[56] The employers were well-enough organised to be able to negotiate with employers in Glasgow and agree not to poach each other's men, so preventing journeymen applying pressure to the masters by moving between cities.[57] At the end of December, the masters accused the men, before the Sheriff, of having entered into a combination, by written agreement. The sheriff found them guilty and ordered them to be imprisoned, until they found caution to work at the old rate with their last masters, for at least a month. A few, who rejected this, were kept in prison.[58]

Again and again, it was in tailoring that the sharpest tensions remained. Clearly the master tailors were finding it difficult to maintain the regulations on hours and wage rates. There were ways round it, with masters paying the regulation shilling rate, but also paying a surplus rate to their regular workers by the month or by the year. The Incorporation also faced growing numbers of masters who were outside its control. As more and more unregulated firms appeared, the Tailors' Incorporation struggled fruitlessly to maintain some kind of control. It took action in the courts against a number of leading staymakers and threatened further prosecutions.[59] This was at a time when the journeymen tailors were asking the courts to reduce their hours to 6 a.m. to 7 p.m., with an hour for dinner. The London and Westminster tailors had recently had their hours reduced to twelve by Act of Parliament, and the Court granted the Edinburgh tailors the same. The issue of the Tailors' Incorporation's control over the staymakers reached the Court of Session in 1770 and there it was ruled that the tailors' regulations did cover the staymakers, because the journeymen tailors frequently worked as staymakers. The master staymakers argued that whereas the tailors were traditionally unruly and mobile, moving from master to master, the staymakers were stable employers with a stable workforce. After much litigation, the Tailors' Incorporation lost and had to pay the staymakers' expenses.[60]

The effect of these decisions seems to have been to usher in a few years of peace in the trade. But a new dispute blew up in 1776, a year when the demand for military uniforms would have been high. The initiative came from the Incorporation, who asked the Sheriff to prohibit keepers of houses of call. The complaint was rejected as 'too vague and general'. In September 1777 the masters announced their intention of prosecuting any tailors paying more than the regulation shilling. When the men sought a rise to 1s.2d. the issue was brought before the JPs. The fact that the approach was to the Justices of the Peace is an indication of the extent to which the boundaries of the royal burgh had become quite irrelevant in the development of crafts. It was futile for the Incorporation to try to maintain regulation only in the burgh when so many operated outside it. The Justices set up a committee, consisting of Henry Dundas, Archibald Cockburn of Cockburn and James Balfour of Pilrigg, to hear both sides of the case. The masters concentrated on the tyranny of the houses of call, while the journeymen pressed for a rise in wages. The committee reported in November 1777 and recommended tighter regulation of the houses of call, ruling that any unemployed journeyman tailor had to be allowed to have his name on the list or slate, at a cost to him of no more than 1d.; that the list had to be made available to any employers, again for a charge of 1d., and that a master could employ anyone he wished from the list. The earlier rule that any unemployed journeyman on the list had to work at the rate of no more than a shilling for any master who wanted him was reaffirmed. Finally, it was laid down that these regulations should extend to the whole county. The Quarter Sessions approved the recommendations of their committee.[61]

The journeymen predictably sought to challenge these regulations by asking for a Bill of Suspension from the Court of Session. They argued that the Acts of 1617 and 1661, under which the Justices had acted, which required them 'to set a price in craftsmen's work' and 'to appoint prices for all handicrafts', referred to the *price* of finished work, not to the wages of journeymen. They argued also that the JPs had the right only to regulate country wages and not those of urban mechanics. Their advocate, having perhaps just read his *Wealth of Nations*, suggested that it was extremely impolitic for JPs to set such regulations:

> Every profession will find its own proper rate of wages in proportion to the state of the country and to the wages of other professions, without any forced regulation of this kind, which cannot have any good effect, and never will for any length of time keep wages below their natural rate. Let judges do what they please, nay let the legislature enact what it will, every man's work will fetch what it is worth.

The masters' case was that although the statutes of 1617 and 1661 allowed JPs to set a price for finished work, 'the power of rating wages must be implied and included under it'. The journeymen got their bill of suspension from Lord Stonefield against the JPs' ruling in February 1778, but it was overturned by the full court in July, when they ruled that JPs *had* the authority to fix the wages of the craftsmen. The journeymen were told to go back to the JPs if they were dissatisfied. But the Court of Session also affirmed its own powers to review JPs' decisions.[62]

Action was taken by the Incorporation before the Sheriff against some of the employers who paid over the rate; but the Court of Session proved none too sympathetic to the Incorporation. It was pointed out that the acts of the Town Council covered journeymen only when employed at the usual hours: 'Extraordinary work was entitled to extraordinary payment'. If wages were to be regulated, it should be done only by the JPs or by local magistrates, not by the sheriffs, who were officers of the Crown, or by the Incorporations. JPs, said the Court, were 'popular, more connected with, and supposed to be more kindly towards the inhabitants'.[63]

Immediately following the 1778 ruling, the journeymen tailors again submitted a request to the JPs for higher wages. After a great deal of litigation a committee of JPs again heard proof from both sides and again ruled in favour of adhering to the old regulations and the old wage rates. The men now tried to get a table of piecework rates introduced, as an alternative to the usual day rate, only to be blocked by the Justices. Once again the issue came before the Court of Session, the journeymen asking for 15d. to be fixed for the day rate or a piece-rate table approved, but the Court upheld the JPs' regulations on all points.[64]

By the 1770s major changes were taking place in Edinburgh. The building of the New Town in the North and development of land to the South was underway, with a demand for skilled building workers of all kinds. But it was not a smooth process: funds were short and it may have been the suspension of work on the Adams' new Register House that triggered the next dispute among building workers. In April 1778 the journeymen masons petitioned for a pay rise of 3d., to

1s.6d. a day. A week later the master builders unanimously agreed not to comply and to insist on a discharge certificate from any journeyman, indicating that his last master had been willing to part with him. The men, in their turn, began advertising their services in the press, directly to the public, while warning men from the country to keep clear, 'lest they incur the displeasure of the brethren'. The masters responded with a lock-out, because journeymen still at work were supporting those who were on strike.[65]

At the same time, the journeymen wrights came out on strike and, like the masons, advertised their services in the local newspapers. The Sheriff seems to have refused to take action against the strikers, though there were warnings about intimidation of non-unionists. Efforts by the employers — joiners, cabinetmakers and masons acting in concert — to import country labour seems to have met with little success. At the end of May, the journeymen, over the signature 'Unity', were thanking their country brethren for contributing towards their support. On 13 June, the masons were still saying that, on the whole, the country men had given financial support and kept men out of Edinburgh. Levels of wages and profits were bandied around in the press, with the employers claiming that wages had risen by a third 'within memory', and the journeymen claiming that they had only gone from one merk to 15d. It was accepted, however, that masters' prices and profits had, if anything, declined because of competition. In June there was clearly the start of a drift back to work, but as late as 17 June a General Society of Journeymen Cabinetmakers, Joiners and Carvers in and about Edinburgh announced that it was raising money to build houses and to set up a factory to undertake cabinet and chair work. Apparently £130 was contributed on the first night.[66]

One has in these decades, from early in the eighteenth century to the end of the 1770s, the emergence of journeymen's organisations among an ever-widening variety of crafts. The pressures that brought about organisation were various. For many, the desire to acquire some security in sickness and old age was crucial and led to the establishment of mutual-aid societies, where a few pence went to a fund to help the incapacitated and widows and orphans. New urban workers, cut off from the security offered by their own kin in their own parish, sought to create their own security. Not unnaturally such organisations were probably based on links at work. Although it was quite possible to have mutual-aid societies that were not confined to particular crafts, it is an indication of the centrality of the craft in the lives of most that they tended generally to be craft-based. The emergence of such organisations was probably an indication of the failure of the Incorporations to perform one of their central functions, and that, in itself, was probably a reflection of a growing separation of master and journeyman and a transition to employer and worker. Incorporations became exclusively masters' organisations with little concern for the plight of the craft as a whole. Indeed, because of the persistence of the incorporations, a feature of eighteenth-century Scotland's industrial relations was the way in which masters acted together. As journeymen frequently pointed out and as Adam Smith noted, masters operated very effective combinations, both 'tacit, but constant and uniform ones' not to raise wages and specific ones 'conducted with the utmost silence and secrecy' to reduce wages.[67] The links formed in the friendly society could lead to collaboration on industrial action. Leaders trusted to look after life savings were likely to be trusted to give guidance in labour disputes. The very fact of meeting to collect and disperse friendly society funds would, one imagines, have encouraged discussion of wider trade issues.

The timing of the emergence of a clear pattern of industrial activity probably, more than anything, depended on numbers. The fact that the most active of the early organisations were among the tailors can only be explained by the fact that this was the trade that was attracting most new workers and seems to have been one of the first to develop a capitalist structure in which employers and journeymen were socially separate. The long credit that came to be expected by customers of tailors must have excluded many, who lacked the necessary capital, from setting up in business on their own. It was the continuing pressure of numbers coming from the country into the city in the early eighteenth century that led the Edinburgh tailors to try to control the quality and number of entrants through their house of call. Here too the industrial side, mutual aid side and social side of the journeymen's activities could intermingle because the call-house was the focus of all three.

The issues in dispute were generally rates of pay. The journeymen, tailors in particular, learned how to take advantage of moments of high demand to push for rises. They used periods of rising food prices to press for adjustment to agreed rates. From the 1740s onwards the demand for skilled labour was increasing steadily and journeymen were taking advantage of it. Traditional masters were trying to resist this upward trend in rates, but they were faced with pressure on two fronts, from the more effective organisation of their journeymen and from the increased competition from new employers moving into the trades.

One of the most striking features of the Scottish pattern is the part played by the courts and the extent to which the courts, at burgh level, at county level and at national level, assumed a role in the development of industrial relations. This was inevitable in a country where regulation of crafts still persisted. The kind of control over crafts that had died out in the English burghs in the sixteenth and seventeenth centuries persisted in Scotland. The incorporations remained a real force, backed by the authority of the magistracy and, while their control over new employers was being eroded, they could rely on the authorities to maintain their control over journeymen. Evidence of a lack of subordination among workmen was seen as a threat to the entire social fabric. One the other hand, it was not always accepted that the employers knew best, and the magistrates and judges did see the necessity for conciliation as well as confrontation. This legal element in industrial relations in itself encouraged the development of organisation among journeymen. Money had to be raised to make a case before the magistrates for changes in wage rates or hours. Lawyers had to be hired and paid, cases had to be prepared for the courts. Particularly when cases reached the Court of Session, a great deal of data had to be accumulated to bolster the argument. Written evidence had to be collected and advocates briefed. All of this required and encouraged leadership and organisation. Although we know little about them, the constant litigation by the Edinburgh tailors must have produced a leadership skilled in the ways of the law, effective in the raising of money and shrewd in the handling of their fellow journeymen.

What is apparent from this is just how accessible the Scottish courts were in the eighteenth century. Indeed the Scots were notorious for their readiness to resort to litigation. The courts were clearly seen, and indeed increasingly seen, as places where there was a chance of righting grievances. And in a city already awash with lawyers there was no scarcity of advocates ready to take the journeymen's brief. The readiness of the journeymen to appeal to the Court of Session is perhaps an indication that the lower courts were seen as less even-handed. As some master craftsmen grew in wealth and status, they could perhaps rely on colleagues on the magistrates' bench to see the world in their way. In these circumstances, the judges of the higher court were regarded as potentially more sympathetic. The interesting thing is that the judges of the Court of Session were willing to take upon themselves a role in industrial relations. Over the next few decades this role was to be greatly extended.

4
Conflict and Conciliation

In three decades, since the end of the 1740s, the foundations for more sustained economic growth had been laid. An adequate infrastructure had been created with road and bridge improvements in the 1760s and 1770s and with developments in banking. This allowed the opening up of new coal and iron works, encouraged further improvements in agriculture and generally stimulated demand. Since the 1740s linen had acted as the leading sector, in the vanguard of growth, bringing into being a rapidly growing labour force with high levels of skill. On to this, from the 1780s, was grafted the cotton industry. The first cotton spinning mill in Scotland was built in 1779. By 1787 there were nineteen of them and the process by which cotton textiles were to become by the end of the Napoleonic Wars, Scotland's major industry was well underway.

All around, in the 'eighties and early 'nineties, there was evidence of a new prosperity. The quality of both public and private buildings from the 1780s is an indication of how a poor, underdeveloped country had been transformed in three quarters of a century. The fine streets of Edinburgh and Glasgow were the most obvious examples, but even in remote Dumfriesshire there was evidence from 1788 of 'an uncommon spirit of building' and of 'a general taste for good houses'.[1]

In no way was there an even distribution of the gains of a new prosperity. Some Scottish workers undoubtedly prospered. There are numerous rose-tinted comments on dramatic improvements. The pages of the Old Statistical Account are full of them, pointing to wages more than doubling between the 1760s and the 1790s. According to the minister of Auchtermuchty, to take but one example from many similar comments, wages had doubled in twenty years and even a common labourer, if 'he is frugal and well-married he can do more than support himself and his family'.[2] This may have been rather truer in rural areas, trying to hang on to labour attracted by the growing towns, but other evidence shows that a similar rise in money wages was taking place there. Sir John Sinclair remarked that such improvements were being achieved on a five-day week: 'many of them riot on Sunday [and] are idle all Monday'.[3] Yet for most workers the situation was not quite so consistently rosy. As was to be discovered at the end of the century even the crises of exceptional harvest failure, with its subsequent shortages and high prices, had not been eradicated. But money wages were rising, especially for those with skill. It was probably in the last twenty years that the gap between the traditionally low Scottish wages and those in the North of England narrowed, with Scots gaining faster rises as employers tried to hold on to scarce labour.[4] But it was also a time of rising prices with all indices pointing to substantial rises from the end

c

of the 1780s through the first decade of the nineteenth century. Despite this, it does seem that, for most Scots workers, wage rates kept pace with price rises and for some there were undoubted gains in living standards.

The most extensive changes took place in the textile industry, with the increased use of cotton and the development of factory production of yarn. We still have much to learn about patterns of factory production in late eighteenth-century Scotland. There were the large mills by the side of fast-flowing rivers, like New Lanark and Catrine and Deanston, using Arkwright's huge thousand-spindle water frames. But alongside these there were many spinning mills using hand-driven machinery. The spinning jenny and Crompton's mule were both in use long after the coming of the water frame.[5]

These technological developments in spinning helped to solve the longstanding problem of bottlenecks in the supply of yarn. There were massive gains in productivity with major implications for traditional patterns. There was now less need for the woman spinner working at home. Some, especially in the linen areas of the East, turned to weaving, while others became involved in the various finishing processes. But for many rural families it must have meant a significant fall in earnings. In the early factories men and women were both involved in spinning. Only gradually, with the application of power and the enlargement of machines, did cotton spinning become a predominantly male preserve, with women and children acting as assistants.

The fine linen weavers of Renfrewshire and Lanarkshire were able to modify their skills to weave the muslins which became a Scottish speciality from the 1780s. There was a great demand for weavers' services, particularly for the more highly skilled who entered their 'golden age'. But good earnings quickly pulled in more workers to the plainer work and weakened the bargaining position of the poorer end. It was a period when work patterns and work-relationships were being constantly altered.

Although their technology was changing little, the organisation of their work was going through frequent and extensive change. There were frequent alterations in the materials being used as manufacturers experimented to find a niche in an often-changing market. This must have meant delays, frustrations and difficulties as the weaver learned to cope with new mixtures. It must have created tensions with the agent if work were disapproved of. Yet the weavers were more and more dependent upon manufacturers and their agents. Few could retain a traditional independence when materials and markets were changing so quickly. They had to become tied to those who knew the ever-widening markets. Weavers were, therefore, conscious of being caught in a process of rapid change over which they had very little control.

There had been signs of organisation among handloom weavers before the 1780s. Paisley had become a major centre of fine linen and, in 1754, there were the first signs of 'organised protest with weavers smashing the windows of those masters who had reduced wages', following the crisis produced by the withdrawal of the export bounty.[6] Weavers had in the past been tightly controlled by the various weavers' incorporations in the burghs and were expected to have served an apprenticeship and to have paid the traditional apprenticeship fee. By the mid-eighteenth century, however, at least in Glasgow, it was possible for the fee to be waived in return for a longer period of service at low rates,[7] and there was growing pressure to get a more rapid expansion of the weaving labour force. The 1751 Act had forbidden weavers' incorporations to charge entry money or to restrict master weavers setting up where they wished. The restrictions on entry to the craft laid down by the Weavers' Incorporation, by which only freemen could be employed by members of the Incorporation, were rescinded by the Trades' House. While all other crafts were still able to supply the needs of the city, the weavers could not, it was argued, 'unless they are left at liberty to employ whomever persons they shall think proper either in Town or Country'.[8] The effect was a great influx of poor weavers into the town most of whom had no links with the Incorporation.[9]

It was to try to maintain regulation and order in the trade that the weavers of Fenwick in Ayrshire formed their society in 1761. It followed many months of severe stagnation in the trade when conditions probably deteriorated badly. An inspector was to be appointed annually to check the quality of work being produced and the prices asked, with fines for those who were irregular. It could be disastrous for a village if it gained a reputation for bad workmanship or late delivery. From a general recommendation about prices being neither higher nor lower than in other towns, the Society, in 1768, moved to actually setting piece rates for the different qualities of cloth.[10] What was being attempted was the retention of traditional patterns of equal rates, in resistance to the competitive pressure that was pushing down the prices paid by the manufacturers.

The Paisley weavers, in 1764, showed a new level of organisation with the setting up of the Universal Trading Company of Paisley. This early attempt at co-operation was presumably a rebellion against the control of both supplies of yarn and of the selling of the finished product by a few large manufacturers. What was proposed was a co-partnery, of no fewer than 600 members, to carry on the manufacture and selling of silk and linen goods. It laid down the rates to be paid and seemed clearly intended to keep up earnings; but it broke up in the following year, when some of the members refused to pay their contributions. The directors sued for breach of contract, but the decision, Barr *versus* Carr, in the Court of Session in January 1766 was that the co-partnery had, in fact, been an 'illegal combination and of a dangerous tendency to society' and could not, therefore, sue.[11]

The beginnings of organisation of weavers in Glasgow seem to have come in 1767 in reaction to organisation among the manufacturers. In 1766 there were moves by London drapers to have the ban on the importation of French cambrics and lawns lifted. They claimed that there was widespread smuggling and that Scottish manufacturers were, in fact, smuggling French cambrics and selling them as home-produced cloth. The Glasgow manufacturers opposed the lifting of the ban and asked for time to increase their output. They won their case and Parliament agreed to retain the ban, but insisted on the stamping of home-made cambrics. To increase the output of cambrics the Glasgow manufacturers agreed to reduce the rates paid to weavers of lawns and to increase the wages paid for cambrics. They decided also to try to tighten the discipline over the workforce. For some time there had been complaints of webs left unfinished and of weavers taking work from more than one master to get the initial payments and then not completing the webs. Now the masters agreed that no master would employ a weaver 'without certificate from his last master'. The switch to cambrics seems to have been successful and prices rose and with them earnings. Even the rates for lawns crept back to the previous level, but this was not how it was seen by the workers.

At some stage in 1767 a protest movement began among the weavers. The moving force was one David Nicolson, 'a man of deep views, much beyond his station in life'. Nicolson launched an organisation to gather funds to resist employers' pressure on earnings, and about two hundred joined. The idea was to collect 6d. a month, which would be used to finance a prosecution against the masters' combination and to pay a salary to Nicolson. It was asserted that the manufacturers were trying to reduce rates by as much as a quarter. Pressure was exerted on those taking work at the new rates, with webs cut from their looms and journeymen dragged by a mob through the streets.[12] Arrests were made and five weavers were brought to trial before the circuit court in October 1767, charged with mobbing and with combination. The case against two of the men, James Raeburn and Andrew Somerville, was dropped, but John Millar and Archibald Hamilton were sentenced to two months in prison and William Wilson to one month for mobbing. They were all bound over to keep the peace for two years.[13] This was not enough to destroy the agitation and, in November 1767, a new committee was formed, with Wilson again as preses to push ahead with the case against the masters. A public appeal for funds was made to pay the cost of summoning the manufacturers before the Court of Session to have their combination declared illegal. The charges reflected how the journeymen believed wage rates should be fixed. The manufacturers had, it was claimed, reduced the wages far below the rates formerly paid, to enrich themselves 'without regard either to prices and profits at which the goods may be sold, or the expense of provisions, and the rate at which the living of the Pursuers must cost them'.[14] The case duly came to court in February 1768, but the outcome has not been recorded. Discontent continued and, in the spring of 1768, women, who were employed in clipping lawns, struck for higher wages and two to three hundred of them marched through the streets of Paisley, accompanied by journeymen weavers. At the end of 1768 several thousand Paisley weavers were complaining to the magistrates about the rise in the price of oatmeal. They received scant sympathy: the hundred or so small stills in the town were blamed for the rise in the demand for grain and the JPs advised the weavers not to buy or drink whisky.[15]

It was, presumably, to deal with the rising cost of provisions at this time that the Fenwick weavers took the decision to turn to co-operative buying. On 9 December 1769 it was recorded:

> This present day it is agreed upon by the members of our Society to take what money we had in our box to buy what victuals we thought fit to sell benefit of our society and

it is Intrusted to the management of William Buntin weaver in finnick town for buying in the said Victuals and it is to be sold again by John Burns weaver in finnick town which he is to serve the members of our trade with four pecks at once and they may serve any other with one peck or two whom they please any member of our Society is not to be denyd of four weeks trust but from any other you will take ready money.[16]

This was probably a not uncommon way for a trade organisation to act. The deacon and managers of the Brechin Weavers' Incorporation before 1766, regularly bought victuals to distribute among their members. The trade incorporation in Dundee was doing the same in 1769 and 1770.[17]

By the early 1770s the extent of textile manufacture had greatly expanded. Over thirteen million yards of linen were stamped in each year between 1769 and 1772.[18] Paisley, in particular, grew rapidly and became a centre of silk gauze manufacture that rivalled Spitalfields. New workers flooded into the trade and it never proved possible to establish a system of apprenticeship in this section. This inevitably led to difficulties in maintaining rates in other areas. It was not just children who were being trained: adults were paying a few pounds to be given rudimentary skills. It had great attractions, since the whole family could be employed, with wives and children in spinning. It meant working at home, independent of masters, perhaps indeed becoming an independent master selling directly. Little capital was required and demand was high.[19] The relentless and, eventually, disastrous influx of unregulated numbers had begun. In this atmosphere it was almost impossible for the weavers to maintain any standardisation of rates, especially since there were also fluctuations in demand. Since the merchant/manufacturers had little of their own fixed capital invested they were quick to lay off weavers if demand fell. The years 1772 and 1773 were particularly bad, made worse by the collapse of the Ayr Bank, and, in August 1773, there were proceedings against a number of Paisley weavers, charged with combination and intimidation. Employers talked of a committee meeting weekly, under Hugh Thomson, which was intended to keep up the price of work. Pickets were put on the yarn warehouse and anyone who took webs at low rates was threatened. One Dalry weaver was warned that if he did not give up working he 'would be used as Bishop Sharp or Porteous'. The authorities were unable to find the ringleaders and the case was dropped, with the masters agreeing to the men's rates.[20] There were similar activities in Glasgow and here the authorities were slightly more successful, with six convicted of mobbing and attacking weavers and five acquitted.[21]

An attempt in 1780 in Glasgow by weavers' clubs to act in unison to secure a uniform scale of prices seems to have come to little.[22] But there was more vigorous renewed activity in 1784, as a result of a campaign organised by the new cotton manufacturers. They were protesting against the tax preference given to muslin and calicoes imported by the East India Co., to the detriment of home production. Dempster, the Glasgow M.P., presented a petition signed by 12,000 operative weavers.[23] Distress in 1786 led to further agitation. Prices of grain in the West were generally higher than those in Edinburgh, but under the terms of the Corn Laws ports could only be opened for grain imports when Edinburgh prices reached the set level. The recently-established Glasgow Chamber of Commerce petitioned against the Corn Laws in October 1786.[24]

In November 1786 the muslin manufacturers reduced wages to, on average, 6s. to 7s. a week, according to the weavers, and, in the summer of the following year, they proposed to reduce them by a further twenty-five per cent, as cheap Indian muslins continued to flow in to the, as yet, limited market. A mass meeting of possibly 7,000 weavers and their families was held on Glasgow Green and it was decided not to take work at the new prices and not to take work at all from three of the manufacturers identified only as H.M., W.B. and D.M., 'in respect of their activity in promoting the said attempt' to reduce wages. In the usual manner the decision was imposed upon the recalcitrant by forcibly removing webs from the looms of working weavers and handing them back to the manufacturers, usually with a very public display of disapproval.[25]

As the dispute dragged on there was also a proposal to try to have a voluntary levy of the handloom weavers in Glasgow and the surrounding areas. The idea was a levy of anything from 5s. to £5 'according to their respective abilities' to raise funds to employ weavers in dispute. To the manufacturers the issue was a relatively simple one of whether the prices paid should depend 'on the *option of the workman*' or 'as in reason it ought, on *the demand of the market*', and they resolved not to give out work until the weavers had gone peacefully back to work and the ringleaders had been apprehended.[26] The strike went on through August, with signs of growing bitterness. Manufacturers and their families were molested and at least one warehouse was burned down. The weavers probably hoped that they could get the magistrates to interfere on the issue of wages, and even as the riots were starting they were arguing the case against a reduction at a time of rising food prices. The climax came on 3 September when a group of Camlachie weavers forcibly removed webs from the looms of weavers who were working at the reduced prices.[27] The webs were paraded through the streets to be ritually burned. When they reached the east end of the Gallowgate they were met by the magistrates and by a detachment of the 29th Regiment. Stones and bricks were thrown and the troops opened fire. Three weavers were killed right away and another three or five died of wounds; several others were wounded. Riots continued over the next few days and further troops were brought in. 6000 attended the burial of the dead weavers in Calton.[28] When the riots subsided a grateful magistracy presented each of the soldiers with a pair of stockings and a pair of shoes. The town also paid the cost of repairs caused by the riots.[29]

The aftermath for the weavers was the sentencing of James Granger, the only one of the arrested activists actually to be brought to trial, since the five others indicted with him all absconded. Presumably because of fear of popular disturbances the plan to hold the trial in Glasgow was abandoned and it was at the High Court in Edinburgh that he was sentenced to a public whipping and to banishment from Scotland for seven years.[30] The events of 1787 were undoubtedly traumatic for the bourgeoisie of Glasgow, instilling a real fear of popular disorder. Schemes were devised for the administration of the City to be completely overhauled, dividing it into twenty-four wards, with respectable citizens to supervise each ward and to report on the condition of the inhabitants. There were demands for a police force and it was no coincidence that the first Sunday school in Glasgow opened its doors to 400 boys in November 1787.[31]

Other groups of craftsmen were also active in these years in Glasgow. There are traces of organisation among journeymen blacksmiths from at least 1748 when they tried to reduce their day by an hour, stopping work at 7 p.m. It was the same campaign that they took up in 1784 and they were prepared to accept a wage reduction to have the shorter day. Their existing 6 a.m. to 8 p.m. day, they asserted, was too hard and gave them no time to go to school. In response, the employers had one of the blacksmiths, John Ballantine, arrested and sent to prison. The journeymen blacksmiths threatened legal action to obtain his release and to get redress from those responsible for what was seen as 'the height of oppression and tyranny'.[32] The employers in reply offered a reward for the apprehension of the combination. Soon after the weavers' riots, the Glasgow bakers tried to break free from their long six or sometimes twelve-month contracts and to insist on employment by the week. The masters tried to recruit country labour, but they found that these were deterred by threatening letters. What the outcome of this dispute was is not known, but it continued throughout most of October 1787.[33]

Employers tried to maintain their journeymen in a state of subordination by a variety of means. Legal action was generally a last resort. More usual was concerted action against other employers who stepped out of line by paying over the approved rates, and by keeping a close check on journeymen by means of the 'discharge note'. Dundee wrights, for example, in 1784, faced with a threat of strike action by their journeymen, agreed not to employ anyone who did not have proof of having 'fairly parted' from his previous employer.[34]

Meanwhile, among Edinburgh tradesmen, traditional patterns continued. There was a strike of Edinburgh compositors in 1785, which was submitted to the arbitration of two advocates. These decided in favour of the masters and the opportunity seems to have been taken to tighten up discipline. A printers' chapel, formed at the printing house of Neill and Co., with the masters' approval, had as its principal aim the enforcing of rules against swearing, wastage of candles and dirtying paper.[35] The tailors were again on strike in 1786 to try to push up the maximum rate and a number of the ringleaders were arrested, as were those masters who had paid over the shilling rate. Thirty of them were fined and warned that the maximum wage law would be strictly enforced in future against both men and masters.[36]

A few months later the Glasgow master tailors, facing a dispute with their men and drawing on the experience of Edinburgh, applied to the magistrates for legal regulation of wages. This was duly granted and it was ruled that no master should pay more than 1s.3d. a day, although, if employment were by the day, then a full day's wages had to be paid. On the other hand, piece-rate agreements were permitted. As in Edinburgh, the magistrates, at the behest of the Incorporation, also laid down that all journeymen who wanted work should be allowed on to the call house list and that the masters should have a free choice from among those listed.[37]

Yet another group in dispute in 1787 were the Edinburgh cabinet and chair makers, who, in March 1787, began to agitate for a shorter working day. The men claimed that a day from 6 a.m. to 7 p.m. was out of line with the practice of all other crafts, where work stopped at 6 p.m. The masters had already some organisation, and as a group they insisted on a discharge certificate from a previous employer before taking on new workmen. This reflected changes that were taking place in the structure of this expanding trade. There were a few large cabinetmakers, seven or eight of them, who each employed six to ten journeymen, but alongside these were a number of small men 'little better than journeymen themselves . . . who had not in their employment above one man each'. It was the smaller masters who adopted the hardest line, and were at the forefront of the masters' organisation in resisting the journeymen's demands. In early April the journeymen struck work. The masters seem to have been willing to concede the shorter hours, but they objected to a 6 p.m. stopping time, since this would give their journeymen the opportunity of undertaking evening jobbing work. The employers wanted a day to run from 7 a.m. to 7 p.m., with two hours off for meals, instead of the 6 a.m. to 7 p.m. as formerly. But the price for this reduction was a day of from 7 p.m. to 8 p.m. in winter and tighter work discipline, 'No tippling time or clubbing to drink in the shop be practised during the working hours, nor any man to quit his work except in cases universally understood, without leave being first asked and obtained of the master foreman or clark'. Times of attendance at meals were to be regulated by the nearest public clock, with fines for late attendance.

The men argued against the new hours on the grounds that it would deprive them of the possibility of education, and against the ban on tippling, on the grounds that they needed to refresh themselves. The dispute was referred to the JPs, who came up with a ruling that pleased no-one. They retained the hours from 6 a.m. to 7 p.m., and allowed the journeymen to refresh themselves alone at their bench, but not in groups. They allowed an hour's reduction of pay for those who came to work five minutes late — the masters had asked only for half hour's reduction — and they ruled that journeymen not employed had to take work that was available. The Justices gave their ruling in July 1787 and the men took the matter to the Court of Session, which eventually, in February 1788, ruled in favour of 6 a.m. to 6 p.m. in Summer and 8 a.m. to 8 p.m. in winter, on grounds of health: 'more work would be performed in that period and to better purpose by men who were kept in health by having proper intervals for air and refreshment'. The masters' appeal against this judgement was rejected.[38]

Among traditional urban craftsmen many of the old patterns still remained in the 1780s and they looked to the courts to settle differences. The number of cases coming to the Court of Sessions was increasing and more trades were involved. Whereas up until the 1780s the initiative for going to the JPs came mainly from the employers, looking to the courts to maintain maximum wage rates and a traditional subordination of journeymen to master, after that date the pattern was different. In cases up to the 1780s it was generally journeymen who were critical of wage regulation. Now, however, as they saw their earnings and status being eroded by a flow of labour into the cities and by the faster-rising prices, especially once war broke out, journeymen began to take the initiative in seeking legal regulation. The remarkable thing is that Justices of the Peace and the judges of the Court of Session were ready to respond to this. Among many employers, on the other hand, there was less and less enthusiasm for control. This was most true among the newer and now rapidly growing trades, especially in the West, and there was much more overt conflict. But even there, the prime concern of the authorities remained the maintenance of peace, and there is little doubt that considerable anxiety was aroused among the propertied classes in 1787 as a result of the riots.

The tensions that were emerging were to be exacerbated in the 1790s by a new political consciousness among some workers in the troubled years of the French Revolution. It took time, however for the effects of the Revolution to be felt and, with rising earnings, 1789, 1790 and 1791 seem to have been years of remarkable tranquillity in industrial relations.[39]

Early enthusiasm for the ideals of the French Revolution was widespread in Scotland, and in 1791 the authorities took action against some publishers of seditious literature. But Henry Dundas, the Home Secretary, was reasonably confident in January 1792 'that many who were formerly most violent, and seemingly most determined have been intimidated by the vigorous measures lately adopted and have withdrawn themselves altogether from the Associations'.[40] Such hopes were rudely shattered in the King's Birthday riot of June 1792. Traditionally a time for boisterous celebrations, it now became politicised. Dundas was burned in effigy and rioting went on over three nights, with at least one rioter shot dead. It was a well-planned event. For days beforehand anti-Dundas pamphlets had been circulating. There were many references to the Porteous riots of 1736 and one handbill, addressed 'To All the Tradesmen in Edinburgh', called a meeting 'when we shall give a general salute in the way it was given to Capt. Porteus (*sic*) of the Town Guard, to Mr. Maitland General supervisor (*sic*) of the Excise'. Maitland was accused of making himself rich on bribes from the wealthy and 'skimming and seizing from the Poor'.[41] Hostility towards the Government was reflected in disturbances and effigy burning in Aberdeen, Perth, Dundee and Lanark. The spark for much of this was the rising food prices of 1792, with the Government blamed for the Corn Law of the previous year, which prohibited grain imports until the price reached 19s. per quarter.

By the summer of 1792, Societies of Friends of the People were spreading. The Perth one was reputed to number 1200. The leaders were from the middle ranks, merchants, a surgeon, a minister and a solicitor, with other 'persons of some little respectability in the Town', but the bulk of the membership consisted 'chiefly of operative weavers, of which there are a vast number' and of 'operative people in the various trades of Perth'.[42] In Edinburgh in July radical reformers, young men of the ranks of the gentry, lawyers and army officers, met to establish a broadly-based reform association, the Associated Friends of the People, 'for restoring our Constitution to its original purity'.[43] The demand was for equal representation and 'more limited duration of parliamentary delegation' and for burgh reform.

Tradesmen and journeymen were associated with the new movement, though it was dominated by professional men. Numerous societies were established in the working-class communities of Glasgow and Paisley, Dundee and Dunfermline.[44] At a national convention in November there were representatives of forty-two towns and villages. The social origins of the participants were apparent in the tone of the proceedings and the desire to emphasise their moderation:

> to *reform* and not to *subvert* the order of society ... To give security to *property* against the fraudulent pretences of those whom caprice, interest, or ambition might instigate to swindle it from them — And not to violate *it* themselves by public robbery of equal division.[45]

Any person found guilty of rioting or of 'creating or aiding sedition in the country' would have his name 'expunged from the books of the Society', though any member 'persecuted and oppressed by the arm of power' would be defended.[46]

There were undoubtedly tensions among the participants. Hostility to incorporation control and to other restrictions on free trade, expressed by some reformers, would not have appealed to all craftsmen. Painite demands for universal suffrage and shorter Parliaments began to appear, especially from smaller industrial villages where perhaps the reform movement was less likely to be under middle-class control. These caused anxiety among the better-off reformers.[47]

By the winter of 1792 unrest was widespread throughout the country. There had been a bad summer and a serious grain shortage was building up. Again, with the wet summer, few peats could be cut and dried, so fuel was in short supply and expensive.[48] On top of this, the government was tightening up on the collection of taxes. Sir William Maxwell in Dumfriesshire noted the insensitivity of the revenue officers who posted notices on church doors listing taxes to be paid, including the 1783 charge on registration of christenings and burials. These had never been gathered in the rural areas of Scotland, and, said Maxwell, 'tho' trifling appear to the Country People to be oppressive'. How far political considerations figured in the unrest is hard to gauge. Maxwell, writing to the Duke of Buccleuch, believed that rural labour understood nothing 'about parliamentary reform, equal representation and other grievances of which the discontent in a higher rank of life complain', but what they did have were 'hopes of bringing about a Division of Landed Property, and of getting ten acres each which they have been told will fall to the share of each individual'. He also noted that Paine's pamphlet was 'now in the hands of almost every Countryman'.[49]

Similar anxious letters came to the Lord Advocate from elsewhere. Lord Dundonald wrote of the Dunfermline weavers who

> with their morning drams of whisky imbibed a spirit harsh and inflammatory as the liquor they swallow. Its effects aided by the fumes of constipated Feces caused by the Profession of weaving, and the whole set fermenting by the characteristic sourness and morosity of Scots Presbyterian Sectaries — I do not my Lord heighten the Picture of many of this class of men. They are enemies to subordination.[50]

From Perth there were even more serious warnings that 'the lower Class of People talk of nothing but Liberty and Equality — No Dundas, — No Bishops — and No King. Nothing but a republic for us'.[51] There were riots in Dundee at the end of 1792, during which trees of liberty were planted, triggered by the custom officers blocking a grain landing at the port.[52]

Most of the authorities kept a cool nerve, though there were growing worries about the reliability of troops. A few, like the Provost of Aberdeen, panicked and suggested the impressment of striking sailors into the navy as an effective way of dealing with 'a tumultuous association of sailors to obtain an extravagant and intolerable advance of wages'. The seamen had seized all the ships in the harbour and prevented their being loaded or unloaded or putting to sea. In the end, uncertain about their ability to impose their authority, the magistrates persuaded the shipowners to accept arbitration.[53]

This is not untypical, and what one has over the next few years is a judicious application of both stick and carrot. It reflected the continual debate among the ruling class about how to maintain order, whether by force or by concession. In some ways, it could be argued, the remarkable thing about these years in Scotland is the limited extent of unrest and the failure of the political reformers to make more contact with the workers. As far as one can judge from the available evidence, there was no real threat of revolution in Scotland in the 1790s and the reform movement most of the time remained small and isolated. Yet workers undoubtedly had grievances. Rapid and far-reaching changes had taken place over the previous twenty years. Many had had their pattern of life transformed, from country into town, from workshop into factory, from independent artisan to wage slave. The organisation of many crafts and industries had been completely altered. New employers, new attitudes and the competitiveness of developing capitalism brought all the changes and insecurities that E. P. Thompson has so graphically examined in England. The transformation for many in Scotland had been equally traumatic. One would have expected more agitation. No doubt some of the docility can be explained by the lack of any tradition of political activity in Scotland. There was a more limited language of political (though not of religious) democracy in Scotland than in England, on which reformers could draw: one sees it in the political declarations of radical groups which were, on the whole, derived from English historical experiences, rather than looking to some free, Scottish past. There is no doubt also that sheer repression played its part, but that more unrest was avoided was at least partly due to a responsiveness on the part of sections of the ruling class to fluctuations in the economic position of many tradesmen in the wartime economy.

But first came the big stick. The early months of 1793 brought a whole series of court cases against reformers. First there were trials of printers and booksellers who were publishing and distributing radical literature, particularly dangerous in a relatively literate population. Then came the first attempt to try Thomas Muir, though he failed to appear, having gone to France, purportedly to plead for the King's life. In March, Dun, a Kirkintilloch minister, was sentenced to three months for having taken three pages from the minutes of the Society for Reform in

Kirkintilloch, when the Sheriffs of Lanarkshire and Dunbartonshire were investigating its activities.[54]

With prices remaining at a relatively high level and perhaps with fears of further shortages there were signs of renewed tensions in April 1793. The mounting hostility towards French expansionism in the Low Countries had finally come to war in the previous month. A continuing focus of criticism in the cities was the Corn Law, and it was believed that the growing distress was exacerbated by the lack of importation of foreign grain. The 1791 Act had prohibited the importation of oats until the price reached 19s. per quarter. What caused particular resentment was the fact that English ports could be opened at a lower price.[55] A serious meal riot in Inverness involved men and women from the hemp factory and the thread factory and journeymen from the different incorporated trades, marching behind their trade banners. They forcibly unloaded a grain ship bound for Grangemouth and demanded that the grain be sold locally at 1s. a peck. The local magistrates were convinced that the price of provisions was only 'the specious pretext for this formidable rising' and reported that 'A Pains Book it is now known has been very industriously circulated among the lower classes of our people, and its damnable Doctrine, eagerly embraced by them — of Liberty and Equality they are constantly talking, and of making Laws and fixing prices, on every necessity of Life'.[56]

From Glasgow there was talk of a 'universal panic', with a run on the banks, as people refused to hold notes, and a shortage of coinage. With the outbreak of war, trade had collapsed and many weavers were out of work. A convention of reformers in April 1793, with many more lower-class participants than previous gatherings, called for peace with France, but there were violent arguments on how strongly worded the petition to the government should be.

Muir of Huntershill was eventually brought to trial in August, and the judges, not just the notorious Braxfield, had no doubt about the seriousness of his crime. The jury was handpicked from among signatories of the Goldsmiths' Hall resolutions, which loyalists had signed in December 1792 in direct opposition to the Friends of the People Association and all it stood for. He received his exemplary sentence of fourteen years' transportation.[57] The trial of Thomas Fishe Palmer, and English Unitarian member of the Dundee Friends of the Liberty, followed at Perth in September, when he received seven years' transportation for publishing a handbill, written by a weaver, George Mealmaker, which 'described the King and Parliament as in League to enslave the country and exhorted the people to combine to take decisive measures in their own defence'.[58]

This onslaught on the reform movement in Scotland brought reformers to Edinburgh for a Convention of the Friends of the People, which gathered at the end of October and the beginning of November. By now, however, the peak of popular unrest had probably passed. Depression had dampened reforming zeal among the weavers, if the Rev. James Lapslie from Campsie, one of the main prosecution witnesses at Muir's trial, is to be believed:

> The weavers in my parish at this moment are a more sober industrious and better

> behaved people when making fourteen pence a day than twelve months ago when they made three shillings — their wives and families share more of their wages, now the Publicans share less.[59]

Delegates from England, Joseph Gerrald and Maurice Margarot from the London Corresponding Society, arrived after the Convention had broken up and it was resummoned for the end of November — 'The British Convention of delegates of the People, associated to obtain Universal Suffrage and Annual Parliaments'. There was excited talk of secret committees and of rallying on the first announcement of the suspension of Habeas Corpus or of a ban on conventions or of invasion.[60] At this point the authorities acted and arrested Margarot, Gerrald and William Skirving, who had been secretary of the Friends of the People in Edinburgh since 1792. Robert Dundas was slightly anxious about the outcome. There was, he reported, considerable clamour at the treatment of Muir and Palmer, and 'If the Juries here take it into their heads that more is done to those gentry than is absolutely necessary, they may acquit where they would otherwise have convicted'.[61] The three arrested delegates, however, received the full fourteen years' transportation.

The sentences handed out were enough to deter most from political activities, but a few stalwarts continued secret activities. There were reports of discussions on arming of radical groups from various places. The authorities unearthed a plan for insurrection in April 1794 in which Robert Watt, a former government spy, sought to subvert the fencibles in Edinburgh Castle and to seize their arms.[62] The execution of Watt and the mass arrest of radicals in Paisley, Perth, Stirling, Dundee, Edinburgh and Glasgow in September 1794 generally brought that to an end.

To judges like Lord Braxfield the real crime of many of the radical reformers was to have roused the 'lower orders' to discuss political questions and 'making them leave off their work' to do so: a not necessarily correct assumption on his part that the industrial unrest had anything to do with the political agitation. Lord Abercromby made a similar point in the Palmer trial. It was all right to present petitions 'in proper form, and in decent language' but 'to call meetings and collect together mechanics and those whose education and circumstances do not entitle or qualify them to judge of matters of legislation — people ignorant altogether of the grievances which they are told they are loaded with, till they are assembled and taught that they are in a state of oppression' was unacceptable.[63]

For at least some groups, wages seem to have crept up in the early 1790s in line with rises in the prices of provisions. With coal, iron, cotton and the building industry all booming between 1788 and 1791 there were conditions favourable to workers, with few disputes. By the Autumn of 1792 more wage demands were being reported in both Glasgow and Edinburgh. Edinburgh shoemakers gained 6d. on the price paid for a pair of boots to 4s.6d. and 4d. on a pair of shoes, to 1s.8d. for men's and 1s.10d. for women's.[64] It came to a sudden end with the financial crisis of the winter of 1792–93. And at least one Glasgow businessman welcomed the stagnation of 1793 as having 'the most beneficial consequences for men of real capital':

> The wages of our labourers had got to such a height that they . . . occasioned much idleness and dissipation and much of the time of our workmen was consequently spent in ale houses, where they become politicians and government mongers, restless and discontented.[65]

By the summer there was unemployment and distress on unprecedented levels, with claims that some people were dropping dead from hunger in the streets of Glasgow.[66]

The Summer and Autumn of 1793 was probably potentially the most dangerous time, with economic distress alongside political agitation. Yet there are few signs that a link was made. Indeed the ruling class could gain some reassurance that the middle-class manufacturers who had toyed with radical reform were now firmly on the side of order. They were also helped by the fact that the crisis was largely a West of Scotland one. Other areas were less badly hit, and even in the West there was a quick recovery.

The situation worsened once again in the winter of 1794–95 and Henry Cockburn noted that, in one day in March 1795, 11,000 persons, an eighth of Edinburgh's population, were being fed by charity, with one loaf per week allowed for each individual.[67] Despite this, the Edinburgh shoemakers were out on strike for five weeks in 1795, pressing for 5s. for boots and 2s. for shoes, and they won. The usual tactic was tried by the authorities: a number of journeymen were seized on the orders of the Procurator-Fiscal and sent to prison, but they were not brought to trial and the employers eventually conceded the new rate. The reason, probably, was that the employers themselves could not hold together. This seems to have been a period of intense competition among shoemakers, with many new employers coming into the craft and supplying a growing export market. Alexander Stewart, one of the masters who prosecuted the journeymen in 1795, claimed that some of the new employers 'because of their inexperience of the Trade as to the little profits they make upon it' were paying as much as 7s. or 8s. for a pair of boots and 2s.9d. for shoes. Their aim also, he claimed, was a 'desire of monpolizing the business'.[68] At about the same time, the Edinburgh wrights went to the courts for an advance of 2d. in the shilling. This was granted, allowing ordinary wrights to earn 12s. a week, but giving the employers the right to apply to the court for a reduction 'when the meall should fall to 13d. the peck'.[69]

In the Spring of 1796 there were reports of an 'extremely formidable' Society of Glasgow shoemakers, with James Elder as secretary. This had links with other shoemakers' societies in towns and villages throughout the West of Scotland. Almost all of them were on strike in July 1796 for a rise in wages. Four of the Glasgow leaders were convicted before the JPs, three getting one month and one a fortnight, but unrest continued.[70]

The summer of 1797, when the Militia Act for Scotland was passed, brought the worst outbreaks of rioting and political agitation since 1793. This statute aimed at conscripting up to 6000 men between the ages of 19 and 23. Many were exempt and it was possible to pay for a substitute. The most vulnerable, then, were the poorer young men in small towns and villages, who had no farmer, laird or employer to exert influence for them or to pay the exemption fee. These were the ones who would be picked out by the parish schoolmaster. Not surprisingly, there were riots the length and breadth of the country, with the most serious results in Tranent where troops ran amok and killed eleven men and women. At least some of the anti-Militia riots had encouragement from activists in a revived reform group, the secret United Scotsmen, whose demands were essentially Painite.[71] Because of the nature of the organisation there is no way of knowing how strong it was during its shadowy existence from 1797 to 1803, though unlikely figures of 9,653 were claimed for membership in September 1797. But, Catherine Burns has identified twenty-six societies, half of them in the Tayside area, and it was particularly strong in weaving parishes and in parishes with larger Seceder congregations. The moving force behind the society on Tayside was George Mealmaker, a Dundee weaver, who had been involved with Palmer in 1792–93, but had somehow avoided prosecution. This time he was not so lucky and was arrested in January 1798 and sentenced to fourteen years' transportation.[72]

These last years of the century were ones of considerable economic uncertainty for many groups. Demand fluctuated erratically depending on the fortunes of war; food prices were rising fast; there were signs of growing discontent. Further industrial trouble arose among the Edinburgh shoemakers in 1798. A number of journeymen were trying to push up rates above the scale laid down in 1795 and were generally gaining advances. They were organised in a Society of United Journeymen Shoemakers meeting in Carubbers Close. Each member paid 2d. per month to help maintain aged members and, reputedly, to support those out of work. According to the employers, there was also a secret regulation 'to support the Journeymen against the imposition of their masters and to receive wages when off work'. There were also attempts to impose a closed shop, with some members refusing to work with those who would not join the union. The Society had links with journeymen shoemakers in other towns since it was a tramping society, providing certificates for shoemakers moving from town to town in search of work. It was also financially sound enough to be able to give cash assistance to striking shoemakers in Hull and in Glasgow. The Edinburgh men, in turn, received help from shoemakers in Paisley. More significantly, however, there were signs of a solidarity that was surmounting craft barriers: the first sign of what John Foster has called a 'labour consciousness' or a 'trade union consciousness'. The shoemakers in Edinburgh got help from journeymen in other crafts, including the curriers, the hatters, the combmakers and the tailors. It was the first indication that the experience of rapid industrial change, affecting so many of the traditional craftsmen, was beginning to forge that sense of common experience and mutual dependence which was to surpass craft exclusiveness.

In response to the journeymen's demands a meeting of master shoemakers made out a new table of wages which they claimed would bring improvements to many. They accepted that the rates proposed were lower than what the best-paid were able to earn, but claimed that they were better than those paid to all but ten journeymen. Clearly, what they wanted was to get back to uniformity of wage rates which the new employers had been undermining. The union rejected the employers' proposals and a strike took place in October 1798. Both sides were called before the JPs, where the masters were sharply reprimanded 'for pretending to fix a general rate of wages by their own authority, which was in fact entering into a combination themselves'. The journeymen were ordered back to work at the scale proposed by the masters, but were told that they were free to submit a case to the JPs for higher wages.

A number of them continued to resist and opened their own shop outside Edinburgh 'where any kind of work would be done', and argued that the JPs, by accepting the masters' scale, were, in fact, reducing wages. They sought a bill of advocation at the Court of Session, arguing that they could not be forced to work, since they were employed by the piece and were free to 'adjudge their services for a given time to particular individuals, without their present consent, and independent of all previous contracts'. The Court ruled that in the meantime the journeymen should work at the agreed rates, but when they were paid on a Saturday evening they should also get a note of the wages held in reserve should the justices grant higher wages. The journeymen still refused to accept this seemingly generous settlement and the strike continued. Now the Incorporation of Shoemakers took action against nine of the strikers, 'who appeared to them to be the ringleaders of the Association'. The Sheriff sentenced them to prison, until they agreed to return to work at the wages laid down by the masters' scale of October 1798. On appeal to the Court of Session, two of the men, Peter Arnot, who was by now a freeman of the Incorporation of Calton and 'would not go back for any wages', and James Henderson, who was now working as a carter, were released, but the sheriff's ruling on the others was upheld. It seems to have been intended as a deterrent and for a time did prevent similar applications from other groups of craftsmen.[73]

The end of the century also brought the final emancipation of the colliers. By the second half of the eighteenth century, serfdom was proving to be a major obstacle to the expansion of the workforce. But that expansion was necessary if the coal industry were to satisfy the growing demand, particularly in the 1780s, from the expanding iron industry. Employers, desperate for labour, were no longer returning deserters and, indeed, were often trying to seduce men away from neighbouring coalmasters. Little new labour was attracted into what had long been an outcast workforce and, as a result, wages rose. The bargaining position of colliers was strengthened as was, probably, their tendency to combine. John Millar and Adam Smith both condemned serfdom as contributing to the position whereby the Scots collier was substantially better off than his counterpart south of the border: 2s.6d. a day as compared to 10d. or 1s. in Newcastle, according to Smith in 1763, 12s. a week as opposed to 9s. in Newcastle, according to Millar in 1771.[74]

In 1775 the first Emancipation Act was passed, which laid down that all new workers would be free and that, for existing bound workers, serfdom would be gradually phased out. The pressure for this seems to have come from those, generally newer, employers who wanted to expand their coal works and wanted to be able to poach labour from other mines; opposition came from those who feared they would lose what scarce labour they had. In addition, these same newer employers, especially in the expanding western coalfields, were the ones who wanted to push down the price of labour to make Scottish coal more competitive. There is not a great deal of evidence of pressure from colliers themselves. It is hardly surprising that there should not have been much wish to alter a situation that gave them an economic advantage, though they were perhaps less willing to bind their children. On the other hand, there *was* a social stigma, and at any rate some, as Alan Campbell has shown, were concerned with their lack of 'liberty' from at least 1762.[75] There was no absence of concerted action among colliers. In their tightly-knit communities they had learned long since to work together to exert pressure on their employers, and, at least from the late seventeenth century, there had been 'brotherhoods' of colliers in operation, with masonic-type oaths and rituals binding one another to mutual support. Collective bargaining over wages and conditions went on. Varieties of working conditions and the appearance of new problems meant that there had to be regular negotiations on the prices to be paid for each creel of coal brought up. Employers had to depend upon reliable and experienced colliers or on specially appointed 'overmen' from within the ranks of the operative colliers to assist in fixing a price for a stretch of coal seam. It did not need much organisation to get community action against outsiders, especially the English miners, whom some employers tried to import. The troubles that the Carron Company faced with this are well documented. For the employers, the 1775 Act was a way of breaking the hold of the bound colliers on the workforce. An influx of new workers would smash the tightly-knit communities that serfdom had created.[76]

The 1775 Act did not bring the end of serfdom. It required an approach to the sheriff for bound men to end their serfdom, and one condition was that they should not have been involved in collective action. Many were, also, too caught up in a circle of debt to their employers to break free. Nor did the 1775 Act solve the problem of labour shortage, though the labour force increased by some twentyfold over the next twenty years, and there were still opportunities for colliers to take advantage of scarcity to push their demands. Disputes continued, with colliers taking advantage of high demand to push for increases. Employers sought to counter this by building up coal stocks before confronting combinations among their men. The men responded by cutting the length of their working day or the number of their working days in order to reduce output: itself evidence of a high level of organisation. In the 1790s there were increasing complaints of the tight 'brotherhood' of colliers that existed in many collieries. In this way the men were able to control entry and prevent employers importing new labour.[77] To keep up prices and wages, many colliers were working only three days a week. In 1798, the Scottish coalmasters, called together by those in the Lothians, resolved 'to put in force the present laws respecting combinations in order to obtain higher wages' and they set up a committee 'to consider whether it will be necessary to apply for a new Act to oblige them to perform regular work as other labourers'.[78]

The outcome was a Bill in 1799 to prevent combinations among miners and to regulate wages. It proposed also that JPs should regulate wages of colliers on a yearly basis and that colliers should be compelled by law to work a six-day week. To limit the high turnover of labour a discharge certificate would be made compulsory, with a fine of £50 on any employer who employed someone without such a certificate. Not surprisingly, it stirred widespread opposition among the colliers, and it is a measure of the extent of existing organisation that 600 Lanarkshire men contributed 2s. each to pay the expenses of a law agent to organise opposition. There were petitions also from other miners at a number of collieries, asking to be heard before the measure was passed. This was agreed, although in the event the second and third readings were postponed twice on account of other business, and the men were not heard. More importantly, however, there was opposition from the merchants and manufacturers of the West of Scotland. They feared that the bill would make the labour shortage worse and stir up more agitation. Also, the western coal and iron masters had no desire to see any restriction on their ability to recruit labour, if necessary from eastern collieries.[79]

A much-amended Bill became law in June 1799, which freed the remaining bound colliers. The proposed discharge certificate was dropped, as were the compulsory aspects of wages' and hours' regulation. Instead, colliers were brought under the 1617 and 1661 Acts of the Scottish Parliament that allowed an approach to JPs to fix wages, if a dispute arose. Because of the strength of opposition from western employers as well as from miners a minimalist Act had been passed, but, significantly, it recognised the role that JPs continued to play in Scottish industrial relations. Although emancipated, colliers were still a long way from ceasing to be treated as outsiders in Scottish society. Their reputation as a close, brutal and brutalised group survived for decades, but, at least in law, they were now treated as free men.

Elsewhere, however, there was an increased use of the courts in the late 'nineties and an apparent readiness by the courts to play a role in industrial relations. At times this was to the workers' advantage, at other times not. The Court of Session had granted Edinburgh wrights a rise of 2d. in 1795 because of the price of meal. On the other hand, the Burgh Court in Aberdeen in 1797 was fining twelve striking tailors ten shillings and giving them eight days in gaol, after which they were bound to return to their former masters, for wages of 7s.6d. a week, and 'shall not leave service without giving the masters one month previous warning at least of their intention to do so'.[80] In Dundee, the journeymen tailors tried to push up their wages to 9s. a week by getting JPs to fix rates. When this failed, they struck again and won.[81] Lothian JPs ruled on shoemakers' wages in 1798, and in Glasgow JPs fixed tailors' wages in 1799.[82] The Glasgow shoemakers were involved in a series of cases between 1797 and 1799 as they sought to push up their wages, until in 1799 their funds were exhausted.[83]

Wet weather wiped out the harvests in 1799, drought burned them up in 1800 and there was a severe social crisis. Between 1798 and 1800 the price of meal rose by 140 per cent in East Lothian, and for many there was near famine.[84] Not surprisingly it brought food riots and unrest. The Glasgow Journeymen Wrights approached the Lanarkshire JPs for the rise on the grounds that owing to the present general scarcity and the extreme price of necessaries of life they find it totally impossible with the utmost industry and economy to provide for themselves and families from the wages allowed them by their master, which upon the average do not exceed twelve shillings per week, and from which sum falls to be deducted the expenses of tools of every kind.[85]

The old struggle between the Edinburgh tailors and the Incorporation reached the Court of Session again, when a JP ruled that tailors should maintain three houses of call instead of one. The house of call was the regular meeting place of the Tailors' Society and the centre of its benefit society. The Society met every Monday and members had to pay three halfpence. One halfpence was claimed by the call master, who provided a bottle of small beer to those present. He ran the house from the drink profits, together with pennies from out-of-work journeymen, who paid to get their names on the slate. Another halfpenny each Monday went to the Benefit Society, to provide 3s. or 4s. a week to sick and aged members. To increase such funds, new by-laws were introduced 'to make attendance at the house of call compulsory'.

In 1793 the Incorporation of Tailors petitioned the JPs to fix piece rates, as well as day rates. The JPs repealed the regulations of 1777 and fixed a new maximum of 1s.8d. They also laid down piece rates on some of the main items of clothes. Employers increasingly preferred to pay by the piece, but, since the Justices had only fixed the price of some six articles of dress, there were frequent disputes on new items and over changes in style. At the end of 1796 the journeymen compiled a list of piece rates for forty-one articles and submitted them to the masters. There was no official reply from the masters, and some paid the new rates, while others did not. When a number of tailors struck work for these rates, in April 1797, a criminal complaint was laid against William Hossack, the callmaster, and a number of other journeymen, who were charged with combining to raise wages and using their house of call for this purpose. But the JPs ruled that, although the tailors were bound to serve their masters at the rates laid down, the rates on articles not covered by the 1793 ruling were still negotiable, 'to be settled by the mutual agreement of masters and men, and not at the discretion of the masters alone'.

Eighteen months later, both men and masters submitted tables of piece rates to the JPs, who more or less accepted the journeymen's rates on more than fifty articles of apparel. While this was to the men's advantage, at the same time the JPs demanded that instead of the single house of call there should be three separate houses, with no more than a hundred names on each list. They proposed a 40s. fine for each name above a hundred. Since the house of call was seen as the centre of the combination, the purpose of the ruling was clearly to thwart the journeymen's organisation and generally to weaken it. The Society of Master Tailors, which existed separately from the Incorporation, had already been frustrated in this sphere, when they had taken action against three or four journeymen for illegal combination 'by passing certain resolutions at their houses of call'. The journeymen had resolved that they would not work with anyone who was not a member of the house of call and that masters should get names from the list in rotation. In 1799, there was at least one incident of men refusing to work with a foreman who was not a member of the house of call. The case, in February 1800, was thrown out because of a faulty indictment, 'as not charging them in a manner sufficiently relevant', and no further action had been taken. The journeymen appealed to the Court of Session against the JPs ruling on the houses of call, arguing that they had no right to interfere in the matter of the house of call, while the masters' advocate argued that Justices 'have a right to interfere for the public interest'. The case went on through 1800 and, in February 1801, the Court of Session ruled that the Justices could insist on three houses.[86] The Journeymen's Society once again petitioned, this time arguing that the JPs were not justified in taking preventative action against something that *might* cause illegal combination, but had not been proved to have done so yet. In December 1801, the full court ruled that 'there is no evidence of the necessity or expendiency of the regulations complained of', suspended the JPs' ruling on the houses of call and allowed them to retain the single house. It granted costs to the journeymen.[87]

Probably the most successful appeal to the courts at this time was from the Journeymen Shipwrights of Leith. Their Society had existed since 1731 and was reputed to have substantial funds. Contributions were 10s. a quarter and disabled ships' carpenters could get 4s. a week. Widows received a small weekly allowance. It may have been organised originally by the employers, but at some stage the journeymen had broken away to form their own body, though that 'seems ultimately to have failed'. In 1795, the 150 or so journeymen, taking advantage of high wartime demand, sought an increase and successfully struck work, winning a rate of 16s. a week for 'old work' (repair work) and 14s. for 'new work'. In August 1799 they applied to the Justices to sanction a further rise, because of the high price of oatmeal. The JPs heard both sides and ruled that while the existing wages were 'reasonable and adequate', because of the high prices of provisions, the journeymen were entitled to an advance,

> from the 2nd day of November inst fourpence per day, to continue till the meal in the Edinburgh market falls to 1s.6d. per peck; and 2d. per day after that, till the meal is at 1s.2d. per peck. But declare, that when the meal is at 1s.2d. per peck, the wages are to be reduced to the same rate as before this application was made.

In this case, we actually know the names of the eight Justices who were involved in the judgement. At least four of them were known, active, anti-radicals, who in 1792 had been members of the Goldsmiths' Hall Association. Three of the Justices had been members of the handpicked jury that convicted Thomas Muir.[88] Such men, violent in their opposition to political change, saw the maintenance of traditional interventionist methods of maintaining loyalty and social order as essential. In many ways, the excessive reaction of the authorities to radical movements in Scotland might be seen as the anger of paternalists who felt that they were being spurned.

It was not until the price of oatmeal fell to 1s.2d. at the beginning of 1802 that the masters sought to bring the rates back down to the level of November 1799. Business was, of course, dull by then because of the peace with France. The men objected to the reduction before the JPs but the Justices upheld the masters' decision. Now the journeymen sought a bill of advocation in the Court of Session in September 1802. Lord Hermand upheld the JPs' ruling. The men next petitioned the full court, on the grounds that repair work was unpleasant, involving standing in the mud and in water for long periods. They also justified continuing the present rates because of the high cost of living. At least some of the judges went along with this and argued 'that other considerations besides the price of meal might influence the rate of wages' and that some increase was justified. They referred the issue back to the Quarter Sessions, asking them to consider all the existing circumstances. A committee of three Justices heard the two parties in March 1803 and recommended an increase of 2d. per day. The Quarter Sessions accepted this:

> The Justices, having considered the foregoing statement and whole process, are of opinion, that the price of oatmeal being the principal food of the journeymen ship-carpenters, should enter deeply into consideration in a question of wage, and, that article being at a moderate price at present, find, that the journeymen carpenters are not entitled to the high wages allowed by the Justices in 1799. But, as the articles of clothing and house rents are higher since the wages were previously fixed, find, that the journeymen carpenters are entitled to a rise of two pence per day, and that their wages are now to be 2s.10d. for old work and 2s.6d. for new work per day.

The award was to be backdated three months to 1 January. The masters approached the journeymen to try to get a joint submission against the backdating or, if not, they would resist the whole judgement. One of the main firms, Menzies and Goalen, dismissed fifteen of their men on the first pay day after the decision of the Justices. Not surprisingly, the men insisted on full payment and, although the masters appealed to the Court of Session, the JPs' decision was upheld.[89]

The Edinburgh sawyers were yet another group who found the magistrates sympathetic at this time. The established rate for cutting timber for most of the eighteenth century had been 2s.1d. per 100 square feet, but in 1803 the master joiners, who employed the sawyers, sought to reduce the rate to 1s.3d. It followed a period of exceptional demand for building workers as new fortifications and barracks, as well as private residences, were being built. Earnings had gone up to as much as 6gns. per pair of workers per week. One old builder recalled the pattern in those years — 'They were paid on Saturday and on Sunday they were confined to bed; on Monday they gathered themselves together, sung patriotic songs, and paraded the streets with fiddles and bagpipes, and military music; on Tuesday they came disconsolately to borrow a shilling, in order to buy a file to sharpen their saw'.

The reduction in wages in 1803 was probably both a response to a fall in building orders and an attempt by the employers to reimpose discipline. The men responded by calling a meeting, authorised by the magistrates, at which they showed that the employers had acted in concert in reducing the rates. The town officer was sent to the masters warning them that such a combination was illegal. In the event the employers seem to have given way and the price in fact increased to 2s.9d. per 100 square feet.[90]

The Edinburgh printers were equally fortunate in their dealings with the courts. This relatively well-paid group, in many cases earning over £1 a week, had not made a claim for an increase during the period of scarcity in 1799–1800. Their conditions were comparatively good, with 'steady, warm employment' and great 'licence' in working hours. In March 1803, with the Sheriff's approval, a meeting of 106 compositors asked the employers for a rise of about a third (according to the employers). When this was refused, the men applied to the JPs, who also turned them down. They then applied to the Court of Session for a bill of advocation.

In the presentation to the Court the central issues of the struggle of competing political economies were spelled out. In the employers' case it was asked,

> How far is it fit, or expedient, or safe for Courts of Law to interfere at all, in anticipating, by legal and compulsory means, that natural order of things, which in due time must produce a fair and just arrangment between masters and journeymen, by the operation of that general principle which pervades all classes to the effect of rewarding workmen in proportion to the improvement made in manufacture, and the extent of the demand by the public.

The men, in their presentation, responded,

> It is easy for a speculative politician to sit in his own armchair and talk about the operation of general principles, as if the interest of human society were the same which form the subject of natural philosophers' inquiries. He may lay it down as a dogma in his system (and perhaps in an abstract and notional point of view not unjustly), that the market for labour as well as for other things will always find its level; that inconveniences and disadvantages come by degrees to be pretty justly balanced; and that wages, when left uncontrolled to the higgling and cheapening of the market, will come to the true proportion which they should bear to the peculiar employment in which the labourer is to be engaged.

This might work, said the men, 'were all the masters to continue individual rivals and bidders against each other in the market for labourers; and were all workmen as separate and unconnected, and bidders, against each other for their masters employment', but this was not the case and the tendency of both masters and men was to combine:

> Combinations must lead to opposition; opposition frequently to tumult and public danger to alarm. The best interests of society, then require the controlling power of the court, to whose unbiassed judgement the parties in such disputes may appeal as an anticipation and preventative of evil. It is necessary that there should be tribunals to whom the parties may fairly explain their situation, and lay open the grounds of their claim, either of abatement or of increase of wages; and whose decisions may be as a law between them.

The wage position of the printers was examined in detail by the Court, with an accountant, appointed by the Court, getting access to firms' wages' books. It was claimed by the men's counsel that apart from a temporary rise in 1792 compositors' rates had not increased in fifty years, though the cost of necessities had risen by at least a third. In December 1805, Lord Cullen granted a wage rise, specifying the rates for the different tasks, for example 5½d. per thousand letters for Session Papers, 5d. per thousand for dictionaries, 4½d. for directories, 5d. for foreign words, double for Greek. The masters were ordered to bear the full costs of the case.[91]

While this tradition of judicial arbitration on wages was clearly persisting among Edinburgh craftsmen, there is not much evidence of its happening very much elsewhere in the country. In other areas the most likely legal actions were criminal cases. Dumbarton County Court heard of a combination of calico printers in February 1803, which reputedly had existed for about a year and was part of a national organisation 'extended to every printing ground in England, Scotland and Ireland'. According to the local newspaper,

> By the regulation of this association any member who conceived himself in the smallest degree aggrieved by his employers, or who was offered by them any price for his work which he considers inadequate, was directed instantly to leave his employment, and was from that moment entitled to receive from the public fund an allowance of twelve shillings per week until he should find a master elsewhere who would accede to his demands.

A number of men were sentenced to three months' imprisonment, with George McFarlane, the district secretary, getting three weeks in prison for prevarication under oath and for contempt of court.[92]

Yet there is no doubt that the courts both at the level of JPs and the higher Court of Session were, if anything, increasing their intervention in industrial relations in these years and playing the role of arbiter. It is evident that among the landed class, from which the bulk of the judiciary was drawn, there was that strengthening of paternalism in the face of advancing industrialism which E. P. Thompson has detected in England. Despite Adam Smith and the pressure of expanding capitalism, there still persisted a belief in the need for wages to be related to what they could buy and what was needed for a decent life, not to the crudity of supply and demand. The need for the state to maintain at any rate the appearance of an even-handedness between worker and employer was still held to. It also reflected a Scottish view of the law as organic and dynamic and concerned with social control. Unhampered by English obsession with precedent, Scottish judges were determinedly adjusting the law to meet the needs of a rapidly changing society. Influenced by Adam Ferguson, and other figures of the Scottish Enlightenment, the law was seen as a way of adjusting disputes between classes and securing peace in society.[93] By judicious use of the law in this way, it had proved possible to prevent that link between well-organised trades and the political movements that might well have proved dangerous to the established order. Undoubtedly there were moments of heavyhanded bludgeoning of dissent, not surprising in a country where there had been no recent tradition of public demonstration or debate. But these were balanced by the evidence that it was still possible for journeymen to achieve some improvement in their economic position by constitutional means. It was a vital safety valve. At the same time, the need to respond to altered social and economic needs was causing many legal thinkers to argue for change, for the overthrowing of older, restrictive, regulatory patterns that had made the rights of property subordinate to the needs of the community. This kind of thinking, following from Smith and Millar, which emphasised the sanctity of property, gained ground in the early nineteenth century and led the judiciary to take a less evenhanded position between the propertied and the propertyless.[94]

It is problematic just how significant these legal judgements were in regulating the rates of wages actually paid. By the 1790s there is hardly any mention of maximum rates. Once the courts had moved into piece rates they were generally talking about norms. Similarly, when relating wage rates to cost of living, the courts are assuming that the rates laid down would in fact be minimum rates. How far all employers went along with this or just ignored them, we do not know. It would have been difficult for the most respectable to do so. In many areas the competition for good labour probably meant that some paid more. If there had been systematic underpayment by employers, one would have expected groups of tradesmen to come back to the courts. There is no evidence that this was happening. Undoubtedly, many employers must have detested such interference with their managerial judgements, particularly since they could see a much freer system in operation away from Edinburgh. The next decade saw the whole system coming under sustained attack.

5
The Attack

As J. L. Gray pointed out in an article published fifty years ago,[1] the Anti-Combination Laws of 1799 and 1800 did not apply to Scotland. Nothing in these Acts took any account of the separate Scottish law and its distinct procedures. Given the quite different pattern of industrial relations, it would have been extremely complicated to have included Scotland in the legislation. There is no evidence that any legislator gave it a thought.

Since so much of Scots law was judge-made law, it is not always clear just what the legal position as regards combination was. Even among experts there was uncertainty. Clearly, from what has been said in the preceding chapters, combinations of journeymen existed and were tolerated in eighteenth-century Scotland. It is also clear that men could end up in prison for being involved in combinations. They do seem, on occasion, to hover on the verge of illegality. As far as one can generalise, it was apparently perfectly legal for a group of journeymen to get together to approach the Incorporation of their trade, or to approach the magistrates or JPs or the higher courts to ask for shorter hours or better wages or alteration in working conditions. That was a central part of the system. It was also acceptable to have a permanent organisation to maintain a charity box. Initially this assertion of independence from the Incorporations had not been popular, but charity boxes spread and, by the second half of the eighteenth century, friendly societies of various kinds, and going by various names, existed, some associated with one particular trade, though most ignoring trade divisions. By the 1790s there were more than 200 such friendly societies in Scotland.[2] Some owned houses and other property and were generally looked on with approval by the well-to-do.[3]

Combination as such was not conspiracy in Scotland and, indeed, Scots law recognised the legal identity of associations. What was illegal was to act against the public good. This concept of *contra utilitatem publicam* was obviously a highly adaptable one, but its interpretation lay with the courts, and was debatable within the legal system. What was undoubtedly illegal was to try to force an employer, by means of combination, to go against the ruling of the incorporation or the courts. And, in the case of the Universal Trading Company of Paisley in 1766, the Court of Session ruled that, since one of the aims of the co-partnery was to try to maintain a minimum wage, then it was in common law 'an illegal combination, and of dangerous tendency to society' and, therefore, it could not sue any members who refused to pay their contribution to the Company's debts.[4]

One of the clearest statements of the legal position was made in 1800, just as there were people around who wanted to change it. Fittingly, it was in a case involving the journeymen tailors of Edinburgh, who had tested the law to its limits throughout the eighteenth century. The Court of Session declared

> that it is only when workmen combine to raise their wages beyond their due and legal rate, or seek a rise in wages at their own hands, without submissive, regular lawful applications to the proper tribunal, or when they proceed to acts of violence, and breach of the peace, that they are obnoxious to the laws.[5]

By the end of the 1790s a number of employers obviously resented the increasing interventionism of the courts, now generally to the employers' disadvantage. They tried to deter the journeymen going to the JPs by having combination branded as a criminal offence. From the end of the 1790s use was made of the High Court of Justiciary, the supreme criminal court, against groups of journeymen. In almost all cases the actions in criminal courts followed an appeal by journeymen to the JPs for an alteration in wages. So, in February 1799, while their wages were being examined at the Court of Session, Peter Arnot and other Edinburgh shoemakers were charged before the Sheriff with unlawful combination and conspiracy. They pleaded guilty, after, it is suggested, there had been some plea bargaining, and they received one month in prison. A further case against a group of Edinburgh tailors was similarly intimidatory, when they were charged with seeking 'to control their masters in the management of their business'. But, perhaps because of the uncertainty of the legal position, the Lord Advocate dropped the case.[6]

In 1805 attempts at organisation among ploughmen in the Carse of Gowrie were nipped in the bud when the Sheriff seized four of the ploughmen, who had called a meeting in Perth to discuss wages and hours of work. They duly recanted and 'expressed extreme sorrow for their conduct'. The Sheriff drew attention to the Combination Acts, which made all such activity illegal, he claimed. Despite this, tensions continued and, in 1808, five farm servants in the Carse ended in Perth gaol for refusing to 'clean and dress their horses every night at eight o'clock'. The JPs ruled that 'the masters' orders were not unreasonable' and, therefore, had to be obeyed.[7]

A crucial case in the use of criminal procedures was that against James Taylor and a group of Edinburgh papermakers in 1808.[8] The Lothian papermakers had an organisation linked with 'similar associations both in England and Ireland, and received money from thence for the purpose of maintaining and forwarding the object of the general combination'. In April 1808, the papermakers in at least ten mills asked for a wages increase and, when this was refused, went on strike. The society had funds to support the striking workers and their families and financial aid came from England and Ireland. A meeting of strikers in the village of Roslin, Lasswade, passed a number of resolutions pledging solidarity and 'that none of them should work as papermakers unless they got the rise of wages demanded, or work along with any journeymen accepting of less wages'. The first indictment against the journeymen had been thrown out on the ground that it talked of combining 'for the purpose of raising their wages' and this was not illegal. It was revised to state 'that it was with the intention of *compelling* their masters' to raise wages, and the public prosecutor made a clear distinction between what he described as 'natural' combination and 'artificial' combination. 'The workmen under the influence of 'natural' combination, will seek relief by peaceably writing, and asking from their masters, which they are entitled to do, an increase of wages.' If this were not granted, then they could quit work or they could go to the JPs for legal redress. If the JPs would not grant an increase, then they could leave work 'but they will do so quietly and gradually as possible, not by a motion all at once, which may glut the general market of labour, by too many hands being thrown idle at once'. An 'artificial' combination, in contrast, involved planning, not going to law, raising funds: 'They make the association *a general one* in distant quarters, and rouse the passions of all of the same class in assay against their masters'.[9]

The extent to which the issue of combination had become debatable was clearly brought out in the judges' dicta. Three of the judges, with varying degrees of enthusiasm, went with Lord Cullen in regarding the employers' action in pushing the matter to the High Court as quite improper:

> They should have followed the course which has always been adopted on similar occasions, and have satisfied themselves with a judgement of the civil courts before they thought of coming here, the more especially that both the sheriff and the justices had indisputably the fullest jurisdiction and power to give every degree of the redress that can be desired, and in a manner more suited to the nature of the case.

Lord Hermand had no doubt that they ought to have applied to the Justices, while Lord Craig declared:

> It is not disputed, that without punishable criminality an individual may ask that his wages be raised, or decline working altogether. I do not see how this action changes its moral quality, and becomes a punishable crime, when two or three, or twenty or more are joined in it.

The three other judges gave the opposing perception. Lord Armadale warned of the ruin that would come to a mercantile community if combination were allowed:

> Suppose all the colliers of a country, the servants of extensive iron works, all striking work, all preventing others from working, coal works drowned, furnaces exposed to destruction, by the mere negative conduct of bodies of people flying to compel higher wages.

Lord Meadowbank spelled out the thinking of the new, younger generation:

> Something has been said as if the indictment should have charged that the wages demanded were unreasonable. But I would be glad to know, what it is that fixes the rate of reasonable wages, except a free market. Mr. Jeffrey speaks as if wages ought to be reduced when provisions are cheap and that they must justly be raised when they are dear. But every person knows that the reverse takes place invariably. When provisions are dear there is more labour to sell; because there are more persons who have occasion to dispose of that commodity, which belongs to many, in order, by the price got for it, to purchase the means of subsistence; and at the same time there are fewer in a condition to purchase it. Hence labour falls in the market; and for the converse reason it rises when the provisions are cheap.

In this case, the lack of a majority for such a view was sufficient to save the papermakers.[10]

Hume's *Commentaries on the Criminal Law in Scotland* had made no mention of combination among workmen being a crime. In 1810, two years after the papermakers' case, John Burnett, in a major commentary on the Criminal Law, devoted a substantial section to 'illegal combination' and, in reference to the papermakers' case, concluded that 'the soundness of this decision is extremely questionable . . . And were a similar case to occur, we think it not improbable, that a different result would follow'.[11] Thus, as Professor Mitchison has shown in the case of the Scottish Poor Law,[12] reforming lawyers in Scotland, by describing the law in their new law books as they would like it to be rather than what it was, tried to shape and alter the law in the early nineteenth century.

At the beginning of 1810 the Procurator Fiscal of Ayr brought three journeymen shoemakers before the Justices, charging them with combination to raise wages. Two of those charged absconded and only one, Thomas McNeillie, was brought to trial. It was claimed that McNeillie was a 'principal actor' in a body that received money from Glasgow. The Justices ruled 'that such combinations are exceedingly dangerous, and ought to be suppressed to the utmost', and, specifically under 39 & 40 George III, sentenced McNeillie to two months in prison and a fine of fifty shillings.[13] In doing so they could cite Gilbert Hutcheson's *Treatise on the Offices of Justice of Peace &c in Scotland* published in 1806. Hutcheson accepted that, because of its phraseology, some of the regulations of the 1800 Anti-Combination Act could not be carried into effect in Scotland, but he *did* accept that, except where clauses were explicitly limited to England, it could be applied to Scotland. He had also declared, in another example of writing the law books to achieve change:

> By the common law any one workman may refuse to work till he be paid the price he pleases to fix upon his own labour: But if two or more enter into an agreement of this kind, the common law will punish such associating as being injurious to the interests of the public.[14]

Another case against journeymen shoemakers came up in Glasgow in 1811, when Matthew Chambers, John McDonald, George Emery and Francis Orr were charged. They pleaded not guilty and argued that they had committed no crime 'as they had made use of no force to compel their masters to give the rise, but had only left their work, when their demands were not complied with, which was common practice when masters and servants disagreed respecting wages'. They were defended by the Whig advocates, Francis Jeffrey, Henry Cockburn and John Clerk, but the Court found

> that though relevant matter might be selected from the charges made in the indictment, to infer criminal punishment, they stand too complicated and embarrassed in the detailed statement of them there, to afford that clearness precision and simplicity, which is suited for criminal association and jury trial.[15]

It gave reason to believe that, barring exceptional circumstances, the judges might be more inclined to reverse the papermakers' judgement.

This was a period of considerable industrial unrest, especially in the West of Scotland textile trades. Spinners, weavers and finishing trades were all involved in organising. There was a new level of activity among handloom weavers, who were feeling the sharp impact of falling demand and over supply of labour.

There had been, as has been shown, sporadic activity among groups of weavers in the eighteenth century, and in a number of areas there were weavers' friendly societies, co-operative societies and societies for renting reeds to weavers for setting up their webs.[16] In 1792, at the height of the most prosperous period for weavers, representatives of operative weavers and of the leading manufacturers agreed upon a table of wage rates for the various fabrics.[17] It was the gradual breakdown of this table of prices, starting in the late 1790s, that brought growing discontent among the Scottish cotton weavers. There were too many small manufacturers around, dependent upon the smallest profit margins, vulnerable to every dip in the trade cycle, some at least not averse to dealing in embezzled yarns, for the price list to be fully implemented. It soon became no more than 'a nominal standard of reference'. The prices paid began to fall in the 1790s, but, to an extent, this was hidden by some technical improvements allowing faster output and as long as demand remained high. Not until the sharp food-price rises of 1799 and 1800 was the full effect of the decline apparent. At that point there were more frequent disputes, with individual cases going to law for settlement.[18] A number successfully petitioned Parliament to have a formal system of settling disputes between weavers and manufacturers in the cotton industry. The Act (43 Geo III c.151) covered Scotland, which had not been included in the 1800 Arbitration Act, and it allowed a JP to nominate two referees, one a master or freeman, the other a workman, to conciliate. This was passed in 1802 despite the opposition of the manufacturers to 'the obvious impropriety and danger of laying any restrictions on an intercourse, which is, and ought to be, in its nature mutually free and voluntary'.[19]

After a few years of relative stability, the weavers began to suffer from dramatic fluctuations in the level of their earnings and there was a claim that since 1806 'many families have been so reduced, that formerly held respectable rank amongst other Mechanics [that they] have been under necessity of flying their creditors, and abandoning their families to the charity of the Public'.[20] The handloom weavers were being caught in a vicious spiral from which they were not again going to escape. It was a crisis of over-supply and of over-production. When prices were reduced the weaver had to struggle even harder to maintain his income by increasing output, by working longer hours or by bringing more of his family into the trade with a resultant addition to the surplus of cloth. By 1811 it was claimed that rates had fallen to a third of what they had been when the table of rates had been agreed in 1792.[21]

There had been fairly persistent agitation from 1804 amongst Lancashire weavers for minimum wage regulation, with considerable support from some of the larger manufacturers, who were feeling the effects of undercutting by small men. Succumbing to this pressure in 1808, the Vice-President of the Board of Trade went so far as to bring in a bill to regulate the wages of cotton weavers. Its rejection in June of that year led to riots in Stockport, Rochdale, Wigan and Manchester, with a sustained strike in Manchester.[22] One of the grounds put forward by opponents of the measure for its rejection was that there was no general demand from all parts of the country for such regulation. It was in response to such comments that the Scottish weavers began to move to organise a petition for a minimum wage.

The first meeting was held on 25 June 1808 in Glasgow, with John McIntyre, a Calton weaver, as chairman and John Wood of Tradeston as secretary. A committee was appointed to confer with the manufacturers on the cause of the 'present unexampled low and inadequate price at present paid for weaving'.[23] From the manufacturers they got some sympathy, but little else, and blame was placed firmly on the activities of the 'small corks', on 'pilfering practices carried on in the Trade, by innumerable bands of illicit manufacturers, by whose fundamental means the fair trader is undersold'.[24]

Almost immediately the decision was taken to recruit in other areas. In August, a meeting organised by what was called the 'active committee' was held at Deanston in Perthshire, with McIntyre and Niven Ferguson, two of the original Glasgow members, present. There was already correspondence with England, which McIntyre was appointed to handle. A week later it was decided that 'the first opportunity we have of sending a letter to England and we will ask their opinion of the propriety of making exertions to obtain co-operation of the Irish'.[25] In September, McIntyre reported that he had been in contact with the Paisley weavers, while news came of organising in Govan and in Barrhead.[26] Wood, the secretary, was despatched to Ayrshire in November to organise and recruit there and, after a former secretary of the Perth weavers got in touch with the Glasgow committee suggesting that a delegate be sent to Perth, there were reports of organisation among the Perth weavers.[27]

The aim of the Glasgow Committee was to have an organisation based on district meetings, from which delegates would be sent to a general committee. It was to be financed by a levy of 6d. to 1s. per loom for general funds, to defray the costs of petitions to Parliament.[28]

Since a number of Bolton manufacturers had given support to demands for wage regulation in England, there were hopes of getting support from Scottish manufacturers. A petition was submitted, by the new association, to the Deacon of the Glasgow Weavers' Incorporation, seeking a general meeting of the trade to give backing to the minimum price demand, 'fixing the price of weaving upon a more equitable and permanent Basis, corresponding to the advance of provisions in general'.[29] The Deacon took no action and the weavers found that, although the manufacturers expressed themselves generally favourable, they would not take the initiative in calling a meeting. In the end, the Glasgow committee abandoned the attempt to get the manufacturers to sign the petition, after it had been passed to and fro between some of them, with each saying that he would sign if another did so first. But, helped by a donation of nearly £13, collected by the Lanarkshire Militia, the petition was submitted to the House of Commons.[30]

By the end of 1808 the Glasgow Committee was able to produce details of the number working and the number of idle looms in 149 areas and the organisation was obviously spreading.[31] The Perth Committee was given the task of organising the area north of the Forth, in the Ochil Hillfoots from Doune to Dunfermline, and they were encouraged to make contact with Fife and Kinross, and to extend their influence to Aberdeen.[32] In other words, it was never the intention to confine the organisation to cotton weavers, it was open to all handloom weavers. Kilmarnock too formed a central committee, corresponding with the Ayrshire villages.

There was a major setback in April 1809 when a committee of inquiry into the running of the Association found some irregularities in the financial accounts and decided to prosecute the treasurer, McIntyre. Eventually he was imprisoned and his furniture seized, presumably for debt, until some friends put up money to secure his release.[33] None the less, the organisation kept going. An extraordinary meeting was held in May, with delegates from Perth, Aberdeen, Langholm, Lanark and Kilbarchan, as well as from the Glasgow area. Here plans were launched for restricting entry into the trade by means of an apprenticeship scheme and a new committee was appointed, with Thomas Smith as secretary and Archibald Buchanan as treasurer.[34]

In establishing an apprenticeship scheme, the weavers were following the advice given to them by Mr. Curwen, the MP for Carlisle, and by Samuel Whitbread.[35] The aim of the scheme was that no one should serve less than a five years' apprenticeship, while those who took up their apprenticeship under the age of twelve should serve a full seven years.[36] Until then there clearly had been considerable variation in the time served. From Lanark it was reported that those under twelve did only five years, and those over twelve four years. In addition, there were reports that some master weavers gave time off indenture in return for half the apprentices' earnings.[37] Also, in practice, many weavers were coming into the rapidly expanding labour force with no recognised apprenticeship. By the new rules of the Association, it was intended that no journeyman should instruct more than two apprentices at any one time and no female apprentices, unless they were members of the immediate family. Any linen weaver could switch to cotton, *in his own district*, but in any other district he had to serve for a year under the direction of a cotton weaver and pay 'his instructor the sum of five pounds or one third of his earnings, with two thirds of his light and loom hire during his agreement'.[38] The great attraction of handloom weaving for many parents had been that it was possible for children to enter the trade as an apprentice long before any other trade and they could earn more. Apprenticeships were often finished before they were fourteen or fifteen years of age. Belatedly, the weavers were trying to come to grips with the excessive ease of entry into their trade.

The position of the new organisation was formalised in June 1809, with the setting up of the General Association of Operative Weavers in Scotland, at a meeting in Glasgow. Rules were discussed and agreed over the next few months. There was a general committee, consisting of delegates from all the associated districts who chose to attend, and also a corresponding committee, which was given the task of drafting a table of prices and sending it to the newspapers.[39]

Despite reorganisation, however, the Association was clearly going through a lean period at the end of 1809, when for the last two months receipts were £10.1.6d. and expenditure £9.16.5½d. Most of the expenditure went on the distribution of handbills advertising the agreed statement of prices.[40]

Some renewed activity seems to have been stirred by the arrival of an English delegate, reporting a 'high state of organisation in Carlisle' where the Association also included weavers from the southern counties of Scotland. In February 1810, Thomas Smith began visiting several districts: first, the East End of Glasgow, then, with the English delegate, Paisley, and, finally Stirling, Perth, Edinburgh and the smaller villages on the way.[41] Presumably because of renewed activity there, the Perth district had their books and papers seized for examination by the Procurator Fiscal.[42]

By the summer of 1810, the corresponding committee was in contact with some 100 districts, which contained around 40,000 looms, though what proportion of these were operated by union men is not clear. Perth had a separate organisation, with 2,100 looms, as had Edinburgh and its surrounding villages, with 1500. In Paisley, which remained aloof from the General Association, there were 4,500 looms.[43] In spite of paper numbers, however, the financial situation remained precarious and they were having to tell the Carlisle people that they might not be able to send a delegate to the convention of weavers being held there. The Edinburgh Association, however, did send a delegate. The aim of the Carlisle gathering was to try to get uniformity of regulation for weavers throughout the United Kingdom, with a fixed seven years' apprenticeship. There was some debate on this issue in the Glasgow committee, who seem to have believed that their own more flexible scheme would be more effective.[44] However, a delegate meeting eventually agreed to the Carlisle proposals and in addition gave financial assistance to some imprisoned weavers in Carlisle.

The delegates of the General Association, in November 1810, also launched an ambitious plan for providing work for unemployed members. With foreign trade severely restricted by the results of Napoleon's decrees, conditions were particularly bad. There had been a spate of bankruptcies and there was a great deal of unemployment and underemployment of weavers. The plan was that each member should contribute £2 to establish an organisation whose funds would be kept separate from the weavers' association. When the funds reached an adequate level a delegate meeting would be held,

> to arrange the order of procedure, fix the prices to be paid by the Society for the respective fabrics of work they intended to manufacture, and to appoint some central Agency, for the convenience of country districts to execute their orders for material, clearing and disposing of the finished goods &c.

They were to concentrate on those branches of the trade that were in most demand. It was also intended to set up a permanent factory ('manufacturing concern') in Glasgow with fifty or sixty looms, which would be the joint property of the districts. The aim was to obtain some of the gains of a profitable industry: 'And who can have a better right to the profits of our industry than ourselves?'

After all, it was argued, most of the new designs 'are the offspring of our ingenuity'.[45] There is no evidence that it came to anything.

It may have been the threat posed by such a plan that stirred opposition among the employers. More likely it was only one of a number of signs of growing conflict between craftsmen and their employers. Typical was the shoemaking trade, where thirty-six Glasgow employers combined to resist an annual wage demand. They agreed to introduce a discharge certificate and not to employ union men. They also proposed to abandon uniformity of wages and 'in future pay for trade according to merit'.[46] The winter of 1810–11 was particularly bad with unemployment among various groups 'never been known so bad'. Half of the stonemasons of Glasgow were reported out of work and a third of the cabinetmakers.[47] It was a time of tension with sporadic violence against non-striking workers. At the end of 1810 the Sheriff of Lanarkshire and the Procurator Fiscal seized the papers of the Weavers' Association. At the same time a series of resolutions, emanating from the Trades' House, called on other bodies to join with the Incorporated Trades in endeavouring 'to procure a Legislative enactment to suppress Combination Societies'. There were complaints of a breakdown of 'the natural and just legal order that ought to subsist between master and journeymen'. As the master boot and shoemakers declared,

> Innovations of this kind are making such rapid progress among every class of mechanics, which seem to subvert all order in society, and threaten to overthrow in ruin every Manufacturing Department in the Kingdom, and call loudly for interference of the legislature.

The master cotton spinners complained that recent court decisions, which made clear that the Combination Act of 1800 did not apply in Scotland, had made it impossible for employers to have resort to law.[48] There were fears among the journeymen that the aim was to go even further:

> It is evident that they wish for an act, prohibiting, under severe penalties, the meeting of operatives as such, an act by which the landlord of any tavern or public house will forfeit his licence where such meetings are held; and the possessor of any dwelling house, workshop, or schoolroom to be subjected to fines and imprisonment; and the operative attending to transportation. And also prohibiting, under certain penalties, any manufacturer or employer to admit into his work any journeyman who cannot produce a certificate from his last employer, that said journeyman was not, to his knowledge associated with any operative body.[49]

The result was a meeting of delegates from different trades, in February 1811, in an unprecedented display of workers' solidarity. The occasional financial help across trade lines had been transformed, by experience and by the united front presented by employers, into a new kind of collaboration on the part of journeymen's societies. All the organised trades saw themselves as threatened by this united action by the employers. The solidarity of the masters had produced a new solidarity among the men. It was a sign of yet a further step in the polarisation of employers and workmen. It was agreed to organise a petition should such a bill be introduced.

> which, were it to succeed, would rivet the chains of slavery on the necks of all who earn their bread, under the employment of another; thus dividing the population of the country into two classes, the one tyrants and the other slaves.[50]

They asked a contact in London to report at once on the first moves in Parliament to introduce such a measure. A committee, consisting of delegates from weavers, spinners, tailors, masons, carpenters, cabinetmakers, chainmakers and blacksmiths, ready to respond to any legislative proposals, remained in existence at least for some months.[51]

Some hope of legislative intervention on weavers' wages still existed for, early in 1811, the three Scottish areas of Glasgow, Perth and Edinburgh, following the initiative of Bolton, petitioned the Board of Trade against the exporting of cotton yarn. Unlike the Lancashire men, however, they also protested against the introduction of steam looms: Smith claimed that there was now a large number of these in Glasgow. It is not clear if they actually wanted them banned, but it was probably about this time that a further article was added to the rules of the General Association:

> Steam-loom Weavers, whatever time they may have been employed in that department, cannot be admitted as common loom weavers, without serving, as other apprentices, the full term of seven years; and Weavers who undertake to instruct boys or girls in managing steam or power looms, can never be admitted into the Association.[52]

They made one final attempt in 1811 to get Parliament to accept a bill for the limitation of apprentices and they had the backing of other trades. When Thomas Smith and James Harley, a cabinetmaker, gave evidence to the House of Commons' Committee on Handloom Weavers' Petitions they came as delegates from 'the mechanics of Glasgow', stonemasons, house carpenters, blacksmiths, tailors, cabinetmakers, chairmakers, cotton spinners, 'in short the whole of the trades of any consequence in the town'. They claimed to be speaking for the trades in general when they asked for the Quarter Sessions to be given the power to settle disputes: 'whenever it [trade] is good or bad, let an umpire settle the wages'.[53]

It was with the failure of this application that the Association turned to the magistrates. They were encouraged in this by the decisions made in cases in the Glasgow Circuit Court in 1811, involving charges of intimidation. The judges made it clear that there were remedies for working men who wished to improve their wages:

> . . . the ancient Parliament of Scotland had provided a clear remedy for this precise case; that it had established Justices of the Peace, with express power to regulate the wages of workmen; that they were possessed of local knowledge, and an unlimited power of holding courts; and therefore, were peculiarly fitted for the investigation of business like those; that a temperate discussion of their claims, before a regular court, was calculated to bring the parties to reason, or, at least, to show the public which of them was not unreasonable; that though the masters could never be obliged to give more employment than they chose, it was useful to have some impartial standard of payment, to which both parties might refer; and that, if the standard set up by the

> justices was in favour of the workmen, but would not be conformed to by the masters, then it was time for the former to leave their work; and that, in whatever numbers they might do this, after such a decision so treated, they could never be justly accused of criminal combination.[54]

It was a ruling that paralleled that of the Court of Session in the papermakers' case.

In February 1812, the weavers submitted a table of prices for weaving to the Glasgow magistrates and to the Sheriff of Lanarkshire. It was claimed that earnings had fallen by forty per cent since 1792, a result of cuts in piece rates. In addition, manufacturers had pushed down rates in some fabrics by as much as thirty per cent by the device of re-labelling them as cheaper fabrics. The master manufacturers met and approved a different table. Both sides were brought before the Lord Provost, the magistrates and the Sheriff, with eight members from the Committee of Manufacturers and an equal number appointed from the operative weavers. The weavers objected that the employers' prices were not adequate, that the relation between the different prices was unsatisfactory and that the list did not cover a sufficient number of fabrics. Since the manufacturers refused to make any alterations to the existing price list, the conference broke up.

The weavers now took their case to the Justices of the Peace for Lanarkshire, arguing the case for a just wage,

> that those who choose to employ them, shall according to the laws of the country, and the dictates of common justice, reason, and religion, pay for their industry such a price as may enable a weaver, with fair hours and proper application, to feed clothe and accommodate himself and family, as industrious men of other mechanical professions are enabled by the rate of the wages to provide for their families.

Their case was that there was a legal obligation to give a reasonable wage, 'and that any wage that is not proportioned to the rate of provision, *that is*, wages that will not afford a moderate subsistence, is highly unreasonable, as well as illegal'. The employers' case was that 'The wages ... must be regulated by the demand for the commodity; and in the case of cotton weavers, by the state of the foreign market, with which the justices cannot be sufficiently conversant'.[55]

The JPs took evidence from some 130 witnesses, two for each fabric, and they made comparisons with wages paid in ten other trades, which were on average 18s.4½d. per week.[56] They approved a list of prices that was reasonably close to the weavers' demands. The employers took the judgement to the Court of Session, seeking a bill of advocation, against the JPs, on the grounds that they were not competent to fix wages. A number of the judges did express serious doubts. Lord Bannatyne thought, 'These laws may have been suited to the times, but they do not seem applicable now'. Lord Meadowbank argued that 'the power of the justices ought to be sustained to the effect of inquiring into the circumstances, declaring a reasonable rate of wages, and affording the workmen a remedy where they suffer any injury', but he was anxious about the combinations of workmen that 'threatened to usurp legislative functions'. The Lord Justice Clerk, Lord Boyle, thought that 'all former rules will be unavailing here', because the cotton trade depended 'so much on foreign relations'.[57] They had, however, no doubt that JPs could regulate wages and they referred the issue back to the JPs, who again confirmed their earlier decision.

Even before the ruling from the Court of Session, the weavers were pushing their campaign hard. At a general meeting on 3 June it was resolved that

> no apprentice, having served his time with an unassociated Master, can be admitted to work as Journeyman, unless in the way of first engaging and serving with an Associated Instructor, whatever time his former Indenture may have been deficient of the terms specified in the general regulations at the time said Indenture was agreed upon, besides six months additional service.

Posters were issued warning parents and journeymen weavers of the resolution.[58]

The Justices issued their interlocutor in November 1812, 'declaring the Table of Rates claimed by the Operative Weavers, moderate and reasonable'.[59] On that same day, the Lord Advocate was informing the Home Secretary, Lord Sidmouth, that the Sheriffs of Lanarkshire and Renfrewshire were hoping to collect evidence against the weavers, in order to start criminal proceedings.[60] The masters now refused to give out work at the new prices, while the organised journeymen declined to work for less. One hundred and fifty delegates from ninety-eight districts attended a meeting to consider the JPs' interlocutor and 'unanimously determined to take out no work below the prices declared by law to be moderate and reasonable'.[61] Indeed, according to Alexander Richmond, the issue at stake was less one of money than one of principle. The weavers wanted to assert the principle of judicial intervention on wages and they would have been agreeable to the masters coming forward and presenting evidence that the trade would not be able to afford the new rates. All along they were concerned to emphasise the legality of their activities. The Procurator Fiscal of Lanarkshire actually attended this meeting by invitation.[62]

Once the decision to refuse to take webs was made, the Association had the task of persuading their more cautious or more needy fellow operatives to give up working and to return webs that they had been given at the old rates. They blocked carriers taking out new webs and there was intimidation of non-strikers. By going around in crowds and collecting the revels necessary for setting up the webs they were able to stop the recalcitrant from working. Some of the manufacturers were clearly willing to pay the new rates and the committee advised that 'every Weaver, who can find employment at the full price, should without a moment's hesitation, proceed with the work'.[63] There were ritualised protests, with parades of striking weavers through the streets of Glasgow carrying webs removed from looms. The men's organisation developed as the strike progressed: subscription sheets were sent round and a number of friendly societies pledged funds; credit was organised at various grocers' shops and the treasurer of the Association issued printed credit slips for different values.[64] Altogether some £3,000 was expended by the weavers during the strike and there seems initially to have been some optimism. The Glasgow committee stressed the need for full and continuing organisation. Trying to persuade the Linlithgow weavers to join, they warned 'that altho' we had the Manufacturers brought round to our present measures, there is every chance in the world that without a strict and close association there would be no prospect of keeping the advantages we have or we may have gained'.[65]

The authorities were obviously getting extremely anxious about the turn of events, and not altogether without reason. The year 1812 had not been a year for those of nervous disposition. Throughout the year there had been outbreaks of Luddism among the stockingmakers of Nottinghamshire and Derbyshire and among the shearmen of Lancashire, Cheshire and Yorkshire. The prices of foodstuffs had been rising throughout the Summer and there were food riots in Edinburgh in August. Things were little better over the Winter and, at the beginning of the New Year, a mob of rioters in Montrose prevented a ship from carrying grain from there. Perhaps more worrying was that the example of the Lanarkshire weavers was now being followed by those in Edinburgh, Perth, Stirling and Renfrewshire, who now approached the magistrates in their counties. The Home Secretary was relieved when the Perth magistrates declined to intervene. Outside Scotland, the operatives in Preston also approached the JPs and asked the Glasgow Committee for advice on how to proceed.[66]

The authorities in Lanarkshire now sought ways of exerting pressure on the striking weavers. Firstly, they tried to force the weavers to complete webs already in hand at the old rates, though the General Committee complained that this was irregular and illegal. This brought an intervention from the Lord Advocate, the Solicitor-General, a former Solicitor-General and the Dean of the Faculty of Advocates, all of whom asserted that the rates fixed by the Justices on 10 November did not apply retrospectively and that there was nothing even now to prevent manufacturers entering into contracts with operative weavers at a rate lower than that fixed by the JPs. Then, they announced, following from these first two opinions, that

> ... any persons, who may, directly or indirectly, attempt to prevent Operative Weavers from entering into bargains with their masters for weaving webs at rates lower than those sanctioned by the Justices, or from implementing such bargains when entered into, will commit an illegal act, and will be either liable in damages in a civil action, or be punishable upon criminal prosecution, according to the circumstances of the case.[67]

Armed with these opinions, the sheriffs, magistrates and justices of Lanarkshire and Renfrewshire proceeded to criminalise activities which, until then, had been regarded as perfectly legal. They issued proclamations declaring their intention to crush the attempt to maintain 'a GENERAL COMBINATION AMONG THE OPERATIVE COTTON WEAVERS IN SCOTLAND, to enforce an advance of the Rates or Price of weaving by illegal means' and 'to suppress all such illegal Meetings, plans of Combination, and violent and outrageous proceedings, and to bring to immediate Trial and condign Punishment, all such violations of the Laws of their country'.[68]

Although the Authorities talked of 'violent and outrageous proceedings', a feature of the dispute was the relatively peaceful manner in which it was being carried out. There was no attempt to keep the proceedings secret and an English observer commented that weavers 'act in concert with wonderful unanimity, and they seem to have established an interior system of police in order to prevent disturbances or breach of the peace by individuals'.[69] There were odd hints of latent violence, as when the Association warned at one point

> . . . that rather than submit to the incessant drudgery and insupportable privations they have quietly submitted to during the last thirty months, they will imitate the glorious example of Alexander of Russia, who burnt his capital to save his empire. And to the many sacrifices already made, they will add another, and at once save themselves and their children from degradation, and a perpetuity of wretchedness, by consigning their unprofitable looms and utensils to the flames.[70]

There was also some destruction of webs and intimidation of backsliding weavers. But the same English visitor reported that 'they seem particularly cautious to avoid Luddism'. At the beginning of 1812 there had been an attempt to destroy the power looms in Findlay's mill at Deanston and there was fear of trouble at other mills; but, in fact, power looms were not yet too serious a problem. There were probably about 1,400 women and children engaged in powerloom weaving, but in none of the weavers' publications is it directly suggested that power looms were a cause of handloom weavers' difficulties. There were some approaches from Nottingham Luddites, and some of the minor delegates seem to have been impressed, but the committee distanced themselves from these overtures. Some, however, complained that the existing leadership 'were not sufficiently vigorous'.[71]

The government, in the shape of the Lord Advocate, Alexander Colquhoun, and the Home Secretary, Sidmouth, seem to have feared Luddism less than a recurrence of political unrest, since there were increasing reports of political activities. There was wind of some revolutionary movement called 'the Defenders', which had contacts with England and Ireland, and there were worries that French P.O.W. officers on parole were making a favourable impression on the populace, with the result that 'they have begun to consider the statements of the rapacity and cruelty of the French in Portugal and other countries they have devastated, as fabrications — and to believe them to be people by whom they would not be injured or oppressed, even were they their masters'.[72] There were also discontents among the militia and worries about communication between members of the Association and the militia. J. Dunlop, a leading businessman, writing to the Lord Advocate in February 1812, warned of the dangers:

> Your Lordship must consider that the whole arms of the local Militia of Lanark and Renfrewshire, sufficient to arm all these men are lying in detached warehouses, where they could be seized by the weavers in an hour the greatest number of whom either are, or have been local or regular militia men, volunteers, or disbanded colours and being accustomed to the use of arms are far more formidable than the undisciplined rabble of former days and besides they know perfectly well where every firelock is deposited.

Some of the troops were transferred to England and English ones brought North.[73] But the immediate cause of anxiety for Sidmouth was the presence in

Scotland of Maurice Margarot, the former chairman of the London Corresponding Society. Margarot had returned to Britain in 1810 unrepentent after his fourteen years' transportation and, at the end of 1812, closely watched by government agents, he was in Scotland, renewing his contacts with former colleagues in both Glasgow and Edinburgh. He also established contact with operative weavers in Paisley. The Sheriff of Renfrewshire believed that he was working with Major Cartwright in setting up Hampden Clubs.[74] There was talk of the need to legislate to remove the right of Justices to intervene over wages, but Sidmouth's correspondent, J. J. Dillon, warned that no-one could be sure of the consequences if a bill to this end were introduced. 'Parliament, I perceive', he wrote, 'has nothing to *spare* of credit with the people, and *very little* would induce the body of the weavers to join with the friends of parliamentary reform in England.'[75]

In the middle of December, the papers of the Weavers' Association were seized by the Sheriffs of Lanarkshire and Renfrewshire, and some of the leading members of the Association were apprehended. The local magistrates may have acted precipitately, since the Lord Advocate had been in favour of caution, urging the Lord Provost, Kirkman Finlay, not to take action unless there were acts of violence. He regretted the arrest of the weavers. According to the evidence of Alexander Richmond, one of those arrested, the masters were beginning to make overtures for a settlement, but, when the leaders were arrested, they pulled back.[76]

With the arrest of the leaders, the Association did not fall apart, but continued to exert influence. Since the Association controlled most of the tools necessary for beaming, that is setting up the webs in the loom, they were able to ensure that only webs at the new prices were prepared and only by weavers who were members of the Association.[77] There seems to have been a belief that the Lord Advocate did not intend to bring the men to trial.[78] But, as the weeks passed, the strike began to crumble and, to all intents, was over before the arrested leaders were brought to court. The trial of William McKimmie, the president, Thomas Smith, the secretary, James Johnstone, the treasurer, and Charles Christie and James Granger, two members of the Committee, took place in March 1813. Smith had fled and was outlawed; Johnstone was sentenced to eighteen months, McKimmie to nine months and the other two to four months each. Another four weavers, including Alexander Richmond, were up for trial on the following day, but only one appeared. All the rest had fled and were outlawed. The one who remained pleaded guilty to the charge of combination, but denied any association with acts of violence and was sentenced to two months. Finally, there was a third trial, when two weavers pleaded guilty to combination and were sentenced to five months in gaol.[79]

The verdicts in the McKimmie case seemed to have brought a new crime of simple combination into the law of Scotland. The weavers were charged with the crime of combination, aggravated by threats, abuse and violence, but they were found guilty only of 'an illegal combination or conspiracy as libelled'. No notice was taken of violence and intimidation in the verdict.[80] When Francis Jeffrey for the defence confronted the Lord Justice Clerk with his early stated opinion that once JPs had declared a price fair and reasonable and the masters failed to comply, then journeymen 'had the right to strike in any numbers'. Lord Boyle acknowledged that he had been in error and that Burnett, whose *Treatise in the Various Branches of the Criminal Law in Scotland* with its lengthy section on the illegality of combination had just been published, had given the correct view.[81]

Four months later the statutes on wage regulation in both England and Scotland, dating back to the sixteenth century, were repealed. Within months the past was being rewritten. In 1814, Sir John Sinclair talked of the 'antiquated statutes' by which JPs had regulated wages, and he wrote, 'It does not appear . . . that this authority was often exercised; these magistrates, with much wisdom have commonly left the price of labour like any other commodity in a well-regulated market, to find its own level'.[82] Gilbert Hutcheson's handbook for JPs asserted in its revised version of 1815 that 'it has not for a long time been the practice of justices of the peace to settle or enforce tables of wages at quarter session, whether relating to agriculture or any other country labour. To interfere in matters of trade, now carried on for home and foreign consumption to a great extent would be still worse and indeed impracticable'.[83] The Handloom Weavers' Association was effectively dissolved by the court cases and by the debt claims which were subsequently raised against members of the weavers' committee.[84]

A second group of textile workers active in these years were the calico printers. Their discontent, at least in some areas, was related to the introduction of women workers or 'grounders', who could do the lighter kind of block work. They were paid a third less than the men and the male printers saw their craft in danger. There was growing bitterness as the number of women 'grounders' increased.

Organisation among the calico printers had existed for some time. There had been a major violent dispute in the Vale of Leven in 1790, following the introduction of piece rates and the increased use of cheap apprentice labour. The activities, which included parades of masked white-shirted figures armed with cudgels, were claimed to be organised by a West of Scotland committee. They were strong enough to exert some control over entry. In 1804, it was reported that anyone seeking work would apply to the journeymen first to see if work was available.[85] They had also been involved in a petition to Parliament in 1804 to limit the number of apprentices, and, by then, a system existed whereby an unemployed printer seeking work would get 1d. from each journeyman in a works he visited, on production of a ticket from the union. The Select Committee that heard the evidence from the Calico Printers produced a remarkably sympathetic report:

> Your committee may venture to throw out for consideration of the House, whether it be quite equitable towards the parties, or conducive to the public interest, that at one part there should arise a great accumulation of wealth, while on the other there should prevail a degree of poverty from which the parties cannot emerge by the utmost exertion of industry, skill and assiduous application, and may, at an advanced period of life, notwithstanding perpetual labour, be obliged to resort to parish aid for the support of their families.[86]

It was, of course, the last that most concerned the representatives of the landed interest, since the burden of poor relief fell on them. In 1809 there were reports of an organisation linking calico printers in Denny, Thornliebank, Perth and Linlithgow. At the end of 1810, the Master Calico Printers introduced a 'bond' for their workers to sign, dissociating themselves from the trade society. The issues of conflict that this highlighted were the rights of masters to employ whom they wished on the terms that they wished. They wanted, for a start, to reduce the length of apprenticeship from seven years to four.[87]

The period from December 1810 to May 1811 was later referred to by the journeymen as the 'Reign of Oppression'. It ushered in a long period of industrial conflict.[88] In March 1812 three Glasgow printers were sentenced for mobbing and rioting 'with a view to promoting a conspiracy of operative manufacturers, to subvert the lawful authority of their masters'. They were fined £15 each and £35 expenses and ordered to be held in prison for a month.[89] Far from weakening the men's organisation, this seems to have had the effect of encouraging its growth. By 1814 there was a national organisation with various districts — the Farenese District (Renfrewshire), Leven, Campsie, Kilmarnock, Denny (which covered Linlithgow) and Perth, which went as far north as Aberdeen. There were contacts with similar associations in England and in Ireland. The secretary, Alexander McGregor, was a printer and an innkeeper from Anderston, who was paid 1gn. per week for his services. In 1814, he and three others, Dugald McPherson and John Dichmont, both of Tradeston, and John MacGibbon from Campsie, were indicted for illegal combination and conspiracy to compel masters to raise wages, to impose arbitrary and illegal rules and regulations on employers and other workmen, for supporting workmen on strike and preventing workmen working.[90]

The third group of textile workers who organised in these years were the cotton spinners. Cotton spinning, in rural areas by fast-flowing streams, had been around since the 1770s, but the industry was transformed from a rural to an urban industry with the application of steam power in 1792. Glasgow, with its rapidly rising population, attracted increasing numbers of mills. By 1819 there were to be fifty-two of them.

Spinning now became a male job that required a great deal of strength and skill gathered from experience. There seems to have been extensive resistance on the part of the native population to entering the cotton mills and, unlike the experience in the North of England, Irish labour, mainly from the North, fleeing in the aftermath of the unrest of 1798, found its way into Glasgow mills.[91] There are traces of a short-lived organisation among spinners in the 1790s pressing for an advance of wages and there was sporadic activity between 1804 and 1806. But it was in 1809 or 1810 that an effective organisation appeared.

Compared with many of their fellow workers, the cotton spinners were among the better off, probably earning more than £1 even after their piecers had been paid. It was a desire to maintain this élite position that brought about trade-union organisation among them. A Society of Lanarkshire Cotton Spinners was recognised as a friendly society by the local JPs in 1810 and there was a similar one in Renfrewshire and another in the town of Johnstone.[92] It is clear, however, that the main concern of the society was not to collect money for widows, orphans and the sick, but to keep up wages and to keep others out of the trade. Attracted by high earnings, increasing numbers were making their way to the Glasgow mills. The Union's concern from this time onwards was to keep 'incomers' out of the Glasgow mills.

In 1810, the master cotton spinners associated formally for the first time, in an attempt to break the power of the spinners' society, which was, reputedly, trying to insist that only union members be employed. The associated employers proscribed the society and required all employees to sign a document dissociating themselves from it.[93] It is doubtful if this action succeeded in breaking the spinners' union and there were still sporadic strikes at individual mills, but adverse trade conditions were not conducive to trade-union advance.

These early years of the nineteenth century were crucial ones in changing old patterns. They were years when the heart of Scottish industrial growth switched, very clearly, from the East to the West. The rapid development of the cotton industry and its increasing concentration in the West was a major change. The development of the textile industry brought new employers, new workers and new organisation. These, in themselves, inevitably brought changes in attitudes and in relations between employers and workers. Well-established patterns that were applicable to the world of craft workshops were seen as a threat and a barrier in the new world of capitalist industry. The new manufacturers, committed to change and to rapid growth, were not prepared to accept the restrictions imposed by traditional patterns. They regarded trade societies not as a legitimate mechanism by which workers could debate with their employers before the courts the need for adjustment in wages and conditions, but as conspiracies against the 'necessary advance of industrialisation'. Such employers did not see the courts as sympathetic to the new industrial society and, therefore, were determined to break free from the controls of the JPs, and to criminalise trade societies. Initially, they were faced with magistrates and justices who believed that it was necessary to maintain and, indeed, develop older patterns. The same mentality that had passed the deterrent sentences on Muir and his associates for the unforgivable offence of stirring up the lower orders also sought to ensure that some hope of improvement was possible through the regulated system. As long as the use of the courts was confined to traditional groups of Edinburgh tradesmen, then it might have been tolerated. When the workers in the new industrial world of the West learned from the tradesmen and when they too began to use the courts, it could no longer be accepted. However, the advocates of the change, the supporters of a new industrial society, who believed that the needs of the economy were paramount and that levels of wages were to be regulated solely by market forces, had their supporters within the legal profession. The ideas of Smith, the arguments for *laissez-faire*, undoubtedly influenced a younger generation of legal minds. It would have been odd if they had not been influenced, given the seriousness with which Smith's ideas were treated within the universities. When these men began to produce the new law books, their interpretations were towards a legal system that was in tune with what were seen as the needs of the modern world. Anything which was a barrier to economic growth, anything which smacked of an older, regulated, paternalist world had to be swept away.

The remarkable thing is the speed with which old attitudes were abandoned. The attack on them from employers, politicians and ideologues was swift and devastating. The assumptions of decades would be overthrown in a moment. Up until 1808 there operated within the courts a clear concept of a social economy that accepted ideas of reasonable wages and hours of work, that used measures to fix wages which after nineteenth-century shibboleths about supply and demand, were to seem sophisticated again in the twentieth century: measures such as comparability, arduousness, level of profits and a cost of living index which went beyond the price of oatmeal to include rent and clothing. But, by 1813, what had seemed a rational way of settling differences and making adjustments now became 'impracticable'. Rights to seek redress through united action now became 'dangerous'. Judges who had operated upon one set of assumptions could rapidly adjust to the new. For the Scottish craftsmen it was a traumatic turnaround, and they were a long time finding alternative ways of pursuing their claims. They were left with the frustrations and dangers of political radicalism and, as we shall see in the case of the handloom weavers, a persistent hankering after legal regulation of wages of which they had been so arbitrarily deprived in 1813.

6
The Years of Distress

The end of the more than twenty years of war with France brought great distress in its wake. Viewed all over, there is considerable evidence that the decade from 1813 was one of rising living standards. Workers were able to maintain their existing levels of money wages, while prices were entering a period of fall. But such gains were for those fortunate enough to remain in employment. In Scotland there was widespread unemployment as war demand fell off, and demobilised soldiers and an influx of poor from the North of Ireland added to the problem. Food prices rose sharply in 1816 and 1817 and both tradesmen and factory workers suffered. For handloom weavers the decline was a dramatic one. According to the indices compiled by T. R. Gourvish, a Glasgow handloom weaver's real wages were more than halved between 1815 and 1818.[1] Examples of what was happening were given by Alexander Richmond. The 1400 jaconets that had paid 9⅓d. per ell in 1812, by 1816 paid only 3d.; 1300 gauze had fallen from 16d. per ell to 6d.; this at a time when wheat cost between 90s. and 100s. per quarter, and oatmeal 2s. a peck.[2] While other groups were less badly off, particularly those with money to spend on those goods whose prices were falling, there were few real gains in the postwar years for the majority and the most poorly paid suffered the most.

There were also other problems. Many friendly societies, which had proliferated with legislative encouragement after 1793, came to grief in these years. Sometimes this was a result of mismanagement and fraud, but more frequently it was because of over-generous payments. Initially, friendly societies had been charity boxes where members decided if one of their number needed a charitable hand-out. There was no right to relief and sickness and infirmity, in themselves, were not enough: need had to be proved. Nor were there any set rates of relief: the amount given out would depend on the amount in the funds at that particular moment. Over time, perhaps as a result of competition between societies, this had given way to fixed allowances and an assumption that relief was not a charity but a right of members when they were sick or aged. Subscriptions, however, were rarely raised and remained at the kind of level they had been at their establishment. Also, the young men who had set up the societies in the eighteenth century were now the old men making claims.[3] Many societies went under and distress deepened. Added to this, the abolition of income tax, in response to middle-class pressure, meant that essentials — salt, tea, tobacco, sugar, shoes, soap and candles — were made to carry the burden of taxation, much to the disadvantage of the less well-off.

There was a serious riot among the poor in Glasgow on 1 and 2 August 1816. A soup kitchen in Calton came under attack, together with a 'steam loom' manufactory. The cavalry was called in from Hamilton.[4] The fears aroused, however, stirred action. Relief works were established by the Corporation, for the 'industrious poor', using the residue of funds collected to deal with distress in 1811 and the money raised by poor assessment over the previous two years, though the idea of an extraordinary assessment was rejected. The work given was the levelling of Glasgow Green.[5] In Edinburgh the want among the poor was the worst since 1797 and, here also, work was provided from public funds, clearing Bruntsfield Links of whins and old quarries and making walks along Calton Hill and the base of Salisbury Crags.[6]

It was a period of political unrest, stimulated by the visit to Scotland of the indefatigable reformer, Major John Cartwright, in the summer of 1815. Cartwright made a tour of Central Scotland and, although his meetings went unadvertised and unreported in the pages of a cowed Scottish press, he succeeded in attracting substantial audiences. He left behind a network of Hampden Clubs to gather signatures for petitions to the Prince Regent in support of parliamentary reform. At first any interest in the movement was among merchants and shopkeepers, but with a worsening economic situation in the Autumn of 1816 support for the petitioning campaign widened.[7] Handloom weavers, in particular, conscious of a dramatic destruction of their once comfortable way of life that no trade-society action could prevent, began to involve themselves. They were well represented at the largest political meeting to date in Scotland, held in October 1816. The meeting of between thirty and forty thousand was held on the land of tobacco shopkeeper, James Turner at Thrushgrove, just outside the city boundary, after permission to use either the Trades' Hall or Glasgow Green had been refused. Marching behind great banners, with bundles of rods, symbolising unanimity, large brooms, to sweep away corruption, and caps of liberty, the protesters called for reductions in public expenditure and in taxes, by cutting the army, the abolition of pensions, sinecures and grants 'not merited by public services', rigid economy and radical reform of Parliament.[8] The idea was to present a programme that would have the widest possible acceptance among reformers.[9] It succeeded in attracting large numbers of workers on a scale that earlier movements had not.

Despite the fears expressed in the 1790s about radical reformers stirring up the 'lower orders', there is not much evidence to indicate that they were very successful. It was the middle ranks of society — merchants, shopkeepers, professional men — who heard the siren calls from France. The political awareness among workers was slight. A few, no doubt, did play a part in underground, pseudo-revolutionary groups like the United Scotsmen in 1797,[10] and that tradition was still there in 1813 when Margarot tried to revitalise his old contacts and when there were hints of a mysterious group called 'the Defenders'.[11] But, again, if numbers are a measure, they were of little significance. However, the activists of the 1790s had given Scottish reformers a tradition, which until then had been markedly lacking. While the Scottish covenanting tradition was a democratic one, in the sense of being anti-establishment and anti-patronage, it was not a popular one. Few wanted to replace the authoritarianism of aristocratic rule with theocratic authoritarianism. But from the movements of the 1790s, Scottish reformers had their own version of an essentially English democratic tradition. Elements of both traditions were to be found in Joseph Gerrald's prayer at the break-up of the Scottish convention in 1793:[12]

> O Thou Governor of the Universe! We rejoice at all times, and in all circumstances, we have liberty to approach Thy throne; and that we are assured that no sacrifice is more acceptable to Thee, than that which is made for the relief of the oppressed. In this moment of trial and persecution, we pray, that Thou wouldest be our defender, our counsellor and our guide. O! be Thou a pillar of fire to us, as Thou wast to our fathers of old, to enlighten and to direct us; and to our enemies a pillar of cloud, of darkness and confusion.
>
> Thou are Thyself the great patron of liberty. Thy service is perfect freedom. Prosper, we beseech Thee, every endeavour which we make to promote Thy cause; for we consider the cause of truth, or every cause which tends to promote the happiness of Thy creatures, as Thy cause.

It is significant that this was the one piece of evidence that was found of a politically radical element in the cotton weavers' movement in 1812. A copy of Gerald's prayer was among Thomas Smith's papers, seized by the Sheriff.

The period after 1812–1813 was a watershed. The old paternalist pattern had been swept away. There was now no independent group who could be looked upon to right wrongs and ensure some measure of fairness. There were now no means by which the local state could take ultimate responsibility for the needs of the community. The cold blast of the *laissez-faire* message was blowing strongly. A new harshness was evident in attitudes to the poor. The pressure from the law was for excluding the able-bodied from the right to relief: the pressure from a middle-class public was to cut all poor relief.[13] In 1812 a Society for the Suppression of Public Begging was established in Edinburgh 'to check public mendacity, and to avert charity from supporting it'. The message that Thomas Chalmers was soon to preach from his pulpit in St. John's Parish in Glasgow, that a system of legal assessment for poor relief would in fact create pauperism, was already being heard.[14] These changed attitudes had produced a new level of cooperation among trade societies, at any rate in Glasgow, and the experiences of growing distress and a new harshness of tone at the centre created a new political awareness among many workers.

Weavers, in particular, were well represented at the Thrushgrove meeting. It was addressed by some journeymen printers as well as by middle-class radicals. While radical demands for universal suffrage and annual or triennial parliaments were the main feature of popular demands, there were also, according to a contemporary, those who favoured 'a division of property'.[15] At least some of these were likely to have been *agents provocateurs*. The movement was infiltrated by spies in the pay of the Provost and the Town Clerk, although, as the historian of the radical movement of these years has shown, the authorities had tremendous difficulty in gathering accurate information and were dependent on rumour and on the far-from-reliable snippets that came from informers.[16] The best known of these informers was Alexander Richmond, who had been outlawed in 1813 when he had failed to appear to stand trial for his role in the weavers' strike. He had fled to Manchester but was eventually allowed to return. The price he paid for his return seems to have been that he would keep the authorities informed about activity among the weavers. By 1816 he was playing an active role in the radical movement and generally 'making inflammatory speeches'.[17] According to his own account, it was a period of intense class bitterness:

> Rank, and everything previously held sacred and venerable, was laughed at to scorn; the minds of the people were completely inflamed; a line of demarcation was drawn between the different ranks of society, and rooted antipathy and a ferocious spirit of retaliation was engendered in the minds of the labouring classes.[18]

There were other meetings in Paisley, Dundee and elsewhere. Generally the tone of these meetings was moderate, although there were occasional hints of the possibility of violence. The Sheriff Substitute of Renfrewshire reported 'that the contagion is spreading among the working classes, but they are taught coolly to contemplate the application of violence'.[19] Societies began to be formed, some secret, others more open, to campaign for reform. One in Tradeston established in December 1816 was followed by one in Calton and another in Camlachie. Links were made with Hampden Clubs and with middle-class committees. The aim was to involve the trade societies by encouraging workshop organisation, for example, among the cotton spinners 'so that when one spinner in the mill took the oath he would bring all the rest into the same situation before two days', and among the cabinetmakers who were 'in the same state of combination against their masters'. The idea was to have a general committee in Glasgow linking district societies of no more than sixteen members. Like comtemporaneous movements in London, the inspiration for some of this revolutionary movement was the ideas of Thomas Spence, with their call for land reform, reduced taxation and republicanism. It was broken by mass arrests in February 1817.[20]

The way in which economic distress could be politicised came out in the statements of many of those arrested in February 1817 and charged with sedition. Hugh Dickson, a thirty-four year old weaver from Co. Tyrone, who had come to Scotland in 1800, said in his declaration 'that the stagnation in trade, and the recent distress in the County was attributed by the declarant and those in his neighbourhood to the corn bill some time ago passed and to them not having universal suffrage and annual parliaments'. John Stewart, a thirty-two year old weaver originally from Aberfeldy, had attended a reform meeting for the first time and found himself arrested. He

> was prompted to do so from his destitute circumstances, not having earned more than six shillings a week since May last. That he has received from the Charitable subscription committee by weekly payments of half a crown and three shillings about twenty-three shillings and sixpence in all ... that he has read Cobbett's Register many times of late which is circulated about the neighbourhood.[21]

The *Political Register* was undoubtedly influential in spreading ideas about reform and pinpointing discontents. One ten-year old son of a weaver reported that his father read the *Register* at times and 'that Cobbett's paper is sent from house to house and is paid for by a club, each member paying one half penny in the week'.[22]

The political demonstrations were also linked with a demand from unemployed weavers for relief for their families from the Barony Kirk Session. This had been refused and there was a march led by the Calton weaver and radical activist, John McLachlan, to the house of Dr. Burns, the minister, to present an application.[23] There was a court case in progress to argue the case for relief. This issue seems to have been the one that caused the greatest bitterness among the weavers. According to Richmond, by this time the weavers 'had fallen into the hands of some furious fanatics, with just a sufficient portion of ability to give them influence over the very lowest class'.[24] Meetings of unemployed workmen in Glasgow and in the surrounding villages built up a high state of excitement among the Lord Provost, Kirkman Finlay, and his associates. There were real fears of an extensive conspiracy to overthrow the government by force. It was at a meeting on the right to poor relief that arrests were made in February 1817, apparently on the express orders of Sidmouth.[25] They came at the end of a month of growing alarm in government at activities around the country. Parliamentary committees had reported on the existence of secret corresponding societies in the main industrial cities. Two days before the Glasgow arrests a bill to suspend Habeas Corpus had been introduced in the House of Lords and passed in three days. The Glasgow arrests and the Lord Advocate's assertion 'that there were many of the higher orders of society engaged in the conspiracy' overcame what doubts there were about suspension.[26] There were mass arrests. In Glasgow the arrested included a teacher, William Edgar, John Keith, the manager of a Calton cotton mill, James Finlayson, son of a coalmaster, and William Simpson, a spirit dealer. The rest were weavers and cotton spinners.[27] They were charged under the 1797 Act against the taking of unlawful oaths, the same that seventeen years later was to be used more effectively against the Tolpuddle Martyrs. The relevance of the indictments was vigorously challenged by the seven or eight Whig advocates, including Cockburn and Jeffrey, who had volunteered their services to the arrested free of charge. It took a number of drafts before the Courts would accept the indictments.[28] After six months, for some spent in Edinburgh Castle, all but two, Andrew McKinlay and John Campbell, were released. These two were brought to trial, but when it became public that the Depute Lord Advocate had tried to persuade Campbell to turn King's evidence, the case collapsed and McKinlay escaped with a not-proven verdict.[29] The whole case had been handled with the most extraordinary ineptness by the Lord Advocate's department. As Kirkman Finlay angrily pointed out, by going for capital charges of treason the Crown had effectively ensured that the accused would not be convicted.[30] Despite acquittal, with Habeas Corpus in suspension, many others were detained without trial during the summer of 1817. The later arrest of Neil Douglas, an itinerant preacher with his own universalist church, who was accused of comparing the Prince Regent to Nebuchadnezzar, was equally badly handled. He was acquitted for lack of adequate evidence.[31]

By the time Douglas was arrested in March 1817 the petitioning movement had faded. Cobbett, who had been a major influence, had fled to the United States, and no-one had yet taken his place as the publicist of reform and the scourge of corruption. None the less, the political reform movement of these months of 1816–1817 had been important, particularly in Scotland, where there had been so little tradition of the public expression of political opinions. It had brought meetings and demonstrations on a scale never before experienced. It had brought workers, and especially handloom weavers, into contact with reforming political ideas. At least some had come to accept that political action was perhaps the only possible way of reversing their economic decline. It left a residue of organisation that could be reactivated in the future.

The years 1816 and 1817 were also years of industrial agitation among different groups, some of whom had been organised in the past, others organising for the first time. The summer of 1816 saw a two-month strike of boot and shoemakers in and around Glasgow, following moves by five of the leading employers to reduce wages. The main activists among the journeymen, James Henderson, Thomas Sandylands, John Mitchell, David Wanlass, Joseph Cockfield and Alexander Burnett, were arrested, but, according to the Procurator Fiscal of Glasgow, they received 1gn. a week from the union while incarcerated. The union had been revived about two years before, after having been disbanded soon after the 1809 strike as a result of rumours of embezzlement of the funds.

A central issue, as so often in these years, was that of apprentices. Up until 1809 it had been the rule among journeymen cordiners that they would have only one apprentice at a time, whose indenture would last for five years. Only in the last six months of that apprenticeship would a journeyman be permitted to take a second apprentice. He could also have one 'scholar' in addition to his apprentice. If a journeyman broke these rules, he would be brought before a meeting of the trade and tried and fined. If he did not accept this, then he would be declared an 'illegal man' and all the other journeymen would be expected to strike from the workshop until he was turned out. These rules had been officially dropped by the Society for fear of prosecution, but 'it was considered as a matter of honour among the journeymen that they should be observed'. Since 1809 there had been pressures against the restriction on apprentices as employers sought to expand production, and, significantly, the five firms involved in the 1816 strike tended to be the largest firms, each employing around twenty or thirty workers.[32]

The Glasgow Typographical Society was also formed either at the end of 1816 or the beginning of 1817. At first it was intended as a friendly society, though the newspaper compositors in particular wanted to have a trade role. This soon came about. It decided it could not impose standard rates on all journeymen, since this was 'on the whole rather of a delicate nature', as the first minutes circumlocutarily put it, but a black list was kept of those who worked at under the established rates and who did not join the Society. Their names were sent to societies in other towns and there was a determined effort to weed out 'irregulars'.[33]

The Association of Operative Cotton Spinners in Glasgow also reappeared in

February 1816, and seems to have succeeded in building up a powerful organisation. Wage rates were higher in Glasgow than elsewhere, presumably because of a high demand, and a skilled spinner could earn as much as 30s. per week clear, after having paid perhaps 16s. to his piecer. With the example of the handloom weavers as a warning of the ever-present threat of unregulated entry into trades, the spinners set out to maintain their earnings by trying to restrict entry, ideally to their own family. As a disincentive to 'outsiders' an admission fee to the Association of £5 was charged and a reputation for violence towards non-unionists began to emerge.[34] An attempt by the firm of James Dunlop to break the combination by building a mill with small mules that could be worked by women spinners was successfully frustrated in 1819,[35] but the struggle was to go on and become more embittered.

It was a weaver, from Barony Parish in Glasgow, who was the key figure in the Colliers' Association which appeared in 1817. His name was John Fauldhouse Wilson. There had been moves among colliers near Edinburgh early in February 1817, which the authorities had considered treating as a combination. But they had taken no action, though at least one collier master believed that there was 'a deep-rooted combination amongst the whole of the colliers in Mid and East Lothian'.[36] However, it was in Lanarkshire that the most effective organisation appeared, probably starting as a friendly society.

Miners were a well-paid group whose earnings had risen from an average 4s. a day c.1799 to a peak of 5s. a day in 1815. A twenty-six year old at Greenend Collier in 1817 claimed to be earning, without assistance, 4s. to 4s.6d. a day, and another, with the assistance of a thirteen-year old boy, claimed to earn 10s. to 12s. a day, five days a week. However, from 1816 there had been a substantial decline in earnings for many as the demand for mining labour in the coal and iron industry of the West of Scotland stagnated. As the men complained,

> It requires the same exertion to put out a ton of coals now as ten or twenty years ago . . . formerly your industry and labour procured such a remuneration equivalent to satisfy all demands for the comfortable subsistence of yourselves and families. But alas, very different now the poor collier.[37]

A group of coal-hewers in the Glasgow Tollcross area had approached Wilson, as presumably someone who could write, to get his help in petitioning the coalmasters for a rise in wages. They paid him £1. 4s. per week. A Glasgow and Clydesdale Association of Operative Colliers was formed, complete with printed rules. The aim of the rules was to regulate entry, by admitting only sons of colliers free and charging high dues for outsiders or 'neutrals' as they were called. They were intended also to control the amount of work that young trainees could undertake. Not until a young man was seventeen could he become a full member of the Association and be allowed to work the full 'darg'.[38] Although an initiation oath was taken, there was obviously no attempt to keep secret the existence of the organisation and the Tollcross men were successful after a three weeks' strike.[39] As a result, Wilson was approached by some Ayrshire miners to organise there. The coal trade in Ayrshire, dependent on foreign markets, was dull during 1817 and, with prices down about a third, wages were reduced from 3s. a day to 2s.6d. The issue, however, was not just over wages, but over a series of grievances, such as a reduction in the size of the measure box used for taking the coal to the pit head. The men wanted to be paid for the creel of coal they brought up at the full price 'whether it contained sufficient measure or not'. They also wanted to ensure that no new men were admitted to the collieries and that only a certain number be employed. In addition, they wanted the working day reduced by a fifth, and earnings increased to 4s. or 4s.3d. per day.[40]

In September 1817 the colliers embarked on the old tactic of reducing output to push up prices. In October, the Glasgow and Ayrshire Associations amalgamated, on the grounds 'that the interest of both counties lying in the same export market, what affects the interest of one must be felt by the other'.[41] Employers agreed to negotiate and proposed an advance of 4d. per ton, but no changes to the measure. At the end of November the associated colliers all struck work. After about two weeks, the employers offered another 2d., an advance of 6d. per ton, and the men began drifting back.

The counter-attack came in January 1818 when all the colliers at Dixon's Greenend Colliery, after a strike of ten weeks, were charged with combination and lodged in the Glasgow Tolbooth, 'in the felons' department', for six weeks, before they were eventually granted bail. Wilson and Charles Banks, a miner from Stevenston, were charged with illegal combination. The accusation was that they had threatened to strike, and the men's advocate challenged the validity of such an indictment. But the court ruled that 'in the case of a colliery ... where the interruption of a single day may be attended with great damage to the owner, as well as much inconvenience to the neighbourhood, a threat to strike work is a true and substantial compulsory measure'.[42] By the time this had been settled in May 1818 the strikes were over and the prosecution was not proceeded with. Trouble rumbled on in the coal areas and there was an indictment of Tranent miners for illegal combination in October 1818.[43] But between 1818 and 1824 any activity in mining was sporadic. A reduced demand for coal pushed wage rates down to 3s.6d. a day, and at many points during 1819, 1820 and 1821 miners were on a three-day week or even less.

With the sedition trials of the spring of 1817, the parliamentary reform campaign had declined. The working-class section had been torn with suspicion, as accusations were tossed around about the presence of spies and *agents provocateurs* in the events of the previous few months. Richmond was publicly accused. The middle-class reformers returned to the rather safer ground of burgh reform. The winter of 1818–1819 brought real distress, especially in the West of Scotland where, added to unemployment and low earnings, there was fever ranging in Glasgow. The King's birthday was again celebrated with a riot, and public works schemes were inaugurated. In June 1819, a meeting of weavers demanding action for relief of distress was held on Glasgow Green. The main proposals were for assisted emigration, but voices were once again heard calling for political reform.[44] In the same month there was a large radical demonstration in

Paisley, which rejected the proposal for a petition to the Prince Regent in favour of an address to the nation and, in August, there were reports of numerous meetings of workers and radicals in Glasgow and rumours of a plan for a general rising, linked with disturbances in Yorkshire, Manchester and Stockport. These rumours pre-dated Peterloo, though Melville could confidently write, 'I have no apprehension of any general disturbance in this country or in England'.[45] It is clear, however, that few others in authority shared Melville's complacency. Glasgow Town Council borrowed £30,000 from the Treasury to build a new drydock at the Broomielaw, using unemployed weavers as labourers. Numerous other public and private schemes were inaugurated, as the local landed class grappled with the problem of how to maintain order without adequate means of coercion. As one newspaper, encouraging further such schemes, put it, the hope was that if the poor were helped, then 'the cry for Radical reform . . . would be succeeded by the cheering sounds of gratitude'.[46] Cockburn reflected a general view that the 'sedition of opinion . . . was promoted by the sedition of the stomach'. There were also grievances among perhaps potentially the most dangerous group, discharged soldiers, who could find their pensions cut as a result of some relatively minor misdemeanour.[47] But there were also intellectual changes. Wooler's *Black Dwarf* now circulated widely, replacing the *Register* as the main source of radical information and ideas, and it was altogether more vigorous than Cobbett's journal. Thomas Paine's ideas were again around and, as one young Kilmarnock radical later recalled, Paine's *Age of Reason* 'played sad havoc with the settled opinions of many a previously orthodox Kilmarnockian'. The names of Cartwright, Hunt and Carlile were, he asserted, 'Household words' among a group, mainly of weavers, who met three nights a week in the house of Willie Semple, a cobbler, to read papers on reform. Among them there were at least some who wanted equal division of property, but all could agree 'that there should be no king, no lords, no gentry, no taxes'.[48] In Glasgow, Andrew Hardie, soon to die on the scaffold, had no doubts about why he took up arms — 'I went out with the intention to recover my rights'. When asked what rights he wanted, he replied 'annual Parliaments, and Election by Ballot':

> Question — What reason had you to expect these rights? Answer — Because I think Government ought to grant whatever the majority of the nation requested, and if they had paid attention to the people's lawful petitions, the nation would not have been in the state it was at present.[49]

In the aftermath of Peterloo there were riots in Paisley, after constables tried to seize banners at a meeting of some 12–18,000 people (substantially fewer than had attended a reform meeting in July). The meeting called for a boycott of taxed items like tea, tobacco and spirits. Two days later rioting spread to Bridgeton, where windows were smashed and JPs and special constables attacked. There were signs of growing hostility to the clergy, who were blamed for failing to provide relief.[50] After unemployed weavers were refused relief there was a riot in Stonehouse in Ayrshire. At a large meeting in Glasgow on 26 September, according to the *Scots Magazine*, religion came under an unprecedented attack:

> It was asserted that the clergy gulled every government, and that it was their infamous combination with the landed proprietors which had cheated the poor of their rights. All those who attended church were denounced as hypocrites, because they went to hear clergymen discant on charity, morality, and virtues which they well knew the preachers themselves never practised.[51]

The writings of Paine and of Carlile were widely read, despite the efforts of the authorities to seize as many as possible. The preparations for this meeting to petition against the happenings at Peterloo had aroused extreme trepidation among the respectable. Troops were called in, Samuel Hunter of the *Glasgow Herald* raised a volunteer force of 'Glasgow Sharpshooters', and yeomanry from as far afield as the Lothians, together with a company of hussars complete with field pieces, were brought to the city. According to a hostile witness, the anxiety was not misplaced. A few pistol shots were fired off at the end of the procession and some of the long poles may have been pikes.[52]

In November, there was trouble in Airdrie when a mob prevented special constables being sworn in.[53] Radical reformers were reputedly drilling, demanding annual parliaments, universal suffrage ('every man over 21') and vote by ballot. There was also now a Glasgow radical newspaper, *The Spirit of the Union*, produced by two Glasgow printers, Gilbert Macleod and Alexander Rodger, that circulated among the radical groups in the towns around Glasgow, as far south as Ayr. It only survived for eleven issues before the authorities suppressed it,[54] but it was important in a country so bereft of means of publicising criticism of government.

By the end of the year rumours of impending risings abounded. The authorities, armed with the recent 'Six Acts', banned all public meetings of more than fifty, and began to move vigorously in search of arms. The military certainly believed that 'the people are rife for rebellion as ever, and only in sullen and sultry silence waiting for a more convenient opportunity'.[55] Hostility towards the military came into the open with stone-throwing incidents against troops.[56] Anyone who had shown radical leanings in 1793 was the object of suspicion. The main groups in what was now a predominantly weavers' movement, with very little middle-class participation, were organised in small Union societies, generally of ten or a dozen members, inspired by the missionary activities of Joseph Brayshaw of Yeadon, who, since the end of 1819, had been campaigning for a boycott of tea, beer, spirits and tobacco.[57] Taxation was, according to many radicals, the means by which labour was exploited. It increased the cost of food, it reduced what was available in the wages fund and, therefore, it kept down the level of wages. The additional attraction of the boycott was that it was against the physically harmful tea, drink and tobacco, and this element, linking political to moral reform, seems to have had a particular appeal to the Scots. Yet other groups, however, had links with Thistlewood and his Spencean associates in London and, as far as one can judge, there was an underground movement which at least, *thought* in terms of a more violent overthrow of the system. A select committee reputedly organised small underground groups throughout the West of Scotland and, on 22 February 1820, the day after Thistlewood and his friends were seized in Cato street, a general congress of delegates was held near Paisley to prepare for action. Some thirty of them were seized and imprisoned by sheriff's warrant.[58] There were anxious letters between Boroughreeve of Manchester and Henry Monteith, the Lord Provost of Glasgow, keeping each other in a state of agitation about the extent of radical conspiracy. On the other side, there were contacts between reformers in Glasgow and in Manchester and mounting rumour. On 20 March, the authorities had a story of a plot to set fire to the city,[59] and there was anxiety that clearance riots in Ross-shire would stir the popular agitation.[60]

The 'rebellion' came in the week beginning 2 April with the issuing of the declaration announcing the establishment of a Provisional Government of Scotland. The key figures in producing the Proclamation were three Parkhead weavers, Robert Craig, James Armstrong and James Brash. How much of a part in the projected rising was played by *agents provocateurs*, keen to bring the activists into the open, will never be known, but Dr. Roach convincingly argues that their part was slight and, judging from the pattern of arrests made later, the authorities really had very little knowledge of what was actually going on. How broadly based the support for an uprising was is impossible to assess. The insurrectionary activity in Glasgow itself was limited, though on 4 April most of the cotton mills were on strike. The weavers were at the forefront of the movement while, apparently, most of the mill workers had in fact turned up for work on the 3rd,but 'threatening visits', according to the *Glasgow Herald*, had brought them out. There was a similar pattern in Paisley.[61] Only a few showed any inclination to take up arms, though there were some pikes and swords around among the young men of the weaving community. The 'uprising' was largely confined to a number of small weavers' villages in the suburbs and around Glasgow. Stewarton in the South and Balfron in the North both had their radicals armed and ready to march, though with little heart to confront the troops.[62] At some of the villages around Paisley attempts were made to force farmers to give over their arms, and one radical was shot trying this.[63] At any rate the authorities, who had been expecting trouble for so long, were well prepared. Large numbers of troops were stationed in areas like Paisley that might have proved difficult to control.

There seems to have been an expectation that uprisings would take place in the North of England, and the Glasgow radicals waited in vain for the sign — the mail coach from Manchester failing to arrive — that the South was up in arms.[64] When that failed to happen, rather belatedly, on 5 April, a group of radicals, twenty or thirty of them (again mainly weavers), after a meeting on Glasgow Green, decided to march to Falkirk to seize the Carron Iron Works as a source of armaments. They were joined by a few on the way, at weavers' villages such as Condorrat, and they set off at a remarkably casual pace towards the East. It ended in the bloody skirmish at Bonnymuir. Only a few had joined them on the road, though some of the Camelon nailers had come out.[65] The final act of uprising was when a group of Strathaven radicals, including the veteran of the 1790s movement, James Wilson, marched towards Glasgow, in the belief that they would join a radical army on the Cathkin Braes. With confusion, uncertainty and foolhardiness, the hardy band of about eighty set off to find no radical army and no uprising.[66]

There had been no leadership and little planning. The assumption seems to have been that the first sign of movement in Glasgow would trigger risings all over the country. Undoubtedly there were fantasists among the reformers who believed that a few pikes would be enough or that somehow the old system would collapse when the 'people' showed their will. But there was no commitment to real confrontation of the authorities by force. Yet there clearly were many groups who had vague hopes of revolution, who would have been prepared to play some part in it if others had taken the lead and borne the bloodshed. The fact remains that workers did strike in the cause. There *were* parades in the streets of Bridgeton, when it was thought that there had been an uprising. As late as 7 April, when more and more troops were being poured into the West, some forty Bridgeton men *did* set out for Kirkintilloch to help those they thought were up in arms there. These and the many other pockets of activity do indicate that support for a vigorous show of force was by no means lacking. Any coherent plan of what precisely to do in the event of it happening was, however, totally absent.

Unrest and the occasional 'outrage' against authority continued for some weeks, but these can have been no more than frustrated rage. The authorities very effectively mopped up all who showed signs of radical sympathy. There were widespread arrests: 'persons have disappeared not previously suspected of taking part in revolution', noted the *Herald*. They were kept out of the way for a week or so and then bailed.[67] Any radical workers were excluded from employment. It was a splendid excuse for employers to act against trade unions. A number of employers on 11 April unanimously resolved, 'That no person whatever shall be employed by any of the subscribers who is, or shall become, a Member of any Secret society, or of any Society to which the Employer shall not be invited to become a member nor will they employ any person who shall subscribe or contribute money for any secret purpose whatsoever'. It may have had only limited success. When workers at the mill of Messrs. Barr & Co. at Greenhead returned to work, they faced a reduction of eight per cent on their wages. The regular workers refused and held out for six or seven weeks, effectively frightening off blacklegs until the company took back the union men.[68]

The aftermath was a series of treason trials. Altogether eighty-eight were indicted for treason at courts in Stirling, Glasgow, Dumbarton, Paisley and Ayr, though only thirty actually appeared. Far and away the largest number were weavers, twenty of them in Stirling, eleven in Ayr, four in Glasgow, three in Paisley. There were also five nailers and a wright from Camelon near Falkirk. The rest, smiths (2), shoemakers (4), tailors (2), a cabinetmaker, a bookbinder, a schoolmaster, a grocer, a slater and a flesher were among those identified.[69]

At Stirling Andrew Hardie and John Baird were both found guilty and sentenced to death. The others were encouraged to change their plea to guilty but all eighteen at Stirling were sentenced to be hanged, beheaded and quartered.[70] In Glasgow, Wilson suffered the same fate, less for the actual role he played in the march from Strathaven, which was a minor one, than for his reputation as a father figure of popular radicalism since the 1790s. He was known to the authorities, the actual activists were not. By now a shrewd decision seems to have been made not to press too hard for blood sacrifices or, perhaps, it was a recognition that it might not be possible to get them. The jury in the Wilson case had urged clemency and there were many public appeals for his life.[71] But Sidmouth was determined upon a victim. However, at Dumbarton, after one acquittal, the prosecution decided not to proceed against a group of Duntocher men.[72] At Paisley the jury would not convict. In the end only three were actually executed, Wilson, Hardie and Baird. Another sixteen rebels were despatched to Australia.

Economic distress and the sense that there was no alternative way to improvement had pushed many workers into political action. For the first time, in these years after the War, the demands for reform articulated by middle-class reformers found a widespread response among the workers. Judging from the language used and from the radical papers read, Scottish workers were deeply influenced by events in England. There is not much to indicate a distinctive Scottish series of issues and, in spite of the efforts of Berresford Ellis and Seamus Mac A' Ghobhainn, there is little to show that there was a nationalist element in the activities. We shall never know how far the events of the night of 1–2 April 1820 were the results of a hoax or the work of *agents provocateurs*. That groups did turn out, in the expectation of revolution, is an indication of the reality of the underground movement for radical change that existed. That the numbers rallying were relatively small tells us that these were tiny groups. There are no obvious links between the trade unions and the radical movement of these years. An anxious middle class tended to assume that all organisation among workers was radical and a threat to property and order. No doubt some of the leading activists in trade societies were the politically aware involved in reform campaigns, but there are only isolated examples that come to light to support this. For many, political activity was an alternative to trade-union action when the possibilities for the latter were greatly restricted. But the riots, the strikes and the attacks on troops are indications of an undercurrent of popular discontent that was potentially dangerous. The authorities were probably justified in their worries that disorder would spread, but in 1820 they repeated none of the mistakes that they had made in 1817. While many were arrested, only a few who had been caught in the act were brought to trial. When there were signs, after the initial capital sentences, that there would be difficulty in getting convictions the prosecutions were gradually dropped.

As long as the trials went on there were tensions, especially in places where troops were conspicuous. In the summer of 1820 the 13th Regiment, stationed at Glasgow, had to be removed to Stirling after two incidents in which drunken soldiers and locals came to blows. In one incident in Greenock soldiers opened fire on the crowd and two police watchmen and a third person were killed. The first anniversary of the 'uprising' was celebrated with a riot on Glasgow Green when soldiers and the band were pelted during the King's birthday celebrations and the wooden railing in the park was pulled up and turned into a bonfire.[73] However, with the return of improved economic conditions political tensions faded.

In addition, the Whig reformers of the East reasserted their leadership of the reform movement. While having no sympathy with the democratic aspirations of the Lanarkshire and Renfrewshire weavers, the Whigs did retain some credibility with them by acting as defence lawyers in the courts. They were able to present themselves as 'the friends of liberty', as a party who, if they achieved power, would bring reform. From August 1820 they focused on the irrelevancy of the Queen Caroline affair, blackening the character of the Monarch without undermining the institution of monarchy. They were able to give enough of an impression of being reformers to defuse a beaten and demoralised reform movement. For the rest of the decade, what political reform movement there was was essentially middle-class.

7
Conflicts over Control

The 1820s brought striking contrasts in experiences for many groups of workers. The first half of the decade saw a sharp improvement in the state of the economy after the bleak postwar years. Textiles, coal and, to a lesser extent, iron were all expanding, and in these and in the building industry there was an extraordinary speculative boom in 1824–25. Demand for labour was high. Even without the intimidation of the treason trials, these conditions, in themselves, were likely to bring a reduction in the tensions that had been so prevalent since 1815. But the increased need for labour also gave an opportunity for revitalisation of organisation and for the pressing of renewed demands. Aiding this, but not causing it, was the repeal of the Combination Laws in 1824. There is little doubt that the publicity given to repeal made trade unionists bolder in pushing their demands, but in most sectors the revival or organisation predated the 1824 Act.

The second half of the decade is in marked contrast. The bubble of the 1825 speculation burst in the Autumn, crisis and bankruptcies spread. Unemployment and wage cuts were the lot of many for the rest of the decade. Employers, battling to keep their heads above water, seized the opportunity to reorganise and rationalise many of the practices in their industry, to gain a control over their workforce that they had either lost in the early 1820s or had never before achieved. There were crucial battles over who should control the processes of work.

For the handloom weavers any improvement in the early 1820s was slight. Their union organisation had not recovered from the events of 1812 and 1813 and energies had been directed into what had proved to be the *cul de sac* of political radicalism. Large numbers still flocked into the trade and were prepared to work at low rates. In addition, from about 1818, powerlooms began to be introduced in increasing numbers. Experiments in the use of power looms had been made at Catrine and at Deanston from 1807 and there were about 1500 in operation by 1813. But it took time to overcome many of the technical problems. The introduction of powerlooms did not immediately make the position of all Scottish handloom weavers any worse than it already was. The early looms were quite unsuitable for the complex patterns or the fine muslin work, in which many specialised.[1] What they did hit was the poorest section of the weaving labour force, those producing the heavy cambrics and plain printing cloths. In the long run cheaper powerloom products were to replace the better-quality cloth, but this took decades. However, from 1818 to 1825 there was a marked increase in the number of powerlooms, a fivefold increase in a decade. What created special hostility towards the powerloom was the fact that these lighter machines could be worked by women. They could readily be identified as outsiders by handloom weavers, conscious now for a decade or more of the problem of numbers in their craft. Not surprisingly, therefore, handloom weavers and powerloom weavers continued to feature in much of the unrest, both political and industrial. They were well-represented in Glasgow Green riots. They played a dominant role in one of the most spectacular riots in Glasgow of the 1820s when, in July 1823, three or four thousand workers turned up to demolish 'Harvie's dyke', a wall built across a right of way on the banks of the River Clyde. It became so serious that the dragoon guards had to be called. Of those arrested, twenty-seven were weavers, eight were cotton spinners, three were colliers and the other five were tradesmen of various kinds.[2]

Perhaps linked with this disturbance, since it was taking place at the same time, was an industrial dispute among powerloom weavers. At the centre of it were the tenters, the loom turners who supervised the girls operating the powerlooms. On 22 July, the day before the Clyde wall riot, a youth, employed as a tenter, was dismissed for bad attendance and replaced. A few days later, the replacement was assaulted by some of the women weavers and by boys. He was splashed with vitriol, in what was an early example of the kind of assault that was to become notorious in Glasgow disputes over the next fifteen years. The victim identified two of the weavers as having been responsible and they were dismissed. A deputation to the manager got nowhere. He refused to re-employ the two dismissed weavers and he announced that there would now be new regulations that any worker arriving later than fifteen minutes after the engine had started would be liable to dismissal and would forfeit all outstanding wages. Some of the tenters now went on strike, but they too were replaced. Inevitably the violence escalated and when one of the replacement tenters was enticed into an alley and had vitriol thrown on his back, seven of the tenters were arrested, including Robert Airken, who was identified as the key figure in the tenters' union, with the weavers under his 'charge, controul and direction'. Five of the seven were sentenced to fourteen years' transportation.[3]

There seems to have been remarkably little outcry against such harsh sentences, which were quite regularly handed out for offences involving mobbing or rioting. But, perhaps, Australia held fewer fears than it once had. Broadsheets with information on the transported men of Bonnymuiur circulated in Glasgow in the early 1820s, painting a not unattractive picture of life in Botany Bay. One, consisting of a copy of a letter from Thomas McCulloch, one of the Bonnymuir rebels, asking his wife out to join him, mentioned the radical printer, Gilbert McLeod, who had produced *The Spirit of the Union* in 1819 until he was arrested and sentenced to five years' transportation, 'very well, and is acting as a schoolmaster'. Another, a letter from Andrew White, reported that his sentence had now been reduced to seven years and that after three he could expect to get a ticket of leave and could go to work on his own behalf.[4]

The authorities had been determined to make an issue of the tenters' union, because it was seen as part of a threatening and spreading combination of textile workers. It must have been a grave disappointment for employers to find unions emerging so quickly among the new operators of powerlooms. There had been a number of strikes at cotton mills, some accompanied by violent affrays, and the united employers had once again imposed the 'document'. To deter activists further the authorities were determined to have the case brought before the High Court of Justiciary, where heavier sentences could be handed out. According to the Sheriff of Lanarkshire, 'the use of vitriol is the means by which the Combination (now existing to an alarming extent) has not only kept together the Combination, but is the engine by which it exercises its vengeance on those who chuse [*sic*] not to join it'.[5]

Trouble continued, however, and, later in the year, there were attempts to shoot two managers of powerloom factories who had taken on new operatives after a strike. The issue was who should be employed and there were hints of conspiracies to keep out new workers. There was talk of 'nobs' and of 'sodgering' them and, it was claimed, in this 'they might depend on the support of the cotton spinners'. Such language and such tactics were later to be associated in the public mind with the Cotton Spinners' Society.[6] Who was learning from whom on this occasion is not known. With the development of powerloom weaving factories, in many cases near to spinning mills, the two groups had probably close family relationships anyway. In Calton, in Anderston, in Tradeston and in other parts of Glasgow, tightly-knit communities of textile workers were growing up.

The authorities found it extremely difficult to obtain any evidence of assaults on non-unionists or on strike breakers. They tended to explain this wall of silence by blaming intimidation, linked with the taking of secret and, it was assumed, bloodcurdling oaths, when in fact they were probably up against such a deeply-entrenched community solidarity that it did not require a great deal of intimidation to maintain. 'Nobs' are almost always described as 'bad men', as of 'indifferent character', 'offensive', given to violence against women or piecers. Because of this, attacks on nobs, in many cases by women, were seen as morally justifiable. One Anne McGregor, for example, was given a 'fine silver medal' from her neighbourhood on her release from prison after serving a sentence for intimidation of strike breakers.[7] To break such community solidarity was to court trouble, especially since strike breakers were likely to be incomers into the community. Nor was condemnation of violence by people *outside* these working-class communities necessarily always unquestioning. It proved very difficult to get juries to convict, even in cases involving violence. There was a revulsion against the excessively harsh sentences imposed and, although there were employers who went around calling for even harsher sentencing policies and the extension of capital punishment, the authorities generally recognised that this would be counter-productive and would result in more acquittals.

At a period of rapid growth and change in the cotton industry, there were inevitably disputes over issues of discipline and over who should be employed on particular tasks. For management and for workers new experiences were requiring a pragmatic approach. Employers, through their managers, were trying to impose a discipline in their mills, clamping down on, traditionally, rather casual patterns of work which had been imported from domestic labour into the mills. As Maxime

Berg has argued, 'workers adapted their own culture and rhythms of work to new contexts so that the factory never became the capitalist controlled and utterly rational form of work organisation' that employers wanted. There were efforts to eradicate drinking, a major problem in the city mills. In country mills, like New Lanark, such problems could be largely avoided by ensuring that no public houses were allowed in the community: in Glasgow, with its extensive supply of drinking houses, no such restriction was possible and there were well-established patterns of drinking at work.

As part of their effort to bring tighter discipline the system of fining began to be extended, and it was this trend that brought conflict among the cotton spinners. By this time they numbered around 800 in the West of Scotland and had a union organisation with a central committee made up of two delegates from each of three districts. The spinners' union dwelt at length on 'capricious managers' who 'blamed and dismissed men for frivolous and imaginary faults'. In 1822 there were strikes demanding the dismissal of spinning masters who had behaved 'oppressively' by levying 'intolerable fines'. Indeed hostility to fining was precisely because of the power it gave to overseers. Particular resentment was reserved for overseers, foremen and managers who had been recruited from the ranks of the spinners. There were frequent suggestions of the incompetence of managers and their poor knowledge of the various tasks, and accusations that they bestowed favours on those who plied them with drink, while victimising those who 'declined to stoop to their irregular desires'. At the mills of James Dunlop, where so many of the disputes were to focus, it was claimed that fines could mean deductions of anything from 3s.6d. to 11s.8d. each pay day. In 1822 the men claimed that they preferred dismissal to fines, presumably, at this time, confident that plenty of work was available. At the same time, aggravating the issue, were the attempts by a few employers, again with Dunlop prominent, to make use of women spinners.[8]

In April 1823 a strike broke out at the large Houldsworth mill in Anderston. Partly it was about fairness: the operatives wanted the quadrant and reel that measured the length of yarn adjusted, since they believed that they were being defrauded. Largely, however, it was again about discipline and regulation: they wanted fines abolished; they wanted foremen who were 'too vigilant' to be dismissed and a reduction in the number of foremen. What was being resisted was new management techniques that gave the spinner less independence as to how he carried out his work. There was resentment at the assertion of authority by the foremen over piecers, who were, after all, paid by the cotton spinners themselves. Finally, it was about who should be employed. Trying to control entry into the trade was from the start a major concern of the Spinners' Union. It is a good example of a group of 'new' workers adapting the techniques of traditional craft workers. Although one feature of the Scottish cotton industry is the large influx of Irish into spinning at the end of the 1790s, by 1816 the Spinners' Association's prime concern was to keep out 'incomers'. All kinds of ways were tried: a £5 admission fee to the Union; the use of assisted emigration for unemployed spinners (£3 could get you a one-way passage to New York); the clearly laid-down rules that union members were not to instruct anyone in the art of spinning 'except such as are the sons or brothers of a spinner'. The strikers also wanted no 'indifferent characters' in the works, by which they meant those who had refused to contribute to the Society; and they wanted two men, dismissed for drunkenness, to be reinstated. In addition, tension was caused by proposals to introduce payment by tokens and with it, presumably, the spread of truck.[9] Houldsworth was prepared to make concessions on a number of the men's claims, such as adjusting the quadrant and reducing fining. But he was determined to retain firm control over appointments and dismissals. After his spinners had been out for a month, other cotton masters locked out their workers, weavers and finishers as well as spinners, in all some four or five thousand. This general lock-out lasted for only a week, but the strike at Houldsworth's went on for nearly ten weeks.

The employers' association, reformed, or revived, at this time, remained in existence, but the strikes during the rest of 1823 and 1824, of which there were a number, were confined to individual mills. However, in September 1824, there was another dispute at Dunlop's Broomward Mill, with the operatives demanding the dismissal of a foreman who had taken to himself the power of interfering with the spinners' work methods, such as changing their pinions, and who also regularly abused piecers. There were other issues. Dunlop had been pushing up the deductions for 'wear and tear of machinery' and clamping down on drinking. The spinners' aim, they declared, was 'to make ... management as just and bearable as possible'. To the employers it was a matter of the crucial, and non-negotiable, issue of the prerogatives of management.[10]

Dunlop's men struck on 3 September and, a week later, the associated employers announced a general lock-out, provoking matters further by declaring that any loss that this involved would be paid for by a twenty per cent wage cut. The aim, clearly, was to break the union.[11] Strike breakers were brought in and there was sporadic violence. A number of 'nobs' were shot at and a cotton spinner, John Kean, was publicly whipped and transported for life for one such incident when a loaded pistol was discharged at one of Dunlop's new spinners.[12] That there was intimidation is undoubtedly true, but how far the violence against strike-breakers or against employers was organised is impossible to know. The authorities certainly believed that it was an integral part of trade unionism and they claimed that the Spinners' Association had a secret oath that involved swearing.

> that I will execute with zeal and alacrity, as far is in me lies, every task or injunction which the majority of my brethren shall impose upon me in furtherance of our common welfare; as the chastisement of knobs, the assassination of tyrannical masters, or the demolition of shops that shall be deemed incorrigible.[13]

But, of course, the authorities were largely dependent for their information on the evidence provided by the excluded or disgruntled, and while the oath may well have reflected the activities and the sentiments of the union, it does seem rather unlikely that any secret oath would have been drafted in such precise terms. There may well have been a tendency for those seeking to ingratiate themselves with the authorities, or to escape the consequences of their own misdeeds, to feed the authorities what they wanted to hear.

In fact, since the lock-out continued until February 1825, in some ways the remarkable thing is the lack of violence. The concern of the Crown Agents was at the lack of cases reaching the courts:

> I must in general observe that the very small number of instances of such violence having been offered at Glasgow during the last four months is not a little surprising; and that unless some stronger cases occur before April the proceedings at the next Circuit in so far as regards this crime will doubtless be pounced upon by those who support the repeal of the Combination Laws.[14]

After five months there was a steady drift back to work. During their long dispute the spinners had received some financial support from other unions in the city, though the authorities could find no evidence of co-ordinated action.[15] They also had aid from the Manchester Spinners' Union which, at this time, was keen to pull Glasgow into a union covering the three kingdoms. In fact, however, the bulk of the Manchester spinners had no enthusiasm for the tactics of the Glasgow Association. They believed that to attempt to dictate who could or could not be foremen would lead to a re-imposition of the combination laws.[16] The employers, now faced with a union at least partly broken, were able to push down wages at one mill after another. Economic crisis intensified the pressure. Reductions of wages continued in 1826, first 15½ per cent, then another 7½ per cent. Those who tried to keep the Association alive found themselves dismissed, and it was perhaps some of these Scottish spinners who were reported as active in Carlisle and Belfast at this time, trying to push the idea of a general union of spinners.[17]

The same period brought about the revival of organisation among the handloom weavers, the General Association of Weavers in Scotland. Its emergence predated the repeal of the Combination Laws and was probably related to the extensive unrest in all areas of textiles at this time. The Association had many of the features of the old 1812 Union: a general committee made up of delegates from affiliated districts; a union open to all handloom weavers throughout Scotland, irrespective of the fabrics in which they worked.[18] The aim, as always, was to try to cut down the flood of new recruits into the trade by imposing an apprenticeship, but they were also seeking to improve the organisation of the trade by eliminating any weavers who were likely to embezzle cloth or to abscond with webs, problems that manufacturers had always blamed for the plight of the handloom weavers. The weavers were also seeking to standardise the prices paid, to eliminate undercutting.[19] Conflict, when it occurred in 1824, however, came with one of the largest of the Lanarkshire manufacturers, Peter Hutcheson, who, when he brought in new materials, would not agree to pay top rates for them. The Association resolved to work toward 'thrusting Mr. P. Hutcheson out of the trade',[20] but the effect of this seems to have been that Hutcheson and others began to push more of their work to Ulster.[21] Yet, despite this and the arrest and imprisonment of two of the union's officials, the Association continued to grow, claiming 13,066 members in mid-September 1824.

During 1825, there were signs that the Weavers' Association was in difficulty, presumably as demand plummeted as a result of the spinners' lock-out and the beginning of depression. The attempts to resist reductions in rates brought an unbearable drain on the Association's funds. It tried to keep up out-of-work payments of 7s. a week for a man and wife and 6s. for a single man, but, by the Autumn of 1825, the Association was falling apart.[22] At 'one fell swoop', it was claimed, their wages were reduced by half and from 1826 through to October 1828 they were operating at what were termed 'starving prices'. In October 1828 they were reduced by a third more. Remnants of an organisation still existed which made an appeal to the Home Secretary, blaming 'a few unprincipled individuals' who were taking advantage of the scarcity of work to push down wages and who were forcing the respectable to follow. The crunch in Glasgow seems to have come a month or two later in December. Until then average wages among the 20,000 weavers in and around Glasgow were about 6s.6d., enough 'as could afford them a scanty allowance of oatmeal and potatoes', and 'the industrious and careful among them were able to meet the demands of their landlords'. By the New Year wages were reduced by fifty or even sixty per cent — 3s. was now a common wage and even the most skilled of men could not clear 6s. The magistrates had tried unsuccessfully to persuade the manufacturers to keep up wages, and were reduced to public appeals. The attempt to get a poor rate enforced seems to have fallen through.[23] Groups who had avoided the worst decline in standards earlier also began to suffer. The Paisley silk-gauze workers were badly hit by the influx of French imitation Indian shawls. By the end of the decade their position too was bleak.

Changes in the position of other textiles affected developments in areas outside West-Central Scotland. The framework knitters of Hawick, which, since the 1770s, had grown into the main centre for the manufacture of stockings and woollen underwear, had been organised since at least 1816, when a number of the stockingmakers refused to work at reduced rates. There was an agreement that men wanting to break their engagement had either to give a month's notice or pay 4s. When a group tried to raise a fund to pay the necessary 4s., four of the activists were arrested and kept in gaol for eight or ten days, before being bailed. They were not brought to trial, but the arrests effectively killed the strike. In 1817 there was another small strike when the masters, acting in concert, refused to raise wages. It lasted some seven weeks. Two years later there were reports of another strike against a fifteen per cent reduction.[24] In spite of the repeal of the wage-fixing legislation six years before, the men appealed to the JPs, who seemed to have adopted a sympathetic approach. A number of employers were detained for having 'combined to reduce wages', to levels of about 8s. to 10s. a week, for days of often fifteen hours in length. Six of them were questioned by Sheriff and Procurator Fiscal, but all were discharged. The JPs accepted that they had the right to regulate wages and they accepted also 'that the statement of grievances ... is not overcharged', but they declined to intervene, on the grounds that the master manufacturers were going out of their way to maintain wages at as high a level as possible.[25] In 1822 came the 'lang stand oot', a six months' strike and lock-out against a ten per cent wage cut. The strikers received financial aid from Dumfries, Carlisle and Edinburgh and it was only the arrest of twenty activists that broke the strike. It was the usual tactic. It was never explained on what grounds they had been arrested and they were never charged.[26]

Dundee was a major centre of the flax industry and, in September 1822, there was a successful strike among the flax hecklers against a reduction of 6d. per cwt. in the payments made to them for preparing the flax. This was a trade in which the men still had a fair amount of control over who should be employed, the number of apprentices and the patterns of work, but they were beginning to face new difficulties with a surplus of hecklers coming in from the unregulated country mills in Fife and Montrose and from the introduction of machines that were ultimately to replace them.[27]

A second major group that was particularly active in these years was the coalminers. The Glasgow and Clydesdale Association of Operative Colliers of 1817 and the parallel Ayrshire Association had not survived the arrest of John Fauldhouse Wilson, but united action at collieries still went on, with restriction of output:

> When the colliers wish to obtain an increase of wages, their general mode is by continuing to work, and endeavouring by every way possible to thwart the masters. When they observe a master has a demand for coals, they limit their supplies, and perhaps they will only do half work, and for days decline to raise coal altogether; in this way thwarting him so much that they generally obtain their ends.[28]

There were signs of renewed activity in 1823, when there was a long strike among colliers near Edinburgh.[29] But it was with the repeal of the Combination Laws in the Autumn of 1824 that new miners' associations appeared. It was also a time of booming demand for coal, but at the same time of increased competitiveness among coal owners. The complaint of the miners was that there were masters 'who are constantly running a race in the deduction of wages and are never satisfied unless they are paying below their neighbours, and by forcing the measure far above the common standard, to find a sale and outsell their neighbour colliers'.[30]

In Ayrshire, delegates from twenty-seven pits met on 25 October to draft new regulations on taking in what were called 'neutral men'. The aim was to keep control over entry by means of an apprenticeship system: 'Any person coming into the trade who is not a collier's son must serve a regular term of Three Years, and pay Five Pounds Sterling Entry Money'. While a collier's son could come into the pit at 10 and get full work at 17, the newcomer would not come in until 16 and not get his 'full liberty' until he was 19.[31]

While the rules emphasised that colliers were 'to make no unreasonable demands on their masters', provisions were made for disputes. A miner in dispute with his employer could look to the Association to support him at 7s. a week, and to make sure that no-one replaced him. Within a few months membership had reached 1200 out of about 1400 colliers in Ayrshire.[32]

Similar associations appeared in Glasgow and, by the end of the year, miners in

Lanark, Renfrew and Dumbarton were united in a single association, the Glasgow and Clydesdale Association of Operative Colliers, with local 'private associations' sending delegates to a Glasgow-based general committee. Its aim was 'lawfully, to obtain a fair living price for our arduous labour'. While the association at each pit controlled its own funds, the idea was to coordinate action through the central committee. No strike was to be embarked upon without the approval of this committee, except where it was a case of men being thrown out of work 'for refusing to work under stated wages of said Committee'. Ten shillings a week was to be allowed during such a dispute. Membership was open to 'regularly qualified' colliers who had had the colliers' oath administered to them. This masonic ritual caused much consternation to the authorities, since it was associated with secret words and secret hand grips. In fact it was probably no more than a symbolic entry into a craft and a useful way of maintaining solidarity against outsiders, against what was called 'the neutral world'. William McAllister, the secretary of the Kilmarnock Association, said that secret oaths and signs did not belong to the Association, but to what he called 'the Brotherhood of the Colliery', which was 'the same as Free Masonry'.[33]

The success of the new organisations varied. Some managers bowed to the union's control of labour, others effectively resisted 'interference on the part of the workmen in the management or conduct of the work'. Conditions, earnings and work patterns varied between pits. William McAllister claimed that he had earned on average 11s. to 12s. a week between 1821 and 1823 at the Duke of Portland's collieries in Kilmarnock, but there was a free house and 1s. worth of coal per fortnight.[34] In 1825, at a small pit in Parkhill near Falkirk, it was suggested that an active and experienced collier could earn 10s.6d. a day, from which was deducted 1s.9d. for the drawer, for oil and for repairing tools. The house was rent-free and colliers were allowed 'as much coal from the pit as they can possibly use — free'. In Ayrshire average earnings, it was claimed, were 15s. a week, paid fortnightly, and by the ton (though a ton was calculated at 28 cwts.).[35] Work was usually seven days in the fortnight. The Ayrshire Association at the end of 1824 focused on the size of the measure at the pit-head, which at some pits had recently been pushed up to twenty-nine hundredweights. The men wanted it reduced to twenty-six hundredweights and to have checkweighmen appointed. When this was refused at the Ayr Colliery of George Taylor, who seems to have been at the forefront of owners' opposition to the miners' demands since 1817, the men struck. They lost out, since Taylor was easily able to recruit Irish blacklegs. By March 1825, most of his colliers had given up the Association.[36] Elsewhere, however, the Association was able to win concessions and to continue to control entry.

This union among the miners spread to the recently opened pits along the Union Canal in the Redding and Brightons area of Central Scotland, near Falkirk. There were successful strikes at a number of pits for wage increases of as high as seventy-five per cent, but the largest owner, the Duke of Hamilton, ordered resistance. Strike-breakers were brought in from his Lanarkshire estates and, while at first driven off by the strikers, they were eventually imposed, under the Sheriff's protection.[37]

The strike at Redding, with its high wage demands, became the focus of the efforts of the central committee, now, apparently, linking all the organised districts in Scotland. Some £1500 came in to help the strikers. A system was worked out by which striking miners and their families from Redding were spread among working miners in the West, in Midlothian and in Fife.[38] When delegates from different parts of Scotland gathered at Redding in April 1825 they were arrested by the Sheriff Depute of Stirlingshire.[39] In the end they were not charged, but the strike by then was petering out. Little money was now coming in from the Association and payments to strikers had fallen from 4s.6d. to 2s.6d. to 1s.6d. a week. With the union facing the additional cost of sending witnesses to the Select Committee on the Combination Laws, even this dried up.

Later in 1825 the Association was more successful in defeating Colin Dunlop of the Clyde Iron Works, by calling 300 strikers out for nearly two months; and there seems to have been an effective restriction of output to keep up prices.[40] In the West of Scotland a committee of inspection existed to go round the pits to see that output did not exceed the prescribed quantity.[41] By the end of 1825 there was talk about a possible general strike of colliers, and demands for wage rises spreading to Fife and the Lothians. Some employers were making major concessions. The Carron Company, for example, agreed to pay by weight rather than by the traditional measure and to give a twelve months' contract to their workmen.[42] Inevitably this led to a counter-attack, with arrests of delegates, the dismissal of unionised men and the eviction of their families. Colin Dunlop gained revenge in April 1826 by hiring 'labourers, weavers and able-bodied men of all description' to replace his colliers.[43] Many of the strike-breakers were Irish, who for years afterwards complained of molestation and abuse at the hands of native families. As a manager said, 'It was their wish to compel the Irishmen to leave the works altogether conceiving thereby that they would be enabled to raise their wages'.[44]

By now the economic conditions were no longer favourable to the miners. The sharp financial crisis of the Autumn of 1825 was followed by deep economic depression. Coal stocks were building up and employers were able to resist the union and to push back its earlier gains: more and more unskilled labour was being pulled into the pits. Ironmasters facing falling iron prices and increased competition were determined to break the hold that the Union had built up. William Dixon evicted all his striking miners in his pits near Airdrie, and replaced them with new workers under guard. At his Govan pit, a Friendly and Free Labourers' Society, a company union, was formed which all employees had to join, and which was still in existence in 1838.[45] In a variety of ways the national Association was effectively broken.

Another of the groups who experienced an extraordinary cycle of boom and depression in these years was the building workers. All the main towns were growing rapidly: Glasgow's population increased by 54,000 (thirty per cent) in the decade, Edinburgh's by 24,000 (nearly twenty per cent). These years saw a formerly reasonably stable industry thrust into chaotic instability. As the economy moved out of depression in 1820, and encouraged by the easier credit available following the 1819 Bank Act, there was a dramatic increase in investment in property. Everywhere there was ostentatious display of new wealth in castles, office blocks and houses. Unfinished work on the New Town of Edinburgh was resumed and speculative building began. During 1823 and 1824, small builders were borrowing extensively; lawyers were pressing their clients to invest in property and a building mania was underway. The demand for building workers was unprecedented. In 1815, a period of sharp depression in the building trade, when only one or two houses were built in the whole of Edinburgh, there had been only seventy masons in the city. At the peak of the boom in 1824, more than 3000 were fully employed. Wages rose from 18s. to 28s. per week and workers poured into the city from all around. 'Old masons, who in '15 had taken to keeping provision shops, and in other ways to eke out a subsistence, once more returned to the 'mell'.' Other groups of building workers made commensurate gains. Joiners' wages rose from 15s. to 25s., and plasterers' from 16s–18s. to 24–28s. in 1824. There was a particular scarcity of competent plasterers, so much so that it was calculated that it would have taken Edinburgh plasterers two years to finish all the property put up in 1824.[46]

Such conditions gave the journeymen a powerful bargaining position, which they used to their advantage. Inevitably employers saw it differently:

> There never existed a worse class of men than the masons of that period. They were dissipated; they were idle; they were insubordinate. You could not call in question their work ... if the foreman quarrelled with them they laughed, or if he persisted they swore, if he lost his temper they would fight.

Apprentices were corrupted and a four-day week was common. In a sense these employers were in the hands of their workforce. There was heavy borrowing, competing in a market where supply soon outstripped demand, profits were cut to the bone, and labour 'was the source of success or of failure, of profits or potential bankruptcy'.

However, the gains of 1824 were short-lived and the extraordinary conditions of the period also brought changes with long-lasting adverse implications for building workers. There was an increased use of sub-contracting by builders, hiring building gangs rather than employing tradesmen directly. With country workers arriving in vast numbers, it was no great problem to establish this system, which was emerging in London and Lancashire at about the same time. Similar changes were clearly happening in the trade in Glasgow. Among forty-four builders in 1824, 1744 masons were employed: four of these builders employed over a hundred masons, another seven between fifty and a hundred and eleven of the remaining had over twenty. The day of the general building contractor had arrived.[47] Once established, it was impossible to eradicate.

Signs of a slowing down in the boom were apparent by the end of 1824 when striking masons settled for a wage rate of 16s. per week.[48] The first sign of impending collapse came in the summer of 1825, when one of the speculative builders absconded with the savings of some 1500 of his men, who had formed a friendly society. Credit dried up and work stopped. More than 2000 masons were thrown idle in a few months and, for the first time for a decade, Edinburgh-bred masons were forced on the tramp. At the end of 1827 there were fewer than a hundred masons left in the city and wages were as low as 12s.–14s., less broken time. The pattern in Glasgow was very similar. In 1826 wages were reduced to 15s. per week for the March to October period and to 12s. per week over Winter. With stoppages for wet weather and frost, it was reckoned that average earnings were 11s. per week. Approaches to employers for increases were met with contempt.[49] There was stagnation in building into the next decade and positions won over previous decades were lost. Alexander Somerville has left a telling example from Edinburgh:

> The sawyers objected greatly that my brother should at such a time of depression introduce a new hand; and they were disposed to prevent me from working. They said little to him; but on several occasions they told me I might probably get my head broken, and would possibly be found by somebody dead in the Cowgate Burn. Had it been a busy time, they would have struck work and refused to work for my brother, but it was otherwise so many being out of employment and suffering dreadful privations, they were powerless.

Eventually 'on purchase of whisky' he was allowed 'into the mysteries of brotherhood'.[50]

For the Edinburgh tailors, a decade of relative prosperity reached a peak in 1822, with the visit of George IV to Edinburgh. All those kilts and plaids, hats, dresses and military uniforms required every available tailor. As the gentry flocked to the city the wages of many tailors doubled or more. The foreman cutters were reputed to be on six guineas a week. However, with the excitement past, the pressure on wages and trends towards the reorganisation of the trade returned. The journeymen's society went on strike in 1823 with disastrous effects. The organisation was smashed and, for forty years, the tailors never succeeded in becoming effectively organised again. Ready-made clothing, much made by sweated labour in workshops or at home, came in rapidly. Only a very few firms in the West End, producing for the upper classes, continued with the bespoke trade, but they employed probably no more than thirty or forty journeymen at best.

In contrast to this pattern of deteriorating conditions, there was one group who began a slow progress towards improvement in these years: the bakers. The Edinburgh bakers had always been a notoriously violent and aggressive group, traditionally at the forefront of every mob. Their working conditions deteriorated in the early nineteenth century as demand for wheaten bread expanded and as more bakehouses were set up to replace the public bakehouses that had traditionally been provided. The conditions in these new bakehouses were notoriously bad. Journeymen bakers were engaged by the half year and were paid £2.10s. to £3.00 with bed and board, worse than a domestic servant could expect. They lived in the bakehouses, often foul, rat-infested cellars, and were generally single men, since it would be assumed that there was a high risk of married men stealing bread to take home. Their work was hot, heavy and deforming as a result of having to carry huge metal trays on their heads. They became bull-knecked and brutalised with 'enormous hairy caps and sallow complexions, and fearful language, [that] were the terror of all peaceably disposed citizens'. After the war, they had succeeded in moving to a system of weekly wages — 8s. for first hands, 6s. for second and 4s. for third, but still living in the bakehouses. In 1824 they organised their union in Edinburgh and demanded the right to live outside the bakehouse. They were not immediately successful, though a rise of 2s. per week was granted and a few masters agreed to allow their men to live 'without the walls'. But they had begun a process of liberation from their bondage.[51]

Other traditional craft groups faced familiar problems of the erosion of their position under pressure from growing numbers. The 1820s were also a decade when there was an expansion of publishing: newspapers, books and journals all flourished as never before. This brought demands for printers and bookbinders. Printing firms like Constables and Blackwoods in Edinburgh had grown very fast in the first two decades of the century in the great publishing boom of Scott novels, the *Encyclopaedia Britannica* and political and literary reviews. Newspapers, books and journals all flourished as never before. While this brought opportunities for journeymen, it also brought dangers of the unqualified and low-paid coming into the trade. In Glasgow, the Typographical Society had been offering sickness benefit since 1817. By 1824, a Glasgow Association of Letterpress Printers was trying to ensure that no-one should be employed who could not produce a membership ticket of the Association. There was also a committee to curb the number of apprentices: one firm reputedly had sixty-two apprentices to forty-four journeymen in 1825. The method used was for two or more of the committee 'to call upon the parents and guardians of any youth who may purpose to become an apprentice in one such irregular office, and explain to them the objects of the Association, and represent the evil consequences attendant on such attempts'.[52] To break this, in June 1825 the proprietors of the *Scots Times* led a number of employers against the Union. Printers were given a fortnight to abandon any connection with the Association and there was a threat of legal action against a 'strong and lawless combination' responsible for writing 'anonymous and incendiary letters'. Faced with the risk of prosecution, the Union dissolved in December 1825.[53] In the short term, this might have meant the persistence of some kind of underground organisation among the activists, but it is doubtful if an illicit body could have survived for long.

An Edinburgh Union Society of Journeymen Bookbinders was established in March 1822 'to prevent any of their rights and privileges being encroached upon'. The aim was to try to maintain the seven years' apprenticeship and to take a more aggressive line than the existing Journeymen's Bookbinders' Society. There were complaints that 'so many young men from the country' were getting employment at the expense of time-served craftsmen. It was becoming an attractive trade for the children of the slightly better off, it seemed, and many of those from the country were able to accept lower wages 'on account of their parents being generally in such circumstances as to be able to give some assistance to make up the deficiency of their wages'. There was also an increasing number of small employers in the trade, in many cases journeymen setting themselves up in business on their own, employing too many apprentices and paying low rates. Of the forty master bookbinders in 1825, half of them employed only apprentices: as many as five or six. In other cases one journeyman and seven apprentices were not uncommon.

Some of the country men coming to work at the trade were on only 7s. a week at a time when the regular bookbinders were trying to get a standard 16s. (This compared with levels of 24s. approved by the Court of Session in 1811). Between 1822 and 1825 the bookbinders did make gains through their union. Low-paid groups were encouraged to press for higher wages and, if sacked, were given financial support by the Society. As a result of this pressure, wages crept up to as much as 18s. or £1. Those who would not confront employers were expelled from the Union. The employers tried to recruit from Glasgow, where a Union had been formed only in 1824. To prevent this, a union of the two societies was brought about. In the Spring of 1825 the Edinburgh journeymen tried to abolish overtime or get extra rates and improved rates for those on night work. Initially, this was accepted, but an employers' society was formed and a lock-out ensued. The dispute caught the public imagination and the bookbinders were able to attract support from other trade societies.[54] They also got support from London and, as a result, seventy-seven of their number, 'the Glorious Seventy-Seven', were able to hold out for two or three months until the employers succumbed.[55]

The experience of the two branches seems to have been quite different. In Edinburgh pressure of numbers was pushing down wages and the Society got caught in a bitter struggle in 1825. Nevertheless it survived and continued to be a very active body in giving aid to other workers, though avoiding confrontation with its own employers. In Glasgow, although amalgamated to Edinburgh in the Union Society in December 1824, the position always seems to have been much more conciliatory. One does read of pressure being exerted on employers who took on non-union men,[56] but this seems to have been enough. Looking back in 1831 on six years, the Society could congratulate itself on its friendly-society side, which gave relief to the unemployed of 5s. per week for up to six weeks in a year, whether tramping or remaining in town. As regards the industrial side of its activities, 'in consequence of the considerate disposition of the employers', it was claimed, it had been 'hitherto rendered subordinate'.[57] A successful friendly-society side was probably unusual. Many friendly societies were still very vulnerable to financial collapse in the 1820s. So bad was the situation that the Highland Society instituted a major inquiry and came up with recommendations for reform of the system and level of payments.[58] However, there was little chance of much reorganisation in the second half of the 1820s with so much unemployment and reduction of wages.

The great boom in Edinburgh book publishing came to an end with the spectacular collapse of the firm of Constable and of Ballantynes in January 1826, taking Sir Walter Scott down with them. It was the 1830s before workers in the booktrade regained some strong bargaining power.

Much of the activity of these years may well have been stimulated by the repeal of the Combination Laws at the end of 1824. The campaign for repeal had brought petitions from colliers, boot- and shoemakers, nailmakers, printers, bookbinders, typefounders, cotton spinners and carpet weavers from all over Scotland, but the passing of the Repeal Act acted as a catalyst, coming as it did at a time which was favourable to the bargaining position of workers. According to Francis Jeffrey, the Whig advocate who had over the years defended working men but who was no admirer of trade unionism, 'scarcely were they repealed, when a fearful set of combinations started up in the country'.[59] But it is more likely that the favourable economic conditions were much more important. After all, the laws had not been applicable in Scotland, and although the Wilson and Banks cases of 1818 did have the Court of Justiciary declaring that an illegal conspiracy or combination to compel a rise of wages was a crime, the applicability of the 1799 and 1800 statutes to Scotland was never tested, and the Lord Advocate declined to bring cases on the charge of simple combination. Unions were formed, survived and grew in these years with little interference from the authorities. None the less, workmen were conscious that the laws were there, and there was always the threat of more effective legislation. Henry Houldsworth was complaining to Peel in 1823 that many of the cotton industry's problems stemmed from lack of effective combination laws in Scotland, and he was organising pressure to get legislation brought in.

The early repeal of the 1824 Act and its replacement by the tighter 1825 one may well have been influenced by the events in Scotland, which gained considerable notoriety. A central part of the 1825 Statute was to confirm the authority of employers as to how their business should be regulated and managed. Huskisson made clear that it was in response to an 'assumption of control on the part of the workmen' that was 'utterly incompatible with the necessary authority of the master at whose risk and by whose capital it is carried on'.[60]

Among the groups that petitioned for alteration of the Combination Laws was a general committee of Glasgow trades. This was one of a number of signs of increased cooperation between different trades. A meeting of associated trades' delegates was summoned by the Glasgow cotton spinners in October 1824 during the cotton lock-out. Sawyers, weavers, tailors, colliers, tobacco spinners, stocking weavers, calico printers, cabinetmakers, joiners, curriers, masons, founders, tinsmiths, saddlers, reedmakers, blacksmiths, corkcutters, nailers, brushmakers, coopers, shoemakers, ropespinners, carvers and gilders attended. The Sheriff Depute of Lanarkshire in 1825 believed that most of the trades in the county were in combination and, although he could unearth no firm evidence, he believed that there was a 'complete and concerted understanding between the other trades and the cotton trade'.[61] There had been talk of the need for this step for some time. A letter from an operative in the *Glasgow Chronicle* had called on

> the professors of the numerous trades and occupations in this great commercial country legally to associate themselves into societies, and these societies to form a general union, by which means any single trade may be upheld against oppression or reduction.

Another correspondent, writing on behalf of the Lanark, Renfrew and Dumbarton colliers, had talked of the 'propriety of joining in a 'union of trades'.[62]

It was a deputation from something called the 'Associated Trades of Glasgow' that presented Joseph Hume in October 1825 with a plate for his public services. (The plate was declined).[63] The most ambitious attempts at collaboration, however, came in Edinburgh following the 1825 bookbinders' strike.

While the strike was going on, one of the Journeymen Bookbinders called for 'a Union of the whole trades who have formed themselves into Societies'. Some such body appeared, calling itself the Mechanics' Institution, though not at all linked with the self-improvement body of the same name recently formed in Glasgow. It remained in existence throughout 1826, giving help to the painters in May and to the Rope and Twine Spinners in December. During 1827, however, it clearly faced difficulties. There were disputes over the Institution's funds, held by the individual societies, and when, in August 1827, the Rope Spinners withdrew, they, according to the Bookbinders, were the last remaining society.[64] This was probably one of a number of short-lived schemes for general trades unions or, at least, mutual trades society co-operation in these years. There was certainly one in Manchester at roughly the same time.[65]

In almost all cases in the mid-1820s, especially in textiles and in mining, the underlying issue in industrial disputes was the question of control. Hardly any of the disputes was about wages. They were about who was to have power in the workplace: who was to control entry to the workforce and who was to control the patterns of work in the mill or the colliery or the workshop. It was a crucial struggle central to the whole future of industrial development. The struggle came in the 1820s because of the boom conditions that existed in 1824–25. For the workers it was an opportunity, when demand for labour was high, to try once again to halt what seemed an inevitable decline in their position as a result of the flood of new recruits. They sought to impose regulation over their trade, to maintain some of that artisanal control over the property of their labour. The cotton spinners had managed gradually to build up some of this over the previous decade and to carve out a distinctive area of skill for themselves. For the miners it was a case of trying to regain some of that control over their communities, which, paradoxically, their serfdom of the eighteenth century had allowed them. For artisans it was a question of resisting the encroachments on their traditional regulation.

For the employers the belief was that such control had to be broken if they were to get the necessary fast expansion of their workforces. It was those employers most concerned with getting rapid growth who were at the forefront of the onslaught on the unions. Yet, only in a period of good trade could the employers hang together long enough to effectively confront the unions. After 1825 the position of the unions was much weakened by the sharp depression, but so too was the position of many employers. They were less concerned with expanding their labour force. They were in a sharply competitive situation, less willing or able to confront and, perhaps most importantly of all, not ready to stand united. The collaboration among employers that had been achieved in the early 1820s began to fall apart and unions, surreptitiously, were in some cases able to win back some of what they had lost in 1824–25.

The issue of control was by no means resolved in the disputes of these years, despite temporary setbacks for the unions. The colliers perhaps lost out most, with the break-up of their Association, but guerilla activity continued at individual pits and there were enough incidents of violence against those who were not 'bred colliers' to deter all but the most foolhardy or most desperate from trying to break in. The cotton spinners, while losing specific battles, still remained remarkably strong. By 1827 equalisation of pay rates had been achieved at Glasgow mills. It is clear from the discussion of the delegates at the Isle of Man Conference of 1829, which resulted in the formation of the Grand General Union of all the spinners of the U.K., that the Glasgow spinners had few of the grievances that affected those in Lancashire and were well content with the position their union had achieved. Artisans, particularly in the building trade, were less able to recover lost ground though they had learned to look to one another's societies for mutual support.[66]

8
The Search For Alternatives

The 1820s were the decade that brought the fastest and most extensive changes in the position of Scottish workers. It is true that pressure of numbers, the influx of country-bred workers into the towns, had been going on for decades. But the extraordinary boom of the early 1820s followed by the collapse after 1825 created the conditions for a massive deterioration. General contracting and subcontracting had transformed the building trades. Everywhere there was talk of the 'host of half-bred or indifferent hands' (joiners), 'no attention to character and skill' (lathsplitters), 'apprentices ... brought by the dozen and set to men's work' (painters), a 'system of regular apprenticeship ... fallen into disuse' (cabinet-makers). In tailoring the once powerful organisation of Edinburgh journeymen was broken up and regulation of the trade disappeared. 'Master tailors began to keep cloth; master clothiers began to keep foreman tailors.' Slop work, which had been around for decades but contained 'in an atmosphere of congenial obscurity along with the trade in old hats and second-hand clothing', now appeared in the best shops catering for the middle classes.[1]

Of course, for many this meant there were new prospects: for the country workers who seized the opportunities offered in Edinburgh between 1822 and 1825:

> Provident masons from Perthshire and the north continued to gather a portion of the squandered capital. South country masons who eschewed dissipation saved up half their wages. Sharp men from Aberdeen and Banff made off with their savings on the first sign of dissolution; and lank-haired Presbyterians from Argyleshire ... returned to the barren neuk from whence they sprung, and gladdened the hearts of their poor relations with the sight of more gold than their eyes had ever seen, their ears ever heard of, or this fondest dreams could ever have realised.[2]

For those with skills in wood and iron, machine-building brought new opportunities from the steam-engine makers to the blacksmith, from the patternmaker to the wire workers. For yet others new technology totally altered the nature of their work and put less of a premium on skill. In plumbing, for example, the skilled casting of lead gave way to the fitting of manufactured pipes and cisterns, and while once 'they considered themselves tradesmen; now they consider themselves no longer entitled to the name'.[3] The relentless advance of capitalism brought deterioration in wage rates and, perhaps more seriously, in status for many craftsmen. Now there was no clear social position defined by the term 'tradesman'. New employers and new workers, using division of labour, had effectively undermined the position of the all-round craftsmen. Some, calling themselves tailors or shoemakers, might in fact have a very limited skill, to make only part of an article, and yet be (equally) regarded as tradesmen by outsiders.

While in the radical movements of the years up to 1820 the tendency was to blame excessive taxation and the corruption of government for the plight of the workers, in the 1820s attention switched to the economic structures. This was almost inevitable in view of the theories of classical political economy that were increasingly being propagated by every possible means. The new orthodoxy had been forming for decades, but in the postwar years of unrest there was a concentrated effort to popularise a standard view. In Scotland, J. P. McCulloch was at the forefront of such a campaign between 1817 and 1822, using the pages of the *Scotsman*, which apparently had a readership among 'the tradesmen and mechanics of Edinburgh', and the *Edinburgh Review*, the foremost organ of Whiggery.[4] From pamphlets and pulpits the message was spread. It was believed that it was particularly important to get to the workers, to eradicate the 'violent and unjustifiable proceedings' of the manufacturing population.[5] The Edinburgh School of Arts, opened by Leonard Horner in 1821, and the Glasgow Mechanics' Institute, established in 1823, both had as part of their purpose the conversion of the labouring class to 'sound political economy'.[6]

The message of political economy was that economic forces operated independently of human intervention, guided by 'laws', just as in the world of physical science, which it was impossible, and wrong, for mortal man to try to defy. Any restrictions on freedom of trade or freedom of the labour market by means of government intervention or of trade-union action was to be abhorred as a defiance of such fundamental 'laws' and, at any rate, in the long run was bound to be ineffectual. Only moral restraint or emigration to reduce population size, so that the means of subsistence were not overwhelmed, could bring some improvement for the mass of the people. Without a reduction in the supply of labour, there could be no real improvement in how the fixed wage-fund, out of which wages were paid, was divided.

In response to such arguments there gradually emerged a series of views among working-class radicals that together made up an alternative view to orthodoxy: what Noel Thompson has called 'The People's Science'. This view blamed competitiveness, the very essence of capitalism, for the plight of the workers and for the deterioration in their position, from what was seen, increasingly, as an earlier golden age. As such ideas caught hold, there were those, therefore, who believed that only through finding an alternative to the competitive system could conditions be improved. A search for alternative forms by which labour could be organised was begun.

The most radical of these, in Scotland, was the Orbiston Community. Planned in 1825, this was intended to put into practice the ideas of Robert Owen. Owen had been in Scotland since 1800. As David Dale's associate and, soon, son-in-law, he had the *entrée* into West of Scotland industrial society. He soon took over the running of the New Lanark mills, was on the Board of Directors of the Glasgow Chamber of Commerce, and was generally regarded as a leading industrialist.

After 1812, he began to acquire an international reputation with his experiments in work discipline and in education. It was his educational work, with the provision of a school for infants, that probably first drew the attention of the wider Scottish public to Owen's activities, and he became more and more concerned to catch the public eye. His advocacy of legislative restriction on the hours of children in cotton mills in 1815 can hardly have endeared him to his fellow mill-owners in Lanarkshire, though it helped make him nationally known, an experience he undoubtedly relished. With the dancing masters and musical bands, the drills and the exercises laid on for the workers at New Lanark, he was already coming to be regarded as a dangerous eccentric when, in 1820, he presented his *Report to the County of Lanark of a Plan for Relieving Public Distress and Removing Discontent* to the Commissioners of Supply of the County. In it he built on ideas he had already presented to a House of Commons Select Committee on the Poor Laws in 1817. His fundamental premise was 'that manual labour, properly directed, is the source of all wealth' and 'that, when properly directed, labour is far more value to the community than the expense necessary to maintain the labourer in considerable comfort'. He was no opponent of industrial growth, but he abhorred the irrational and wasteful manner in which the new productive powers of an industrial society were being utilised.[7] He emphasised the need for the poor to be managed and to be trained, and proposed that this could best be done by establishing villages of 'unity and mutual co-operation', where the poor would be self-sufficient. They would be 'able to create all their own subsistence and repay the interest of all capital invested in the outfit of the establishments'. His proposals attracted a local landowner, A. J. Hamilton of Dalzell, who offered to lease up to 700 acres for an experimental scheme.[8]

By now, Owen was attracting a great deal of national attention. George Mudie in the pages of the *Economist* had successfully introduced London to his ideas, and a British and Foreign Philanthropic Society appeared, to propagate his community-building schemes. It was this body that offered to back Hamilton's proposals, when the Lanarkshire Commissioners of Supply decided not to go ahead. Land was bought in 1822, but Owen himself was now turning his attention to the already established community of New Harmony in the United States. However, two of his enthusiastic admirers, Hamilton and Abram Combe, an Edinburgh Owenite and brother of the well-known phrenologist, George Combe, decided to take up the scheme. The two of them had already founded an Edinburgh Practical Society, with about thirty skilled craftsmen, in 1822, committed to carrying into effect 'the New View' that it was possible to find an alternative to capitalism that would give labour a more comfortable share.[9] Reputedly, it eventually had about 500 members. It had attempted to run a co-operative store and a school, but collapsed when the storekeeper misappropriated the funds.

The 'Articles of Agreement' for the Orbiston Company were signed in March 1825. It was to put into practice Owen's views on education and his ideas on political economy. In the preamble to the Articles it was argued

> that it was not necessary that *any portion* of mankind should continue to exist in a

> state of degradation and misery; and that the poverty or want which now exists in the world is not the necessary consequence of deficiency either of the natural powers and inclinations of individuals to create wealth, or of material requisite for that purpose, — but that it arises necessarily from the existing system of competition.[10]

It was the first attempt in Britain by means of a community to try to emancipate the working class by offering an alternative to the dominant economic system. Such a scheme was not in opposition to the technological advances that were being made, but to the way in which they had been applied. A more rational application of the new productive powers presented by machinery, it was argued, would not lead to massive displacement of labour, but rather to a system that would eliminate economic distress. Such a change could only be achieved in a co-operative community free from the pernicious influence of competitive capitalism.

Unfortunately, according to Abram Combe, who was manager of the new community, it almost at once attracted to it 'a population made up for the most part of the worst part of Society', though quite what was meant is not clear. They were, he suggested, concerned with opting out of the consequences of the new capitalist society, rather than, like Combe, fervently committed to moral reformation.[11] Nevertheless, by the Autumn of 1826, the Community had become established, advertising its services in printing and bookbinding, boot- and shoemaking, carving and gilding, turning, painting and glazing, watch-and clockmaking, tailoring, hairdressing and perfumery, upholstery, wheel-carriage making, machine-making, ironfounding, tinwork, weaving and building.[12]

But it was never a united community. The more prosperous sections, such as the ironfoundry, were less than enthusiastic about profitsharing with the not so successful. The general economic climate was far from favourable and there were growing financial problems. It was abandoned in the Autumn of 1827. It failed, like many communities before and since, because its goals were never clear and because its recruitment of members seems to have been largely unregulated. It failed also because it was never self-sufficient, but was dependent upon those who made money in the 'Old Society', and were subject to the pressures of that society. There is no sign that it gained any local support, indeed, far from it.[13] To many in the local area it was a 'Babylon'.[14]

The immediate impact of Orbiston on the consciousness of the Scottish workers was probably of almost no significance. But it did throw up a figure who was to play a vital role in many future developments in Scottish labour over the next forty years. This was Alexander Campbell, a joiner by trade, who in 1822 had been treasurer of the Bridgeton Co-operative Society and became the leading advocate of co-operation in Scotland.[15] At Orbiston, Campbell had been a partner in the successful foundry company and was jailed for debt by the creditors after the community's collapse. However, his enthusiasm for co-operation remained undimmed. As he wrote to Owen, whom he had met when Owen paid a brief visit to Orbiston, 'I can only say for myself that the whole of the proceedings at Orbiston has tended to confirm my mind stronger both as to the practicability and utility of your system over the present arrangement of Society'.[16]

On his release from jail, Campbell travelled around spreading the ideas of co-operation. He believed that the failure of Orbiston would prevent capitalists putting their money into similar schemes, and therefore, any hope had to lie with the 'labouring class' who should be encouraged to form Union Societies to raise funds to establish their own communities. The way to achieve this was by means of co-operative store-keeping. He claimed that it was he who originated the idea that profits should be divided and should be distributed in proportion to purchases.[17] This was much more in the tradition of the old Scottish victualling societies, and his campaigning led to co-operative retailing societies in Glasgow, Paisley, Bannockburn, Cambuslang and other places. Some other co-operative stores were still around from earlier dates, so the ideas that Campbell was propagating were not entirely unfamiliar. A Govan Victualling Society dated from 1777, one in Lennoxtown from 1812 and another in Larkhall from 1821.[18] Campbell clearly had a wider vision of what co-operation was about, though he accepted the trading aspects of the stores as important.

Campbell was behind the Co-operative Bazaar, opened in London Road, Glasgow at the end of the 1820s. This was an Owenite labour exchange, where articles brought by members were priced according to the time spent on their production. By this means, it was argued, the exploitation of labour in the act of exchange could be eradicated and 'the whole produce of labour should belong to the labourer'. Exploiters of labour would no longer be able to add profits to labour costs. The means of exchange were the Bazaar's own notes. In this way, producers and consumers would get together independently of the capitalist, and capital could be created 'for the exclusive benefit of the labourers out of their own transactions'.[19] Unlike the stores, the Bazaar had the aim of using profits 'for the further object of giving employment to members who may be either out of work or otherwise inefficiently employed'. Its ultimate object, as Campbell made clear, was 'the possession of land, the erection of comfortable dwellings and asylums for the aged and infirm, and seminaries of learning for all, but more especially for the formation of a superior character for their youths, upon the principles of the new society as propounded by Robert Owen'.[20]

Just as with the Orbiston Community, differences of view on the objectives of the Bazaar soon arose. Some wanted it to be a business enterprise, others the first step towards the new moral world. The two aims were not always compatible. In March 1831 it split, with committed Owenites breaking away to form their own Society.[21] Although no information exists about the numbers who were involved in these enterprises or who continued to identify with Owenism, there seems little doubt that numbers were small and that they faced a great deal of presbyterian hostility. Laurence Pitkeithly, visiting Glasgow and Edinburgh in 1833, found strong prejudice from 'some regarding your irreligious (sic) some on account as they insist of your advocacy of a community of women'.[22] However, Campbell never gave up and he and others continued with missionary activities. An Owenite Social Festival of the Industrious Classes was held in Glasgow in April 1833, at which Campbell tried to get commitment to a National Association of United Trades that would provide the raw materials for the unemployed of various trades to produce goods which could then be exchanged for labour notes. The profits of the enterprise were to be used 'to purchase land, build houses and workshops and install machinery'.[23] In 1836 there were still Owenite groups in both Glasgow and Paisley, meeting every Sunday to discuss religion and science and 'occasionally the science of society — the principles of which I am glad to say are silently ingrafting themselves on the minds of the people and displacing the old prejudices created by ignorance'.[24] There were even hopes of Owen becoming a parliamentary candidate for the Glasgow constituency.[25] In 1838 Owenite groups existed in Edinburgh, Leith and Dundee. From Paisley it was reported 'that the tenets of Mr. Owen have gained several converts ... and that, in consequence, many stay away from church *on principle*'. By that time, however, the appeal of Owenism was much more as a religious heresy than an economic heresy and, in the Halls of Science which appeared from the end of the 1830s, it was mainly religion that was debated.[26]

Another advocate of co-operation was a weaver from Parkhead near Glasgow, William Thomson. Thomson accepted that 'labour is the true origin of wealth ... [but] it is not the productive portion of mankind, but the unproductive, which reaps the real advantage of labour'. What was needed, argued Thomson, was to eliminate 'the selfishness of man' by 'adopting some better system of social economy'. Thomson propagated his views in the counties of Lanark, Renfrew and Ayr, calling meetings 'by tuck of drum, sound of horn or ring of bell', and left in his wake a number of what were called 'economical societies'.[27] These seem to have had no wider intention than selling goods at wholesale price. He rejected the victualling society idea because they sought to make profits and 'to enrich themselves at other people's expense'. He rejected the co-operative system, 'the design of which is to accumulate property', and what he proposed was 'a plan by which he might go to the very best market, and purchase all they need of the necessaries of life, &c of the finest quality and at the lowest price possible'. There would be no profits and no credit. By the Autumn of 1833 there were twenty such societies.[28]

Alexander Campbell's ideas of co-operating to provide work seem to have been the ones that attract the widest attention. His message was that the workers could improve themselves 'if they would unite, be sober, and exercise a little self-denial for a time'. *The Herald to the Trades Advocate*, launched in September 1830, was to be the means of raising money to finance a stamped working-class newspaper, *The Trades Advocate*, which was to be the vehicle for spreading this message. It was published by a United Trades Committee, whose secretary was John Tait, clerk in an engineering firm, and later a journalist and coffee-house proprietor, and whose main members were leading figures in cotton unions, Daniel Macaulay of the powerloom operatives (Tait's brother-in-law), Joseph Miller, James Nish, both cotton spinners; but Campbell appears to have been the instigator. He had called a meeting in June 1830 and proposed to raise £500 to launch a paper. It was to be a 2d. working-class paper, with the 5s. shares 'to be held by the working classes particularly; they would thus have the complete control of a press of their own', and offer an alternative to a 'prostituted press'.[29]

Proposals for a Trades Union on the model of Doherty's National Association for the Protection of Labour were put forward in the *Herald* in October 1830. The introduction of machinery was blamed for the low wages of many operatives, but there was, it was claimed, no hostility to machinery if 'properly conducted for the benefit of all'. What was needed was the reduction of numbers in the labour market. This was to be accomplished by means of the Trades Union. Every distinct trade would form a union, with a shilling entry and 1d. a week subscription. These, in turn, would be united in the Trades Union:

> ...the great and only object of the whole Union should be to give employment to the idle and superfluous hands belonging to the different trades who contributed to the general fund. By this mode being adopted, the first object to be accomplished might be our intended newspaper, which would be a vehicle of communication for all. As soon as this was accomplished the next object might be the erection of an Operatives' Hall, with convenient committee rooms, extensive bazaar, for the receipt of the produce of the members employed, or the United Operatives' Bank; and last, though not least, seminaries of learning for themselves and their hitherto neglected offspring.

The hope was to have 40,000 members and for workers to 'become your own capitalists and employers'.[30]

Letters of support for the idea of finding an alternative to 'the present competitive state of society' flowed into the *Herald to the Trades Advocate*, with co-operative unions clearly being seen as the means by which workers could be employed for themselves. But there were differences of view. Some of the Trades Committee leaders wanted to distance themselves from Owenism and, when the Glasgow Co-operative Society split, the paper commented, 'This, we are afraid, comes of intermingling metaphysics with the very-day purposes of life. Co-operation, relating entirely to marketing and exchange of goods in the most advantageous manner for those who produce, may be carried on most cordially by persons of every creed'.[31]

Again, it is impossible to assess from surviving evidence how successful any of this activity was, but some were clearly moved by it. On the other hand, it is worth bearing in mind that the idea of self-employment by workers was by no means new and not all of the schemes that appeared in the 1830s were necessarily Owenite-inspired. It was a tactic that had been tried by different groups in the eighteenth century. More recently, the shipwrights in Dundee, after a lengthy conflict with their employers over wages and apprentices, set up their 'New Shipwright Building Society of Dundee' in 1826. They had taken between £200 and £300 from their benefit funds for the initial capital, until ordered by the JPs to replace it. Less encouragingly, the Society went out of business in 1831.[32] An Operative Turners' Society was formed in Glasgow in March 1831, not to support strikes — 'We have seen that strikes have never produced those beneficial effects that had been calculated upon' — nor to oppose masters 'by using compulsory means', 'but rather to raise a capital to purchase machinery and material for our own employment, when we are unable to find work elsewhere'.[33] In May, the Operative

Slaters formed an Association 'for the purpose of employing ourselves upon our own capital'.[34] In July the newly-revived Blacksmiths' Union resolved 'That so soon as a sum requisite for establishing a factory for the employment of idle hands is accumulated, it be commenced'.[35]

By now, however, the hopes of a new newspaper to succeed the *Herald* had collapsed. By the last issue of 28 May 1831 only 1609 shares had been subscribed and money had run out even before it was suppressed under the stamp acts. What probably also killed it was the appearance of Peter MacKenzie's *Loyal Reformers' Gazette*. Political excitement was mounting and Mackenzie's journal offered a more racy style of political comment.

It is probable that there had always been differences of opinion on where efforts should be concentrated: how much effort should be put into political activities and how much on more narrowly defined industrial activities. But these differences were widening as a result of the greatly expanded debate on the nature of political economy that had been taking place in the 1820s. Scottish activists had access to the writings of Thomas Hodgskin, William Thompson and others in the pages of English journals which made their way to Scotland. *The Herald to the Trades Advocate* published some of these. There were still many who clung to traditional, radical views that blamed the fate of the poor on 'old corruption', on the politicians, placemen and pensioners, on the sinecurists and corrupt officeholders who manipulated the state for their own benefit. To them the way to change was still through democratising the political system. Others saw the root of the trouble in an unjust and irrational economic system. Campbell had always leaned to the second of these positions, putting his faith in union and co-operation. As he warned, 'whatever steps the present Ministry would adopt, the interest of the working classes, who now composed two-thirds of the whole population, would be left out, and prevented from having influence on the representation of the country, or any share in making these laws by which their character is formed'.[36] But another group, led by Daniel Macaulay, president of the Trades Committee, were admirers of Joseph Hume and pinned their hopes on parliamentary reform. Campbell had originally played a part with them, and it was he who chaired a meeting in honour of Joseph Hume when he visited the City in September 1830. His message cannot have been entirely to Hume's liking, however, with its emphasis on the need for 'The Working Classes, on whom depend the whole fabric of society', to 'begin to think more of themselves. On them depended all pensions, sinecures and taxes; the army and the navy were upheld by the produce of their labour'.[37] Hume's visit left behind a middle-class Reform Association, dominated by businessmen like Colin and Henry Dunlop and Charles Tennant, many perhaps, like Robert Dalgleish the Lord Provost, less than enthusiastic about reform, but anxious to be involved so that they could control and curb the reform movement.[38] In January 1831, however, a slightly more radical grouping, to link middle class and working class, came together at a Trades Political Dinner. Although Campbell had played his part in this gathering, it was Macaulay and John Tait who came to the fore. Campbell continued to warn that parliamentary reform was not enough and that real change could only come if the workers could find the means of retaining the whole produce of their labour. Nor were the Whig franchise proposals anywhere near adequate, he insisted: women too ought to have the right to vote.[39]

Some twenty-four trades took part in the Reform Demonstration in Glasgow on 2 May 1831, when numbers of between 100,000 and 200,000 were claimed, though it was left to middle-class radicals to declare that 'it was now the Bill or the Barricades. The Reform Bill must be passed or blood would flow'.[40] Later that week the first issue of Peter MacKenzie's *Loyal Reformers' Gazette* made its appearance and there were alarmed letters from Lanarkshire, warning of the high degree of political excitement in the Western counties.[41] In fact, the tone of MacKenzie's paper and of the political activists inspired by it remained staunchly deferential. MacKenzie's frequent references to the radical movements of 1816–1820 were not to paint parallels but contrasts. His exposure of the activities of Alexander Richmond and his accounts of the spy system were part of a process of pinning the blame for the more extreme actions of these years on *agents provocateurs*. This time the emphasis was to be on constitutional reform and on collaboration with the middle classes, 'throw[ing] aside forever that party spirit and animosity which has so long existed in their breasts against their more fortunate brethren the upper classes', as a Glasgow Trades Political Committee put it in August 1831.[42] There were contrasts with 'deluded brethren in the South who went for riot and disorder'.[43]

Political activities continued to dominate through the Autumn and Winter of 1831, when there was something of a marking of time as the Reform Bill trundled its way through Parliament. Edinburgh trade unions, which had been slow to move in the early stages of the parliamentary reform movement, became more active. An Edinburgh Trades Union was formed in May 1832, committed to a most eclectic list of reforms:

> For co-operating with others in the obtainment of Union, Burgh Reform Repeal of the Corn Laws, Free Circulation of Knowledge, Revisal of the Militia Laws, Separation of Church and State, Extinction of all unmeritted Pensions, Free Representation in Parliament, Equitable Settlement of the National debt, Sobriety, Industry, Economy, Improvement of the Working Classes, Employer and Employed United, Abolition of Slavery, Free Trade.[44]

It was this body that organised the great reform jubilee parade in Edinburgh in August 1832, when sixty-three different trades took part.[45] In November an unstamped fortnightly journal, *The Trades Examiner*, appeared urging 'the united trades to be up and doing' to achieve very much the same list of eclectic reforms that had been put forward in May.[46]

In Glasgow, with the collapse of the *Herald to the Trades Advocate* in May 1831, there was a lack of an effective vehicle to put forward a wide range of views. Peter Mackenzie's *Loyal Reformers' Gazette* followed an often idiosyncratic course, depending on Mackenzie's whim. The *Radical Reformers' Gazette*, another weekly, was not particularly sympathetic to trade societies and adopted a traditional interpretation of blaming problems on 'old corruption'. The Glasgow *Trades Advocate* at last made its appearance in June 1832, with Tait as editor. No copies of this paper seem to have survived, but in 1833 it became *The Liberator*, again with Tait as editor. Tait continued to edit *The Liberator* until 1836, when it was taken over by Dr. John Taylor and became the most influential of the Scottish Chartist newspapers.

At the first post-reform election in Glasgow there was no agreement among the radicals about whom to support from among the five candidates. Campbell, consistently with his earlier position, proposed that a working-class parliamentary association be set up to raise money by weekly contributions to return a working-class MP. An attempt at one meeting to select a candidate of the unenfranchised was frustrated by the hall being closed to them and the audience turned into the street. In other cases, the talk of exclusive dealing by the unenfranchised to exert pressure on the voters came to nothing and two candidates, generally regarded as right-wing, were returned.[47]

With political reform out of the way and with economic conditions improving fast, there was a revival of interest in trade unionism. There followed two years of quite unprecedented industrial activity. New societies appeared and old ones revived, with many of them linking up with branches in other towns to form what were really loose federations, although they were usually called national unions. One of the most downtrodden and exploited groups, the bakers, linked their local unions into a federal structure in January 1834 and went on strike 'to secure to themselves an independency'. Their aim was to escape finally from the boarding system and to improve wages and conditions by imposing a closed shop and restricting the number of apprentices.[48]

The building trades, recovering from five years of stagnation, were among the most active. The Scottish United Operative Masons' Society was founded in Glasgow in October 1831 to try to recover some of the cutbacks made in the late 1820s. The new union campaigned for two years for an advance of wages, but got nowhere. However, it was able to build up membership and funds to that it was in a position to lend £400 to the Lancashire masons on strike in 1833. At the end of 1833, they had hopes that there would be less of a Winter wage reduction than usual and the men demanded shorter working hours in Winter. Until then only one hour had been allowed for meals, and now they wanted an extra one for most of the Winter period. More important from the employers' point of view were demands for an agreed code of laws on workplace rules. The men were trying to reimpose order on an industry that the coming of general contracting and its accompanying sub-contracting had, in less than a decade, rendered unstable. What was at issue was control of the workplace. The master builders got together to resist the 'tyrannical attempt ... to interfere betwixt them and their men'. In November 1833, 700 masons were locked out. After a week or two 'a few of our most respectable employers' granted an advance of 2s. a week, and some 200 men went back to work, but the other employers held out. In January 1834, the

Glasgow Masons were appealing for support through the Owenite journal, the *Pioneer*.[49] But the struggle was given up in February when the men abandoned any attempt to 'control' the employers, though an advance of wages was conceded. However, the Union remained in existence and, in 1835, there was a seven-week strike in both Glasgow and Edinburgh which seems successfully to have eradicated a great deal of sub-contracting, despite the arrest of some activists in the course of the strike. In 1837 the Scottish Union had more members than the Union in England and Ireland.[50]

The bricklayers in Glasgow formed a society in 1833 and went on strike for an advance of 2s. a week to 18s. They planned to set up a house of call and to offer their services directly to the public. The Glasgow slaters had a strong union and were able to get an advance of 2s. per week in 1833 from 16s. to 18s.[51] The Glasgow Carpenters and Joiners Society, which had been formed in February 1832 by joiners 'deploring the gradual decline of their trade', rejected the idea of becoming the basis for a general union of all trades, and instead, working with the Greenock joiners, formed the Scottish National Joiners' Association.[52] By the beginning of 1833, they were in touch with Edinburgh, Leith and Falkirk. Their programme was to regulate overtime and ensure that it was paid at time and a half; to get allowances for lodging and for walking time; to get regular fortnightly payments instead of monthly ones and to prevent employers lending workmen to other employers. In August 1833, the Scottish Union linked up with unions in Manchester and Liverpool and became the 'central branch' of a federal union. However, it did not survive long and, by 1835, only the founders, Glasgow and Greenock, were left in the national union. The explanation given for the failure was that too many had been admitted 'without question as to character and achievement'. Glasgow remained in touch with Manchester and Liverpool and, in January 1836, it was again a branch of the Friendly Society of Operative House Carpenters and Joiners of Great Britain and Ireland.[53]

A Scottish National Union of Cabinet and Chair Makers was formed in April 1833 linking branches in Glasgow, Edinburgh, Dundee, Aberdeen and Greenock. Like most of these new unions, it combined an industrial side and a friendly-society side. The 2d. per week payment gave unemployment benefit, insurance of tools and travel expenses of 5s. to £1 for those who were leaving town in search of work. Each workshop had a collector to go round to collect the dues. The Glasgow cabinetmakers were involved in a protracted struggle of twenty-one weeks starting at the end of 1833 and lasting until well into 1834 against the masters, united in a 'Protecting Society'. The aim of the employers was to break up the Union and, at one point there seems to have been real danger of this occuring, as the employers insisted on 'the document' renouncing union membership. But the union appears to have survived.[54]

As in England, 1833–34 was a key year in union organisation for textile workers also, with many groups unionising for the first time. A Women's Power Loom Association covering Glasgow and the surrounding area appeared after a mass meeting of 1000 delegates in February. It was 'for their mutual protection against the encroachment of tyrannical overseers, and the reductions of masters'. The weekly subscription was a halfpence, but the hope was that eventually sick pay and unemployment benefit could be introduced. At Aberdeen, after the managers of the Broadford linen mill reduced the weekly wages of reelers and spinners, 156 women operatives met to form 'a Co-operative Union' and about 1000 women from seven mills turned up to protest against the masters' 'millocratical union'. Despite denunciations by the local clergy, the Aberdeen Female Operative Union successfully held out and forced concessions from the employers. Throughout the struggle they received male support: David Thomson, preses of the Weavers' Union, and William Donald of the Flaxdressers' Union were the main advisers and there was financial aid from the United Trades of Aberdeen.[55]

Some of the bitterest disputes at this time were those among the calico printers. The industry had started expanding rapidly after the duty on printed linens and calicoes had been repealed in 1831. As a result, many new workers (particularly children and young girls) were pulled into the industry. Until this time, union organisation seems to have been fairly effective in the different branches of printing work. The journeymen appear to have controlled entry into the printing works. One pattern designer, taking up an apprenticeship at the Dawsholm printfield in 1818, had to pay thirteen guineas to the journeymen there, and seven or ten guineas was not uncommon among other groups. Regularly indentured apprenticeships seem to have remained the usual practice into the 1820s and then, only gradually, came under threat of erosion. Old customs persisted. Drinking in the workshop, for example, was a regular feature. At most lunch hours, the 'tear boys', the printers' assistants, would be sent out for 'a piggin of whiskey'. The calico printers, indeed, were notorious for a whole ritual of celebrations associated with drink. A block printer's printing of his first handkerchief, or his first garments or his first furniture cloth, an apprentice having his first shave or getting his first tailed coat were all occasions when he was expected to provide a pint of whisky with which his workmates could celebrate. Some of the celebrations of indentured apprentices could last for days with the whisky and rum flowing freely.[56]

From the beginning of the 1830s the pressure for change accelerated. The issue was how far the traditional autonomy of the printers in the workplace was to continue. The blockprinters' union, the Associated Calico Printers, which had built up funds of between £6000 and £7000, by means of monthly levies of 1s.6d. per man and 9d. per apprentice,[57] tried to reassert traditional rules that there should be three journeymen to one apprentice and to fine employers who breached this rubric. In addition, a Workmen's Trade Committee issued a statement of the prices that they believed should be paid for printing different articles, to bring them into line with the higher Lancashire rates and to deal with new lengths of cloth being introduced. In 1833 it was decided to focus pressure on two printfields, one at Milton of Campsie, the other at Partick, but the men were outmanoeuvred by the associated masters and were all dismissed. The employers, simultaneously at twenty or thirty printfields, began to recruit new workers, particularly from among the handloom weavers, and to employ women and children. The process of bringing in new workers began in February 1834, but there had been remarkably little preparation to ensure either order or the protection of the new workers. Protests from the established workmen exploded into violence, against both people and property, with apprentice printers who, because of their indentures were not dismissed, playing their part on behalf of the strikers. The employers, in panic, called for military aid. In many places, strike-breakers had to be protected by troops and were besieged inside the works. There were riots and street battles, attempts to deter strike-breakers by force and attempts to smoke them out, all generally successful since there were neither enough special constables nor troops to guard all the scattered fields all the time.[58]

The trouble was widespread in early February, with incidents reported in Anderston, Milngavie, Campsie and Denny, but it became particularly concentrated in Stirlingshire. There were fears among the authorities that the calico printers, 'if not instantly put down', would set an example to weavers and spinners and other groups of workmen.[59] Hefty sentences of three months or more began to be handed out. By the end of February 1834 the Sheriff of Stirlingshire had gaoled twelve and the Lord Advocate was promising every assistance, with troops to escort the new hands to and from work, as long as it might be necessary. The worst incident was the murder by 'nobs' of George Miller, a nineteen-year old union printer. Two were eventually charged, but one was acquitted and the case against the other was found not proven. According to a writer, not particularly sympathetic to the union, 'certain parties used golden ointment for the palms of some witnesses' hands, which had a wonderful effect over their recollection of the incidents attending the murder'.[60] In another incident a calico printer's wife was sentenced to six months for intimidation. When four rioters were charged at Campsie it was pointed out by the defence lawyers, much to the consternation of the judge, that in the printers' communities what was done was not seen in any way as culpable. It was 'in a glorious cause'.[61]

The strikes and violence continued through the Spring, with sentences being increased in severity and cases switched from the Sheriff Courts to the more formidable High Court. Troops were more and more used to escort and guard strike-breakers. Not until May, after ten months' strike, did the Denny men in Stirlingshire return to work. In some other areas the end did not come until July after around £12,000 had been spent by the Union. Much of it must have come from other unions in Glasgow and, it was believed, Lancashire.[62] There were still sporadic outbursts of violence between old and new hands in September, but, as a sign of settlement, in November all calico printers who had been imprisoned by the High Court from seven to fifteen months were granted a free pardon, thanks to the efforts of their legal agent, Andrew Gemmill.[63] However, many of the strikers were unable to get their jobs back, because strike-breakers were kept on. Machine cylinder printing came in quickly after 1834 and within twenty years blockprinting had almost completely died out.[64]

A new level of violence and bitterness was also apparent among the colliers. New men, outside the traditional brotherhood, were coming in in increasing numbers. Attempts to restore organisation had begun in Lanarkshire in 1830 and, in 1832, there was an eighteen-week strike in parts of the now rapidly expanding

Lanarkshire coalfield. Miners, in disguise, with blackened faces, used cutlasses and pistols against blacklegs. One strike-breaker had his ear cut off, and in another case a miner was killed. In spite of sentences of transportation for life of two miners and for fourteen years for another, strikes and riots at various pits continued through 1833 and 1834, although they appear to have been unco-ordinated and effective organisation was not achieved on this occasion.[65]

Another group to confront their employers at this time were the engineers, the men who built the machines on which the advances in industrial change depended. They are likely to have been mainly builders of cotton machinery. Initially this was the business of woodworkers, but with the coming of steam power iron machines were necessary. At first it had proved extremely difficult to find men with the necessary skills in Scotland and most machinery was imported from England. Even in 1824 Henry Houldsworth told a House of Commons Committee that although the proficiency of Scottish mechanics had much improved, intricate parts had still to be imported. By the early 1830s, a core of engineers, no doubt highly-paid because of their scarcity, were determined to protect their position from an influx of the less-skilled and less-highly remunerated. Organised in the Operative Mechanics' Union, the engineers were largely concerned with restricting the number of apprentices and keeping out 'illegal men'. They wanted a five years' apprenticeship and only one apprentice to every three journeymen, and a 'certificate of legality' from workmen when anyone moved jobs. The men's definition of a legal hand was one who had served a five years' apprenticeship in a machinemaker's or in an engineer's shop. They would not recognise anyone 'who has wrought as a smith in the country, for any period'. A dispute started at Houldsworth's Anderston Foundry in July 1833, when a deputation asked the firm to accept the Society's rules. When it was refused, 108 struck work but, perhaps more seriously for Houldsworth's, they found that work from their cotton mills was blacked, so they could not get spinning machines repaired. Houldsworth was at the centre of an Association of Master Engineers, Millwrights, Machinemakers, Founders and Blacksmiths of Scotland, and the Anderston strike developed into a general lock-out of some 700 engineers. The masters sought to insist that they could employ any workman they wanted, that any workman had to have a discharge note from a previous employer and that there would be no control over the number of apprentices or for how long they should be bound.[66]

With the iron industry expanding rapidly this was a time when skilled engineers must have been in demand and, after resisting for a couple of months, the employers gave way. at least some of them agreed to take back their locked-out men, to employ no illegal men or those who had not been five years in the trade. They accepted one apprentice to four journeymen and abandoned the discharge note. Apparently, they even agreed 'that the men they have engaged shall not work in any of the shops with the regular workmen, neither be employed at any steam engine or machine work'.[67] On the other hand, Houldsworth and some others held out. By January 1834, 323 were still out and being maintained by the Union on 9s. to 12s. per week, but apparently 294 of these had been replaced by new hands. The struggle was eventually given up in February, with the men accepting the right of the masters to employ whom they wished, though in practice intimidation of non-unionists continued.[68]

The handloom weavers too made another try. By now their conditions had deteriorated desperately. Handloom weavers in Airdrie claimed to be on 5s.6d. per week on average, 10d. or 1s. for a sixteen-hour day. Depositions of weaving agents in the Kilsyth area, north-east of Glasgow, showed weekly earnings during the first three months of 1833 of 2s.10d to 3s.4d. after 1s. was allowed for the expenses of loom rent and candles. One who had been in weaving for thirty years remembered a time when 1200 pullicates were paid at a rate of 9d. per ell, now it was 1¼d.[69] Three unions appeared in the early 1830s among the cotton and silk weavers of Glasgow and Paisley — the General Protecting Union, the Glasgow Harness Union and the Paisley Harness Union (sometimes called the Paisley United Weavers). They tried to impose agreed tables of prices on all manufacturers. The Paisley Union, by the mid-1830s, organised some 10,000 fancy weavers in Renfrewshire and Ayrshire, while the General Protecting Union dealt with the plain cotton weavers. Communication among a scattered membership was achieved by means of the *Weavers' Journal*, published by the three unions with the co-operator, William Thomson, as editor. It survived for eighteen months from October 1835. According to the historian of the Scottish weavers, Norman Murray, the unions achieved substantial advances in the three years between 1833 and 1836.[70]

The handloom weavers put a great deal of faith in the formation of trade boards as a way of maintaining a minimum wage. One had been formed in Paisley in 1829. In the weavers' analysis, the cause of their plight was excessive competition, brought about by 'adventurers in the trade' who pushed down the prices paid. As a result, 'the most respectable manufacturers are obliged against their will to reduce the wages of their workmen to the level of their unprincipled rivals'. 'Dishonourable' employers were using 'unprincipled' competition and undermining the position of the 'honourable' employer. They believed that a board made up of a certain number of masters and men would receive support from the better employers and that it could 'equalize, superintend, and regulate the prices of workmanship'.[71] That, together with the union, would prevent the creation of a 'reserve army of labour' that would push down wages. It is no surprise that the Scots weavers were at the forefront of this movement. They could look back to an interventionist period which, in a Scottish context, was not so far distant.

The weavers received support for their campaign from a number of MPs, in particular, John Maxwell of Pollok, MP for Lanarkshire, and Gillon, MP for Falkirk Burghs. These two, with John Fielden from Oldham, were at the forefront of a parliamentary campaign over the next four years. Maxwell reflected the views of handloom weavers in arguing that labour was as much a property as corn or wool or cotton — 'does not labour demand equal protection?' He had regularly brought forward motions in the 1820s for a tax on powerlooms. But Maxwell and his associates were up against a government that increasingly accepted the arguments that industrial capitalism could advance only in an atmosphere of freedom from government intervention in relations between employers and employed. A Select

Committee, at which Alexander Campbell and a number of weavers appeared as witnesses, gave ample evidence of the reality of the plight of the weavers, but Fielden's bill, which came from it, allowing for local trade boards, was defeated in 1835. Maxwell tried again in 1836 and 1837 and Fielden made a final attempt in the same year, but each time they were well-beaten.[72]

There is not much evidence that there was any enthusiasm for the idea of trade boards among the rest of the working class. A meeting of the United Trades of Glasgow did resolve to petition Parliament on behalf of the weavers, but it was not pressed with much vigour and the weavers complained of a lack of interest in their fate.[73] The pages of the *Weavers' Journal* by 1836 were showing growing evidence of despair that trade unionism could do much to halt the relentless decline.

For factory workers, hope of improvement lay in shorter hours. Daniel Macaulay had been at the forefront of this campaign when in 1830, as secretary of the Glasgow Powerloom Operatives' Society, he had written to Peel at the Home Office. The powerloom weavers protested against the fluctuations in employment that had affected most of their members over the previous few years. They specifically rejected the now familiar argument that nothing could be done about it until the market improved. Unregulated competition was unacceptable. 'We would rather see all parties in moderate employment, with a modest remuneration for their labours, than be as we are at present with one party toiling incessantly under the most aggravated circumstances for fifteen hours per day and another strolling in the streets in deepest misery'. They appealed for legislation that would restrict labour in the cotton mills and weaving factories to twelve per day, including breakfast and dinner hours. Only by shorter hours could the available work be fairly shared and the industrious operative be restored 'to the rank which he ought to hold in society'.[74] The *Herald to The Trades Advocate* took up the cause at the end of that year, with frequent condemnation of factory abuses.[75]

Once a national factory reform campaign got underway and Michael Sadler's Bill was introduced in 1831, there was renewed interest in shorter hours among various groups of Scottish factory workers. Dundee operatives formed a short-time committee and, in Glasgow, a number of cotton workers started campaigning. Macaulay, predictably, was active, along with spinners such as James Dunn, James Nish and Peter Hacket. There was also Patrick McGowan, who had been closely associated with John Doherty in Lancashire, and who was now back in Glasgow.[76] Some of the cotton spinners were prepared to confront the employers and impose ten hours by direct action, but this proposal was abandoned when Sadler's Bill was introduced. At the Reform Jubilee procession of October 1832, the cotton spinners carried a portrait of Sadler, and petitioned Ashley and Fielden in support. They put it at the forefront of the Address, 'from various shops, factories and districts, on behalf of a great portion of the operatives of Glasgow', presented to William Cobbett when he toured Scotland in October 1832.[77] Generally, it was an uphill struggle making any impact against the entrenched hostility of Scottish millowners. While James Nish and other Glasgow cotton spinners described the awfulness of child labour in the hot, dust-filled mills of Glasgow, Kirkman Finlay, as spokesman for the employers, voiced the view:

> I am yet to learn of any proof or colour like to proof that shows that the employment of persons in well-conducted factories for twelve hours in the day is unfavourable to health.[78]

As the *Morning Chronicle* commented, 'It appears that the most barbarous of the Yorkshiremen are outdone in barbarity by the Scots'. The struggle was often a personal one: Patrick McGowan, for one, was victimised for his role in the short-time movement.[79]

With less intensity, the issue continued to interest the spinners after 1833. In May 1836, the *Weavers' Journal* carried an article by Henry Dunn condemning those political economists who believed that 'the misery spread over the mass . . . is one of the designs of eternal providence intended for the especial good of our race' and calling for a ten-hour day. One the other hand, the 1833 legislation which protected young children tended to be ignored. According to a spinner, 'It was a matter of necessity: the mills would stand idle if such was not the practice'.[80]

The campaign for state-regulated hours was confined largely to factory workers. It had little relevance to the craftsmen in their small workshops or building sites. For them the ideal was self-employment, setting up in business on their own. Various schemes continued to be floated with that as the ultimate goal. Alexander Campbell was behind most of them. He could press his views as secretary of the Glasgow Joiners' Society and, briefly, in the pages of his unstamped paper *The Tradesman*. This was the successor to an earlier venture, the *Scottish Trades Union Gazette*, an unstamped weekly produced between September and December 1833. *The Tradesman* appeared at the end of December 1833 and survived until the Exchequer Court closed it down in May 1834.[81]

Campbell consistently had two goals. One was to pull together the trade societies into larger general unions and the second was to encourage schemes for self-employment of workers in co-operative production. The *Herald to the Trades Advocate* had proposed a Glasgow and West of Scotland Association for the Protection of Labour whose 'Fundamental Laws' were published in May 1831. It too was to unite different societies and to resist the 'repeated and unnecessary reduction of wages'. Should an individual union not be able to resist a reduction or to settle the dispute 'by a reduction in an amicable manner', then it could turn to the Association and get 8s. a week for members.[82] The collapse of the *Herald* gave no opportunity to press this idea and the existing trades committee got caught up in politics. Campbell tried again in August 1833 when he proposed 'a Union of All Trades for the Protection of Labour'. The idea was that it would establish workshops for unemployed members and eventually build houses for members. The ideal of self-employment as a solution to unemployment had an immediate appeal and a number of trades took it up. In January 1834, delegates supporting striking masons and carpenters in Glasgow backed a motion to raise money to build an Operatives' Hall to give employment to strikers. The potters, in the summer of 1834, started a co-operative concern for their unemployed members.[83] The Glasgow slaters after a strike in April 1834 announced that they proposed to set up in business on their own.[84] The thousand-strong Dundee and Lochee Weavers' Union about the same time resolved 'to make an attempt at manufacturing for themselves'.[85]

Events in the South in the Spring of 1834 undoubtedly acted as a stimulus to such activities in Scotland. Campbell called a meeting of the Glasgow United Trades to protest at the harsh sentences on the Dorchester labourers. Delegates from cotton spinners, calico printers, potters, glassworkers, brushmakers, nailers, joiners and cabinetmakers all agreed to petition and all expressed themselves in favour of the General Trades Union. Thirty thousand in Glasgow signed a petition protesting at the sentences on the Tolpuddle men, and at a mass meeting there were demands for a Consolidated Union of Scottish Operatives. Alexander Campbell again emphasised the need for working-class initiatives. The delegates to the Consolidated Union could be elected and could become a Scottish Parliament of Workmen 'to take the entire management of their affairs into their own hands'.[86] There were contacts with the Grand National Consolidated Union in London, and delegates from it came to Glasgow to explain the events in Derby to meetings of trades' delegates. But the response of Glasgow workers was rather half-hearted. The feeling of the meeting was that it was necessary to get workers in Scotland more extensively organised before joining up and co-operating with unionists in the South, although they resolved in favour of 'consolidating the unions in one grand whole'.[87]

Yet, despite this flurry of activity and despite the rhetoric of confrontation, there was no spark to light this growing sense of self-assertiveness among the organised working class. No conflict triggered off a general strike and the backlash of employers was, for the moment, restrained.

In these early years of the 1830s there was a readiness on the part of different trade societies to co-operate as never before. As well as the various committees and attempts at general union, there were many examples of mutual assistance. The calico printers levied their members to help the cotton spinners oppose wage reductions in 1833; the yarn dressers offered a loan of £500; the spinners assisted the calico printers in their long struggle in 1834. Glasgow joiners, as well as helping fellow joiners in Greenock, Manchester and Liverpool, also supported the striking bricklayers and sawyers in the city. Men trade unionists gave support to newly formed women's groups. Female powerloom weavers, powerloom tenters and powerloom dressers in Glasgow united in one union 'for their mutual protection against the encroachment of tyrannical overseers, and the reduction of masters' in January 1834.[88] There was even talk of a general strike, influenced, no doubt, by William Benbow's pamphlet of the previous year proposing a 'Grand National Holiday and Congress of the Productive Classes'. A resolution on the issue at a weavers' meeting was 'received first with astonishment and then with a burst of enthusiasm'. It recommended

> that they take into early consideration the propriety of fixing a day when the whole shall simulataneously suspend work for one month, or till the rights of labour and

property are properly ascertained and adjusted, a certain provision of the real necessities of life established for the truly industrious to the extent of our national resources, and till every sane and mature member of the community be invested with the elective franchise.[89]

In Edinburgh in 1833 a group of trade societies (the moving force seems to have been the painters' society) got together to publish a *Trades Monthly Journal*, the first issue of which appeared on 1 October. Although no copies of this paper seem to have survived, it was still around in April 1834 when the *Edinburgh Evening Courant* linked trade unionism in Britain with the Lyons riots in France. It talked of leaders 'endeavouring to organise workmen into one general confederacy' and claimed that in the columns of the *Journal* 'the masters and the higher classes generally are reviled as oppressors and tyrants ... The workmen are desired to 'emancipate themselves from the fetters of oppression, which have for so long a time held them the subservient slaves of their employers'.[90] There were undoubtedly differences of opinion on what should be the relationship with other classes. In September 1834 a meeting of Edinburgh trades delegates refused to join in a presentation to Earl Grey, much to the indignation of the *Scotsman* newspaper. But a group of delegates decided to make a presentation of their own, and representatives of thirty-three trades eventually turned out for the procession.[91]

In Aberdeen different trade societies collaborated to provide mutual support during disputes, with the United Trades of Aberdeen co-ordinating fundraising activity, such as during the female operatives' strike of 1834. There were plans also to issue a journal to be called *The Artisan*.[92]

Even the agricultural labourers, undeterred by the experience of the Tolpuddle Martyrs, made another attempt at organisation in these years. Ploughmen in the Carse of Gowrie called a meeting in the Summer of 1834, probably encouraged by weavers who were on strike in Dundee. Two active unionists, James Begg, a weaver, and Edward Buik, a flaxdresser, addressed a meeting of 600 at Inchture, between Perth and Dundee, in June, at which they called for a ten-hour day in Summer and eight hours in Winter 'which are as much as the human frame can bear with due regard to its physical and mental powers'. At seedtime, haymaking and harvest they were ready to work as required, but only on condition that they were paid 'according to the rate of day labourers, for every hour beyond the stipulated agreement'. The idea was to co-ordinate action in time for the feeing market at Longforgan. Farmers probably varied in their reaction: some certainly gave notice to those associated with the union, but others may well have made concessions in order to get workers.[93]

Many signs were there in Scotland by the mid-1830s of that sense of class that E. P. Thompson has identified in England: a class of itself and for itself feeling 'an identity of interests as between themselves, and as against their rulers and employers'. As against that, however, the response of skilled craftsmen to the changes wrought on social relationships by the process of industrialisation was still a very traditional one. The cause of the deterioration in their position was still almost always perceived as coming from other workers, from the 'dishonourable', the 'half-bred', the apprentice and women. Although much attention was paid to seeking alternative structures, none the less the purpose of most of the unions was to control entry and to keep out others. That almost always took priority over the efforts to create a sense of mutual dependence that went wider than the trade.

There was, however, a new determination that the voice of the working class, expressed through trade unions, needed to be heard and ought to be heard. John Tait summed it up in the *Liberator*:

> The Trades no longer wish to cringe, and bow, and blasphemously de-beastify themselves, by protestations, and imploring their fellow men to bestow what they have a right to demand. They wish, by a more decisive course, to work out, on their own resources, their political, and, I may add, their religious salvation.[94]

There was now a clear awareness that capitalism in its very essence was destructive of those aspects of working-class life that were now appreciated as important — community, co-operation, pride in craft, fairness, independence. The search for ways of resisting an erosion that was now becoming overwhelming was a frantic one — co-operative enterprises of a variety of kinds that would allow an opting out; state regulation of wages and hours that would recapture what was seen as a more just distribution; resistance by collaboration in national and general unions. There were those who believed that changing government or the political system would provide a cure, although that view was muted after 1832. There were still those who talked the language of Cobbett and Hunt of twenty years before and who still believed that common ground lay between the radical middle class and the working class against a corrupt, non-productive aristocracy. But, by the mid-1830s, the true attitudes of most middle-class employers towards the working class were apparent in the attempts to break trade unionism by lock-outs and by the imposition of 'the document'. The tone on both sides was one of conflict and confrontation, with, on the unionists' part, a sharper determination to halt the advance of the detested features of capitalism.

In spite of their efforts, the employers were not powerful or united enough to break the unions in 1834 in Scotland. The unions did not get caught up in any great symbolic clash and all the signs were that gains and advances were being made. Perhaps because they had distanced themselves from the more grandiose Owenite schemes of south of the border, perhaps because of the strength of some of the unions, perhaps because of a lack of unity among the employers, there was no great collapse of unionism in Scotland after 1834. Indeed if anything, unions seem to have gathered strength over the next two years.

9
Of Shootings and Sheriffs

Conditions were very good for trade-union growth in the middle years of the 1830s. The Scottish economy, stimulated by the opening up of the blackband iron-ore seams in Lanarkshire, expanded. Trade with the Americas continued to grow. There was a period of relative tranquillity in industrial relations during 1835 and into the Summer of 1836. The first sign of change came, unusually, among unskilled workers. Labourers at the huge St. Rollox chemical works and others were organised in a United Labourers' Society. Their wages were 9s. to 12s a week and, in March 1836, they announced that they would not accept less than 12s. Three hundred came out and there were attacks on Irish strike-breakers brought into the St. Rollox works. The military were called to maintain order and eventually about half the strikers returned to work, while a hundred new labourers were taken on.[1] However, for most workers boom conditions generally persisted through the Summer of 1836. The change came in the Autumn, and at the centre of it were the cotton spinners.

The spinners had recovered quite quickly from the setbacks of the 1826–27 period, when there had been a whole series of wage reductions. When delegates from Glasgow attended the Isle of Man Conference in 1829, which sought to establish a British union, the Grand General Union of All the Spinners of the United Kingdom, the Glasgow men had a few of the grievances of their Lancashire counterparts.[2] But there were latent difficulties. The Scottish cotton industry never fully recovered from 1825. Over the next decade it faced growing problems in hanging on to its export markets and, more seriously, competition from Lancashire in the area of fine yarn, which was the particular Scottish specialism. In order to compete, profit margins were having to be trimmed and there was pressure for higher productivity. In November 1832 there were reports of strikes, again at Houldsworth's, over payment of new sizes, with some violence against blacklegs and by blacklegs against union spinners.[3] There was a notorious case of vitriol-throwing against one Mary McShafferty, who, it was suggested, had been mistaken for a woman spinner, though responsibility for this act was never pinned upon any spinner. Eventually, Patrick McGowan, Doherty's former lieutenant, who seems to have become a dominant and respected figure among the Glasgow Spinners in these years, negotiated a settlement of the dispute with Houldsworth's.[4] There was another violent incident in December 1833, when Robert Millar, the manager of the Lancefield Mill, was set upon and attacked, but again there was no proof that it was connected with industrial grievances. On the whole, however, these were relatively isolated incidents. But, tensions were rising, with fining for poor-quality yarn again on the increase,[5] and the boom of 1833 to 1836 hid the extent to which a crisis was imminent.

Individual spinners played their part in the proliferation of trades committees in the early 1830s and were active in helping other groups, but the spinners as a group were not at the forefront of the various activities. They had few complaints, if the Factory Inquiry Commissioners' Report of 1833 is to be believed. According to that Report, the Spinners' Association was in control of entry into the trade, and was 'carrying things with a high hand' and 'having a complete monopoly of labour'.[6] Wages were considerably higher than in Lancashire. The Spring of 1836 had brought 'an extraordinary and unprecedented prosperity' and the spinners were granted a sixteen per cent rise, the first general increase since 1827.[7]

Hardly had the rise been granted than American economic troubles began to make themselves felt. Prices tumbled and continued to do so through the Autumn and Winter. Two major mercantile houses, deeply involved in the American trade, went down. There was an imminent threat of wage cuts. Since 1827 there had been uniformity of piece rates throughout the city mills, but, in the surrounding areas, a number of employers were undercutting wages and prices. The city employers, agreeing to the wage increase in the Summer, pressed the Spinners' Association to take action against the under-paying country employers. If that were not done, it was threatened, wages would have to be cut.[8] In October 1836, the Union tackled the largest of the country employers, Dunn of Duntocher. One hundred of his spinners struck work and remained out for sixteen weeks. They and their families were maintained by the Union at a cost of over £3000. The working spinners in Glasgow had a levy of 2s.6d. a week imposed to support the strikers. Dunn held out, however, and, in February, the Union, near bankruptcy and very vulnerable, admitted defeat.[9]

Now in a parlous state, the Union faced a new onslaught from the Glasgow employers. The men believed that it was all part of a well-laid conspiracy to weaken the Union as a prelude to reorganisation of the mills. Whether it was or not, circumstances certainly conspired against the Union. The immediate economic conditions stemming from the American financial crisis in themselves were going to cause difficulties. The increasing difficulties that the Scottish cotton masters were having in competing with the Lancashire producers added to the crisis.[10]

The Scottish masters turned to changes in technology. Lancashire manufacturers had brought in a number of technical improvements in the 1820s. In particular, spinning mules were made much larger and 1000-spindle ones were not uncommon. Such innovations had major implications for the spinners. Firstly, fewer of them were needed; secondly, there was a need for more piecers, the children and young people required to crawl under the machines to repair broken threads and generally keep the machines free from dust. For long, most of these piecers had been members of the spinners' families, recruited and paid for by the spinners and drawn from a close community. The spinners had been able to operate an informal 'apprenticeship' system by ensuring that recruitment into spinning was from the ranks of those males who had served their time as piecers.

The requirement for more piecers meant that the spinners had to look beyond their own community for recruits. Thus as technical changes were reducing the demand for spinners, they were also increasing the pool of potential spinners. The imposition of such changes in Lancashire had brought bitter and frequently violent resistance throughout the 1820s.

The Scottish employers had not attempted such innovations in the 'twenties, and mules in Glasgow generally were 200 to 300 spindles in size. Perhaps, with finer threads in which the Scottish industry specialised, the larger machines were a problem. Perhaps the Scottish employers hesitated to confront the powerful spinners' association, though the weakness of its position after 1826 would have given opportunities to the employers. One would have expected the employers to be keen to break the hold of the spinners' union by bringing in new machines. The uniformity of wage rates after 1827, one would think, would have stimulated competition through technological innovation. Whatever the reason, the Scottish industry avoided the bitterness of the Lancashire one until 1837.

The leading cotton masters in Glasgow — Dunlop, Houldsworth, McNaught, Kelly, Oswald, Dennistoun — had long experience of collaborating and, early in 1837, six weeks after the end of the Duntocher strike, a meeting of these employers, under the chairmanship of Henry Dunlop, resolved to reduce wages by sixteen per cent, to the levels of the previous Spring. Three days later the Cotton Spinners' Association decided to resist and called a general strike of spinners. Probably the employers were not unhappy about having their mills lying idle for a time.[11] After a few weeks, at the end of April, the employers met again and agreed on a further series of reductions, up to thirty per cent. They proposed that in future the payment pattern would be on the same lines as in Lancashire, which meant for some a reduction of as much as sixty per cent from their peak in the previous year. Extra allowances won in 1832 for the superior skills required for spinning a particular yarn known as 'shuttle cops' or 'pirn cops' were abolished and, finally, it was announced that new large machines were to be brought in and the old ones were to be doubled-up with only one spinner in charge. But the gains to the spinners from larger machines were to be severely limited. The existing piece rates would not apply. Instead, on machines above 300 spindles, one per cent of the piece rate was knocked off for every twelve spindles. An example of what this meant was that a spinner working a pair of wheels with 300 spindles, making 40 lbs. of twist per week, earned 40s. gross, out of which he would pay 13s.6d. expenses, mainly to his piecers. A doubled machine, with 300 extra spindles, would make 75 lbs., but the spinner would not receive 75s., but twenty-five per cent less than that, 56s.3d. Out of that, since additional piecers would now be necessary, he would pay 25s.6d. expenses, leaving 30s.9d. clear. In other words, despite greater effort and more responsibility, the spinner was only 4s.3d. better off and the equality of payment won in 1827 would disappear.[12] In addition, these new piecers would threaten that precarious regulation of numbers entering the trade that had been the *raison d'être* of the spinners' union.

It was this issue that made the dispute so bitter. It was literally a battle for the future shape of the industry, a battle for the survival of the Spinners' Association.

It was about how rapidly technological change could be brought about and who should gain from the change. It was also about the future of the community of spinners and their families. Not only was there this immediate threat, but there was also the added threat of the self-acting mule, which required much less skill to operate and threatened the whole position of the hand-mule spinners. There had been talk of introducing them in the previous summer, when the advance of wages had been granted, and at least one Glasgow firm had already 'a considerable portion of self actors'.[13]

Tensions mounted during May as more and more strike-breakers were brought in to re-open the mills. The number of incidents of violence increased and there was mass picketing, with as many as a thousand turning up at some mills. After all, not only were the 800 or so spinners on strike, but their action affected thousands of others, perhaps as many as 10,000–15,000. Some of the employers began having guards for their workmen, and those strike-breakers who ventured out were likely to find themselves set upon and chased through the streets. It proved almost impossible to provide strike-breakers with adequate protection. The police force of about 280 covered only the Barony of Glasgow, not the surrounding suburbs. When Sheriff Alison tried to raise one hundred special constables to tackle mass picketing in Bridgeton, only one volunteer turned up and Alison had to make use of the military, not something that was ever popular with the ratepayers who had to pay for it. On 15 May a number of pickets were arrested. One David Keddie was tried and found guilty by the Sheriff, but faced with a massive problem of maintaining order, Alison negotiated with Andrew Gemmill, the solicitor who acted for the Spinners' Association, and agreed to suspend sentence on Keddie and to postpone the trials of other arrested pickets *sine die*, on condition that the mass pickets were called off. This was agreed at a meeting of spinners.[14]

The Union was perhaps looking for a solution. Money was short and in the last week of May only 3s.6d. was being paid to each striker. There certainly was a lull in activity for a week or two, when some talks may well have been going on. The Renfrewshire spinners, who had also been in dispute, accepted the masters' terms. In mid-June, however, the violence reappeared with renewed vigour, and the strike broke out again in Renfrewshire. Attacks on strike-breakers began to occur again, this time in Hutchesontown. Alexander Arthur, manager of the Adelphi Mill, who was taking on new workers (it was a mill that made coarse thread and where only limited spinning skills were required) received a threatening letter denouncing him as the 'low tool or cringing sycophant of a greedy Tyranical (sic) Capitalist' working against those 'engaged in the Protection of their labour, their only capital'.[15] There were now numerous incidents of incendiarism and the firing off of guns at strike-breakers, but there were remarkably few arrests. The violence was probably a reflection of a growing desperation among the spinners. After more than three months strike their plight was dire. Payment to strikers was down to 9d. or 1s. per week, with some oatmeal when the Association could get it on credit. Financial aid had come from Newcastle, Manchester, Belfast, Greenock and elsewhere, but many spinners were reduced to begging.[16]

Negotiations between the Union and some employers to try to achieve a settlement were already going on when on 22 July 1837 John Smith, an Irish strike-breaker, though not a new worker but one who had been at Houldsworth's for four years, was shot in the back. He died three days later and before he expired he reputedly told the Sheriff Substitute that he had received threats from the spinners. Employers and the authorities offered rewards for information and the promise of a pardon to anyone who was not actually a perpetrator of the crime who provided information. On the basis of accounts from two informants, Sheriff Alison led a posse of police to the Gallowgate public house where the cotton spinners' committee held their meetings, and arrested all those present. Most of them were eventually released, but the decision was made to prosecute the officers of the Association, Thomas Hunter, the president, Peter Hacket, the treasurer, Richard McNeil, the secretary, and James Gibb, the assistant secretary, on the charge of conspiring to murder. William McLean was also charged as the man who had carried out the deed. McLean was, by all accounts, a simple 'hard man', with a reputation for drunkenness and for violence: the others were respectable, and respected, working men.[17]

Archibald Alison, who had been Sheriff of Lanarkshire since 1834, was a Tory of deepest hue, whose study of the French Revolution in his *History of Europe* had convinced him that it was the most disastrous of events. He believed that the Whig ministries since 1830 were little short of treasonable and that the 1832 Act had ushered in a democracy that would lead inevitably to anarchy. The failure in France in 1789 and in Britain in 1830–32 had been the failure of the ruling class to stand up against 'popular intimidation'. By 1837, Alison believed that 'Anarchy was rapidly approaching', yet he found 'terror, selfishness and supineness' among the higher classes.[18] Trade unions fitted into his demonology as 'an example of democratic ambition on a large scale', but businessmen were not willing to resist them and appeared wary of giving offence. He had, for example, had little support for his memorial calling for an extension of the police force to areas beyond the city, precisely because it made reference to the use of police in strikes.[19]

Alison was, therefore, convinced that it was crucial for someone to take decisive action against 'the moral pestilence' of trade unionism, which was threatening to 'overturn entirely the social state of the country'. He was probably particularly alarmed that besides the violence of the spinners and among striking miners in Lanarkshire, there was a standing committee of Glasgow Trades Delegates with Alexander Campbell as secretary. It had a voice in the pages of the *New Liberator*. John Tait, who had edited the *Liberator* since 1833, had died in 1836. His paper had been bought over by a wealthy Ayrshire radical, Dr. John Taylor, who relaunched it as the *New Liberator*. It was basically chartist and sought to unite trade unions and political radicals in a demand for universal suffrage. The shooting of Smith gave Alison his opportunity to take decisive action.

The unrest among other groups of workers gave some credence to Sheriff Alison's position. Alison later claimed, with some exaggeration, that the 'whole skilled trades of Glasgow, with the exception of the printers, hand and powerloom weavers' were on strike in 1837.[20] In fact, the worst of disputes had taken place in the winter of 1836–37 when wages started to come under pressure. A three-month dispute among the Glasgow masons, during which the union had been able to pay out 8s. a week to the 300 strikers, ended in March 1837.[21] The bricklayers struck for 20s. per week. The quarrymen, trying to keep non-union labour out of the quarries, were out at the same time.[22] In June 1837, however, there was a serious strike of ironmoulders at the Albion Iron Works which led to further picketing.[23] In Edinburgh there were protracted disputes among typefounders, joiners and cabinetmakers in the Summer of 1837. The most serious, however, were outside the cities in the coal and iron fields, especially those being opened up very rapidly in Lanarkshire.

As with other workers, the good conditions of 1836 had encouraged colliers to reorganise their unions. The same tactics as in the past of restricting output at a time of high demand, by fixing regular days off and holidays, had the desired effect of pushing up prices and securing wage increases. They were helped in this by a powerful cartel of coalmasters, not at all adverse to the rising prices. Once again some kind of national union appeared, not just in the West of Scotland, but in Fife and the Lothians also.[25]

Coal prices began to fall fast in the winter of 1836–37. The men, on 5s. a day, desperately tried to keep up prices by restricting output further, by working only three days a week. While most employers tolerated this, not too unhappy about having their stocks reduced, the Bairds of Gartsherrie, the largest of the ironmasters, decided on confrontation and gave all their miners fourteen days' notice to quit work and homes. Unskilled labourers were brought in to work an open-cast mine of the Bairds, so the furnaces could be kept going. The locked-out men held out for fifteen weeks, but eventually, furniture and possessions sold, gave in. Not all regained their jobs and their houses, since many of these had been filled by the new labourers. Those who did return, according to James Baird, were 'in squalid wretchedness'.[26]

Other coal- and ironmasters followed the Bairds' example. The Dixon collieries in Govan reduced wages by 1s. a day and triggered an eight weeks' strike. Elsewhere, new labour was brought in under armed guard. With widespread destitution everywhere, it was not too difficult to get men to work. Throughout the Summer of 1837 the level of violence intensified. Troops were posted in Airdrie for three months. A company guard was murdered at one of the ironworks. Crowds of colliers attacked strike-breakers and their guards, though by the end of the Summer the resistance to cuts was fading and the union was disappearing. Alison's threat to arrest the union committee, as he had the cotton spinners, finally broke it.[27]

With the arrest of the spinners' leaders, the cotton strike petered out, and the spinners agreed to resume work unconditionally. The strike was in its death throes anyway. Money had run out, distress was widespread, and the employers showed no hurry to settle as long as trade remained stagnant. By now the issue was not about the strike, but about the breaking of union organisation and the imposing of authority.

The difficulty that Alison faced was actually proving his case against Hunter, Hacket, McNeil and Gibb, and proving that they had, as officers of the union, actually sanctioned the violence against the strike-breakers and the assassination of Smith. He had the usual problem, in all such cases, of getting evidence. There was not enough to bring the case to trial at the Circuit Court in Glasgow in September, and only with great difficulty were prosecution witnesses found and a case composed. The prisoners were transferred to Edinburgh and the case was brought before the High Court there. The five accused were indicted for illegal conspiracy to raise wages by threats, intimidation and molestation of other workers; threatening employers; incendiarism, assault and murder; setting up pickets; sending threatening letters; and paying to have John Smith assassinated.[28]

The Crown case depended on the evidence of witnesses, who fell into two categories. First there were strike-breakers who had been mobbed and attacked. Then there were the star informers, mainly former cotton spinners, who had come forward to claim the rewards. They had been held together in protective custody in Edinburgh since August. Extensive accounts were given of some of the violent incidents around the cotton mills, not just in the period between April and August 1837, but over the previous twenty years. Two witnesses, James Moat and James Murdoch, gave evidence that they had attended meetings of the secret strike committee in the Black Boy public house in the Gallowgate, where plans for instigating violence against property and individuals were made. Three engravers gave evidence that the threatening letter to Alexander Arthur had been written by Richard McNeil, though the Lord Justice Clerk in his summing up regarded this evidence as 'extremely weak'.

The evidence of involvement in Smith's morder depended on a most insalubrious witness, Robert Christie, a former cotton spinner, who now ran a spirit shop in Hutchesontown. According to Christie, William McLean had boasted openly, while drunk, that he had murdered Smith, as well as having been involved in various other incidents, and he had claimed that for this service he was to receive some money from 'the committee'. McLean may have been indulging in no more than drunken bravado: all the evidence suggests that he was a man of low intelligence with a reputation for violence. Christie, in making the link with the spinners' committee, may have been deliberately settling old scores. He had a grievance against the Spinners' Association, it was claimed, that when he had given up spinning in 1835 he had been promised payment by the Association, which he had never received. He also was himself suspected of having been involved, with McLean, in a plot to murder Alexander Arthur. He had left town immediately after the assassination and when he returned ten days later he had been arrested. Only when facing possible charges himself did he turn Queen's evidence and implicate the Spinners' Association.[29]

The strongest evidence implicating the Association in violence came from some of the books of the Association which had been seized. These seemed to suggest that there was a policy of paying £5 to Union members for successfully 'unshopping' non-unionists and that 'unshopping' involved threats. Presumably, not too many questions were asked. The minute books suggested that pickets received payments from the Union and, indeed, it may well have been the case that those who turned out when requested on picket duty received more generous relief

G

from the Union's funds than did others. The minutes also showed that lists of 'nobs' were kept and were to be published, 'and a persecuting committee be appointed to persecute them to the utmost'.[30]

The case against the accused committee men was not a strong one. There was no attempt to try to show direct complicity and the prosecution made it clear that what was on trial was the Cotton Spinners' Association. It was a trial for twenty years of intermittent violence. As one of the defence counsel pointed out, the charges related to April to July 1837, but a great deal of the evidence presented by the prosecution referred to the events that happened between 1818 and 1830. The Jury was being asked 'to infer the guilt of the prisoners, of offences committed in 1837, from the guilt of other persons of offences committed sixteen or seventeen years ago'.[31]

Lord Boyle, the Lord Justice Clerk, in a summing up that lasted fourteen hours, referring to these acts of violence, concluded: 'I think most of them are distinctly proved to have emanated from the Association'. On the murder charge, he conceded that the crucial question was whether Christie was a perjured witness, but he did not think there was sufficient proof that Hunter, Hacket, McNeil and Gibb had 'hired, procured, or instigated McLean to commit murder'. The jury followed this guidance. Unanimous verdicts of guilty to conspiring to use 'intimidation, molestation and threats' against non-strikers and of organising pickets were brought in. But by a majority verdict of eight to seven, the eight charges involving murder were found not-proven. The sentences on the other charges made clear that the individuals were of secondary importance to the union, in the mind of the authorities. Lord Mackenzie, delivering sentence, said that what had been proved was 'a conspiracy to deprive the employers and the employed of their undoubted rights, by force and violence, to rob the one class of their rights to employ labourers at such prices as the latter were willing to receive, and to rob the other classes of their rights to dispose of their labour, at such prices as may be agreeable to themselves'. For this, the five were sentenced to seven years' transportation.

That there *had* been violence associated with the spinners was undoubtedly the case. It was a violence associated with the environment in which they worked and lived and with the pressures which they felt themselves to be under. When similar conditions existed among other groups, like the miners or weavers, then similar violence resulted. The factory itself was violent. It was excessively hot — temperatures of 80° to 100° were not uncommon — smelly, noisy and with the air full of cotton dust. Few spinners survived beyond the age of forty in such conditions. The Scottish mills seem to have been particularly bad, and John Arthur Roebuck, the radical MP, who must have seen many factories and workshops and was not a notably squeamish man, claimed that the sight of the Glasgow mills 'froze the blood'. Violence against women and children in the mills was commonplace, and the evidence to the various factory commissions bears testimony. The physical environment outside the factory was also violent. With the rapid growth of the city in the 1820s and 1830s, housing conditions had deteriorated dramatically. In a mere twenty years the population had increased by seventy-five per cent. There was intense overcrowding in the closes of the old town and in some of the newer, jerry-built housing surrounding the cotton mills and the other expanding industries. There were nearly a hundred mills in Glasgow and its suburbs and most of them had appeared in the previous twenty years. Again, the all-pervading features were noise and smells and a general horror, which shook even Edwin Chadwick, who had seen it all one would think, when he visited the city in the early 1840s. Life was short and cheap. J. C. Symons, an assistant handloom weavers commissioner visiting the city in 1839, could not believe until he saw the wynds off the High Street 'that so large an amount of filth, crime, misery and disease existed on one spot in any civilized country' and he concluded, 'It is my firm belief that penury, dirt, misery, drunkenness, disease and crime culminate in Glasgow to a pitch unparalleled in Great Britain'. The chartist G. J. Harney echoed the same sentiments a short time later: 'for undisguised profligacy, offensive brutality, squalid wretchedness, and unbearable filth, Glasgow to my mind excels all'.[32] Over 2000 died in the typhus epidemic in the Summer of 1837 and the typical citywide death-rate in the late 1830s was thirty-two per thousand. In the closes of the poorest parts it was probably two or three times that, although there was no official registration to prove it. To make it worse — or to make it tolerable — there was the 'demon drink'. One in ten Glasgow houses was a public house or spirit shop, compared with one in fifty-six in London. It was not just the quantity consumed that mattered. As someone said, with a lethal mixture of ale and whisky, the Scots, since the end of the previous century, had hit upon a very effective way of getting drunk.[33] Drunkenness was widespread in and out of work with the drinking traditions of the workshop imported into the new factories, and drunkenness contributed to violence.[34]

Violence was endemic, and no conspiracies or secret committees are necessary to explain it. It was the instinctive response of those who found their, always precarious, hold on work and acceptable living conditions threatened. One needs to distinguish between different kinds of violence. There was violence against those who had been unionists, but were now failing to pay their union dues. This was very much the pattern that Sidney Pollard describes among the cutlery trades in Sheffield in the 'outrages' of the 1860s.[35] Just as with the Sheffield union, the Glasgow cotton spinners' union had to be sure of a regular, substantial income. They were not just paying support to workers on strike, but also to idle spinners to keep them out of the labour market and, in the 1830s, they were spending at least £50 a fortnight on assisted emigration. In this category also were those who sought to defraud the union by claiming strike pay while actually working. Only for a short time had the union been able to operate a system whereby anyone moving his job had to get a free line signed by three unionists, saying he was free from debt in his old mill, which he had then to present to the men in his new mill.

Secondly, there were incidents of violence against 'illegal men', non-unionists and strike-breakers — the 'nobs' (with or without a 'k'). The union had at various times a system of paying idle members who were able to 'unshop' illegal men, and keep them away from wheels. The policy was to buy them off, but there is little doubt that this probably contributed to violence and intimidation. But there was more to violence against 'nobs' than just self-interest. As has been suggested earlier, violence had in many cases moral approval by the community in which it took place. The strike-breaker, the stealer of a job, the person who accepted under-rates, was the immoral man. The epithets — 'nobs', 'Knobsticks', 'black nebs' — all implied deep moral disapproval. As even the judges in the cotton spinners' trial admitted, the arrested leaders were eminently 'respectable' men, most of them associated with dissenting church groups. It was the strike breakers who were the disreputable and often drunken, 'bad men', 'low dissipated characters' who when they had money in their hands were 'generally seen in a state of intoxication in the street'. Some made a living as professional strike-breakers throughout the country, prepared to be bought off by the unions. They frequently damaged the machines and acted aggressively.[36] In almost all cases of violence against a specific individual, there was usually some evidence that the person attacked had done something particularly unacceptable. One who had had the vitriol treatment at Houldsworth's Anderston mill in 1823, McKenzie Phillips, was an 'indifferent character' who had tried to murder his brother-in-law. An 1824 case involved one John Graham who was shot at. He was another 'bad character' who had already been 'kneecapped' before becoming a spinner — 'he had been so offensive in his military character that someone cut him in the legs on the public streets of Glasgow'. There are numerous other cases. According to the deposition of James Todd, an umbrella maker, who was not cited as a witness at the trial, John Smith, the 1837 victim, was 'a damned blackguard', who 'had taken indecent liberties and attempted to ravish the young girls who had been employed in the factories as piecers', and had faced a rape charge some years before.[37] As a contemporary writer pointed out, the spinners tended to regard their opponents as aliens and enemies 'upon whom as the public foes of the state every species of violence may be perpetrated without the violation of any moral obligation'.[38]

The spinners, like the colliers, were a relatively well-paid group, who found their position under serious threat in the 1820s and 1830s. Alan Campbell had made use of the concept of the 'independent collier' to explain some of the attitudes among Lanarkshire miners.[39] Relatively free from managerial interference in their daily work patterns, they regulated their own output and the length of their working week. The colliers regarded themselves as independent, skilled men. Like other skilled groups, they sought to regulate entry into the trade through union organisation. The ability to regulate gave them their skill. There was no formal apprenticeship, but the miners imposed their own system of entry, partly in terms of age, but largely by limiting who could be admitted to the 'mysteries' of the trade to those who showed the necessary competence. Like craftsmen, they believed that their skill was a property, to be handed on to their sons. They found their self-status and their economic position under threat, with the rapid expansion of new coal faces and with the appearance of new employers. They were prepared to resist this, if necessary with violence.

The parallels with the cotton spinners are instructive. Here too was a well-paid group, with relative freedom in the work situation. They had lost some ground in the mid-1820s when the issue of managerial control and of foreman supervision had been fought out, but they still retained a great deal of autonomy. It was they, for example, who employed casual spinners to take over *their* wheels if they wanted time off. They employed, paid and trained their own piecers. The fact that they were paid by the piece allowed a certain freedom. Their skill came from experience and they too regarded their skill as a property that should be passed to their sons. Like the miners they sought to impose their own system of 'apprenticeship', by restricting entry, first to spinners' families and then to those who had served their time as piecers in Lanarkshire mills. Finally, they looked for some measure of competence. The threat in 1837 of both technological change and of new workers was to a status that had gradually been won over half a century.[40] It was not going to be easily given up. The resort to violence was a defence of property, just as much as guarding one's home against the thief.

Another parallel with the miners was that the spinners were an outsider group, slightly apart, because of the level of their earnings, from the rest of the working class. They were, as Alison said, 'an aristocracy of labour'. Though obviously less isolated than many of the miners, the spinners were not a particularly well-loved group. While the arrest and the trial of the spinners undoubtedly caused much indignation, there was not that upswell of protest such as the case of the Dorchester Labourers produced in England. There was nothing comparable to the general strike in Oldham in April 1834 after police raided a cotton spinners' union.[41] Although the spinners had given financial aid to many other groups in the past, they themselves had difficulty raising money. They had to look to fellow spinners in Lancashire rather than to unions of other craftsmen. It was five weeks after the arrest of the spinners that the Glasgow Trades Delegates issued an appeal on their behalf. There was only one mass meeting to rally support during the strike and that was addressed by Dr. Taylor, not by any working men, and there was no call for aid to the spinners. The strike was far from popular among the working classes, since it had repercussions for weavers, finishing trades and others associated with textiles, who lacked the resources to provide weekly relief payments to those thrown out of work.

The arrest of the leaders in August 1837 did stir support from the wider trade-union movement. The local trades committee started to raise funds and to organise a petition, which 20,000 signed, calling for proceedings against the spinners to be halted. But, because of the association with violence, it was difficult to project the spinners as new Tolpuddle Martyrs. Delegates from only ten of the city's thirty or forty trade societies attended a meeting in support of them in September 1837. Chartists tried to make some capital out of it. J. R. Stephens, Feargus O'Connor and Augustus Beaumont addressed meetings, though their talk of going forth 'with the dagger in one hand and the torch in the other . . . to wrap in one awful sheet of devouring flame . . . the manufactories of the cotton tyrants' was perhaps counter-productive, if the aim was to raise support from others.[42] At any rate, by the time of the trial the crucial moment of unrest had passed. There was no panic over such views: 'tranquillity and security' had returned to the West of Scotland. After the trial the Trades Committee organised petitions and financial support for the men and their families. They published their own report of the trial in weekly parts.[43] When it was clear that what the trial was about was more than the activities of the spinners, and that it was, essentially, a trial of trade unionism, then the other unions were roused.

Sheriff Alison certainly was prepared to draw from the trial sweeping conclusions about the nature of all trade unionism. He took the sentences as justification for all the accusations that he and others had made. Two months after the trial ended he published an essay on 'The Practical Working of Trades' Unions' in *Blackwood's Magazine*. He went over the accusations that had been made at the trial about the spinners' union's involvement in violence over twenty years. He took it all as proved. He then argued that all unions would inevitably become conspiracies 'exceeding in the tyranny which they exercise, the widespread misery which they produce, anything attempted by the Czar Peter or Sultan Mahmoud in the plenitude of their power'. He presented a picture of trade unions waging war on society with the utmost violence, 'a civil war of the worst and most appalling kind'.[44] At the Select Committee on Combinations of Workmen, Alison gave a very similar interpretation, linking the spinners' union with incidents of violence. In this, however, his evidence was fairly effectively discredited by Andrew Gemmill, still fighting the spinners' case. Gemmill had a sworn affidavit from Mary McShaffrey, the victim of a vitriol attack in 1832, that she had never been a 'nob' and that she had no evidence that her assailants were spinners. In the case of Robert Millar, the manager of the Lancefield Mill, who had been attacked in 1833, he pointed out that there had been no dispute at the time when the attack took place, and so there was no reason to think that the Spinners' Association should have been involved.[45]

The accusations of Alison became the accepted view of what the spinners' association had been about. Unionism had been effectively branded as a violent conspiracy. The spinners' union itself, facing large debts built up to retailers, rapidly lost members. When the Union tried to force members to contribute to pay off the debt, by means of a court action, they lost the case and had to pay the costs.[46] Many unionists were victimised: 276 members of the Union lost their places after the strike.[47] Other unions were aware that this was not a time for exposing themselves to public scrutiny. There were demands for some return of the Combination Laws. Scottish unionism, after a period of unprecedented growth and a period of novel collaboration had, by means of the trial, been branded as violent, drunken, totally disreputable, and a conspiracy against order and individuals. It was an image that was to prove extremely difficult to shake off. For decades after 1838, Scottish unions were weak and failed to attract more than a small minority of workmen. Even relatively strong unions, like the Operative Masons, were unable to prevent the expansion of piecework or effectively to limit entry into their trade and, by the early 1840s, they too were more or less moribund. There was a switching back to political action — 200,000 took part in a chartist demonstration in May 1838, including representatives of seventy trade unions.[48] But, not unconnected with the events of 1837–38, the Scottish chartists went out of their way to emphasise their respectability and moderation, their abhorrence of violence.

10
Conclusion

In just over a century the position of the tradesman in Scotland had been transformed. It was no longer certain that, like Professor Smout's seventeenth-century hammerman or cordiner, 'You could not rise very high ... but neither could you fall very low'. The expanding world of capitalist enterprise had brought about a much less secure world for many. The route from apprentice to independent master was no longer one that many could hope to travel. The restrictions on entry to mastership imposed by trade incorporations had all but been swept away, but the barriers to self-employment were even higher. Few could aspire to it in a world where substantial capital was required. It is true that many of the consumer trades remained unmechanised, but capital was necessary for raw materials and customers expected long credit. Few could become masters without access to extended credit. There were still many small firms around in building, shoemaking, printing and other crafts, but their position was precarious and their survival rates were low. For all but a tiny minority, acquiring a trade was a commitment to a lifetime as a wage earner. It gave perhaps more security than the unskilled had, though not necessarily so. At times of boom, the tradesman was likely to find himself working alongside the 'half-bred' from the country or even the unskilled who had picked up the mere rudiments of a trade. The apprenticeship system in most trades was casually applied and unions found it impossible to impose a control on entry that had disappeared as corporate power declined. At times of slump, the tradesman might well be the last to be dismissed, but he was not safe from unemployment and underemployment, and, perhaps, had even less flexibility than the unskilled in the search for work.

The position of the urban tradesman had been undermined by numbers — most dramatically in the case of the handloom weavers, but in most other trades also. Towns grew in the eighteenth century and pulled into them the young and employable from the surrounding areas who were ready to compete with established workers. The craftsman's position had been undermined also by the increased division of labour, as employers found ways of expanding output rapidly and of making use of the new labour. In the nineteenth century, the position of some began to be undermined even further by technological change. That in its turn undoubtedly created new opportunities, but these again went to the young and the readily trained.

Workers in Scotland, no more than anywhere else, did not docilely submit to these changes. They reacted and resisted, even if they were not always able to comprehend precisely what was happening. They looked for ways of negotiating on the process of change. Trade societies were the most important of the weapons at their disposal.

Organisation emerged in response to the transformation of economy and society that took place in the eighteenth century. But there is no uniform pattern. Each trade had its own timing and its own tactics, though one learned from another. The circumstances of change were never precisely the same and so the responses had to be different. Nor was the transformation of trades along a single clearly defined track. The new capitalists did not have it all their own way: they had to fight to impose changes and workers devised a variety of methods of making their views known. Sometimes one side lost, sometimes the other. More often the interaction produced a new synthesis. Alongside conflict, there was often compromise and even occasionally co-operation between employers and unions.

Initially, journeymen sought mutual support at times of sickness, unemployment and, for their widows, through charitable boxes. These were readily transformed into organisations for industrial purposes when the need arose. In the mid-eighteenth century the development of trade societies among journeymen tradesmen reflected a whose series of changes that were taking place. The incorporations, while still able from time to time to exert considerable influence and to get legal backing against those who ignored them, were losing a great deal of their influence and playing a much more limited role in controlling their trades. The units of production were getting larger. There were more and bigger workshops, where the gap between employer and journeyman was widening. There were fewer formal apprenticeships, which in the past had brought the young worker into the master's home. Now the relationship was becoming essentially a cash one and there was in mid-century much talk of the division between master and man. Socially too the gap was widening as many employers in tailoring, in building and in textiles began to prosper as never before. The expansion of trades meant that customary patterns of wages, recruitment and discipline were no longer applicable. The occasions for conflict, as the pace of change quickened, were more numerous. A debate over wages was both possible and necessary. By the last quarter of the eighteenth century, skilled labour was at a premium in many sectors and employers were desperate to attract it wherever they could. Uniformity of wage rates, imposed by incorporations or by the burgh councils, was no longer realistic. Journeymen combined to defend themselves and to assert themselves. More often than not their combinations were aggressive, aimed at forcing changes in wages or work patterns or to assert greater control. They were vital, dynamic institutions, offensive rather than defensive in their attitude to wages. Many of their trade societies were not ephemeral bodies but had a continuous existence for a number of years. Throughout nearly a century, the Edinburgh Journeymen Tailors' Society formed, divided, collapsed, re-formed, waxed and waned. It disappears from public view for a year or two only to reappear in full vigour and with the resources and coherence to challenge the masters in the courts. We know little of the leaders, but there can be no doubt that there was substantial continuity of leaders and members and that the members of the tailors' community knew to whom to turn to bring their society into action. The house of call provided a base for continuous, collective solidarity. For other trades, a public house as a regular meeting provided a similar base.

The development of trade unionism was also encouraged by the legal position in Scotland. Combination as such was not illegal in Scotland. The law allowed journeymen to combine to approach the incorporation, the town council and the courts to appeal for changes in their wages. It was admittedly a fine line that existed between the legal approach for redress and the illegal coercion of an employer, but groups like the Edinburgh tailors learned to tread this narrow path. The position was strengthened by the readiness of the Justices of the Peace and of Court of Session judges to intervene in industrial relations at the turn of the century.

Conscious of the gains in power and influence that the Scottish landed gentry had made during the century, the lawyers, drawn from the landed class, had no wish to see their position threatened by social disorder.[1] They were prepared to intervene to maintain peace. They welcomed opportunities to strengthen their influence and were free from the constraints of legal precedent to judge what they regarded as necessary for the social good. As a result, they were prepared to regulate wage levels by making comparisons with England and comparisons between trades, and to accept as guidelines measures of the cost of living and of the difficulties of the task involved. The peak of this was reached at the end of the century when social tensions were rising most sharply and when economic and political discontents were coming together. Faced with a middle class that was beginning to demand political rights, the landed class was prepared to pay a price to maintain the loyalty of the lower orders. They saw the tensions created by unregulated industrial relations as a threat to social stability. Just as they had no sympathy with middle-class radicals who sought to stir up the workers through political agitation, they had no great sympathy for employers who caused industrial unrest.

Yet, at the same time, there were contrary pressures. There were those among the landed class who feared the lack of subordination among the poor. There were many who believed that the prime concern of the law ought to be the defence of property against the propertyless. Then there were the intellectual arguments that state intervention in industrial relations was an archaic remnant of an old society, a barrier to the *laissez-faire* that would create a new wealth. The pressure was for assimilation to the English pattern and for an end to restraints on individual rights for some preconceived community good. The greater good, it was now argued, could come only from freedom for each to pursue self-interest. The first decade of the nineteenth century was the crucial period when the force of legal argument swung against the interventionist state.

The greatest pressures for an end to regulation came from the expanding manufacturing sector in the West. The corporate structures had always been modified to meet the needs of expansion, but by the early nineteenth century, the demand for an end to restrictions on growth, on freedom of movement, on wages and on barriers to unlimited competition became very loud. The fact that handloom weavers were prepared to use the courts to maintain regulation and were winning their case was unacceptable to capitalists. They were prepared to defy the court rulings, if necessary. Therefore, the whole pattern of regulation had to be swept away. The fact that trades in England were looking to English courts for redress made the Home Office ready to press the changes.

Denied change through legal action, Scottish unions took time to find a new role. In the West of Scotland, the years from 1813 to 1820 were perhaps the most tense. The cotton handloom weavers found their earnings sliding rapidly. For them and for some others there was an erratically fluctuating demand for their labour. There was a faster movement off the land into the city and living conditions were deteriorating under pressure of numbers and the pollution of industrialisation. That sign of overcrowding and poor housing, typhus, hit Glasgow in 1817. Self-help, through the friendly societies, was proving unreliable, as many societies collapsed under pressure of demand and bad management. At the same time, public help, through the poor law, was becoming more and more difficult to get, as attitudes to assessment and relief hardened. Hopes were pinned for a time on political action and there was an almost millennialist belief that political demonstration and protest would sweep away the injustices of the new order. For a small number only armed insurrection could achieve it. That dream ended in the repression of 1820.

The tension was largely confined to the cotton areas of the West and brought no response from the more prosperous East, where demand for handicrafts trades to build, furbish and clothe Edinburgh New Town and its inhabitants remained high. But, it was in the West that the significant and far-reaching changes were taking place. There, changes in work processes and in organisation of trades continued at a rapid pace, though the tactics of response were not very different. The new factory-based workforce in the cotton mills learned much from their contacts with the artisan tradition. Cotton spinners carved out an area of work for themselves and then learned to use traditional craft methods to protect that area. The whole attitude to new workers among spinners drew on what were essentially craft perceptions of the nature of their 'skill' and the right of themselves and their children to the 'property' of their work. The early factory gave skilled men a considerable autonomy, just as the home-working tradesman had had, and old methods and new practices for long existed side by side. The battles of the 1820s in the mills were about this, about the extent of workers' autonomy and on whose authority changes in work practices could be made.

The cotton spinners were determined to retain, even within the context of the factory, some of that independence that tradesmen valued. They sought to work at their own pace and to resist the ever-tightening factory discipline. They resented the increasing supervision of foremen and managers. The fact that they themselves, as well as being wage earners, were also supervisors of their own piecers and of younger workers, added to their sense of being independent contractors. For employers, it was necessary, at least occasionally, to achieve a 'necessary subordination', to assert their rights to manage. Much of the time it did not matter, but when new technology was being introduced or new work practices were being adopted, authority would be asserted. While the ultimate result of this struggle might be inevitable, the process by which masters obtained mastery was by no means a straightforward one. Ground lost by workers in one struggle could be won back, rarely by direct confrontation, but by a gradual encroachment and reassertion of customary practices. The strike was generally a sign of workers' failure, a sign that employers were reasserting control. The workers' gains were often made quietly in the workplace. How this was done is difficult to get at, since it tends to be only the direct confrontations that get reported.

The same period of the 1820s, with its sharp contrasts of boom and slump, also brought a speeding up of changes in other trades, with few able to maintain effective control of entry and restrictions on apprenticeship. Confronted by the instability of unregulated trades, with the loss of security of accepted status, and increasingly caught in the fluctuations of boom and slump in a capitalist economy, many tradesmen searched for alternatives. Co-operation in community or in production offered an alternative to some, though it was never very clear how the transformation was to be achieved. For others, co-operative enterprises offered a temporary cushion agaist the worst effects of unemployment. Few such schemes could draw on the necessary resources or support to make them viable for long. Set against them was the whole weight of the propaganda of orthodox political economy. From schoolmaster and minister, from politician and editor came the message that there was no real alternative to the capitalist way and that there was no greater community good beyond the pursuit of individual interests. Any check on market forces from trade unions or custom or the state had to be swept aside as a moral evil. The violence of capitalism, when the pressures were strong enough, was brought home to the cotton spinners in the 1830s when the employers co-ordinated an onslaught on their position. But even in 1837 it is doubtful if the masters were strong enough to defeat the men's organisation without the intervention of the state, just as had happened in 1812–13 against the weavers. A very deliberate breaking of union power was undertaken in 1837–38, with the state doing what the employers were unable or unwilling to do on their own.

It was the end of an era. The hand-mule spinners did not disappear, nor did they lose entirely their autonomy in the workplace, but the union never regained that significant, co-ordinating role that it had achieved in the 1820s and 1830s. Like the miners' strike of 1984–85, the implications of the defeat of the cotton spinners went far beyond their own union. It was a turning point for all. The significance of 1837–38 for trade-union leaders was that they could be held criminally responsible for the action of their members. It was a deterrent to vigorous action. The depression of the next five or six years allowed employers to consolidate the assault on trade-union control. In some ways it was merely completing a process that had begun in the 1820s. There was now a substantial reserve of labour. Highland clearances, rural change and Irish immigration provided employers with a ready pool of relatively cheap labour. In almost all cases, in periods of expansion, Scottish trade unions had lost the struggle for control of entry, and they were not able to regain it in years of depression. The Scottish economy was also once again turning in a new direction, with the switch to heavy industry. The shattering of the miners' unions and the opening up of the coalfields to new, unskilled, often Irish, labour smoothed the way for expansion in this area.

Some of the most active of union leaders turned to politics in the late 1830s and 1840s, but it was frequently a politics that was divorced from the central issues of an industrial society. As Iain Hutchison has shown, there was a renewed obsession with the intricacies of church politics in these years that overshadowed other concerns.[2] Even in Chartism, the vital Scottish dimension significantly took the shape of chartist churches. The rest was little more than a feeble mouthing of English issues. The self-confidence of Scottish trade union leaders, so apparent in the first half of the 1830s, had all but gone. In Scottish Chartism one can detect two conflicting pressures: one of which was still a search for the millennium, for a way of making industrial society tolerable, in this case through religion, or of opting out of too much concern with the things of this life; the second was the emphasising of respectability and collaboration with the middle class. The religious issues of the 1830s and 1840s allowed sections of the working class and the middle class to combine against the landed class. The landed class became the focus of hostility both in church politics and in social politics. It was firmly identified as the exploiter, as the cause of distress and of clearance in the Highlands which led to distress, poverty and unemployment in the towns. Significantly, the Scottish bourgeoisie were among the first to see the attractions of a campaign against the corn laws. The arrival of increasing numbers of the Irish added to the anti-landowner arguments. They provided an identifiable scapegoat on whom many ills could be blamed, but, at the same time, here too was a problem created by the landowning class. The fact that despite industrial developments Scotland remained overwhelmingly an agricultural society further strengthened this analysis of the country's ills. For eighty years or more the Liberal middle class in Scotland were able to keep the focus of the workers on the wicked landowner, while, at the same time, of course, the links between landed class and middle class were in reality being forged even tighter.

This has not been 'the Making of the Scottish Working Class'. The focus has been much more narrowly on trade unions; a focus which can be defended, since this crucial area of working-class activity has never been properly examined in a Scottish context. There are many areas of work and leisure, of culture and political action, that still require a much closer exploration. Workers use many other forms of response to industrial change than just their trade unions. We need to know much more about the Scottish public house, so different in Scotland from the social meeting places of the South, about the role of dissenting meeting houses and about many other aspects of working-class life. There is much to be done in all such areas.

Meanwhile, Thompson's classic work cannot be ignored. Inevitably it is there in the background of any study of this period, and some of the questions that he poses have shaped the approach to this work. We are left with his central question. To what extent had the experiences of industrial change and all the accompanying social, political and psychological changes created a working class in which 'some men . . . feel and articulate the identity of their interests between themselves, and as against other men whose interests are different from them and (usually) opposed to theirs'?

As the eighteenth century progresses, one sees the start of an awareness of different interests between many groups of journeymen and their masters. Employers were being identified as a group whose interests were frequently in conflict with those of their journeymen. The persistence of trade incorporations or informal employers' organisations, acting in the interests of master tradesmen, strengthened the feeling of separateness. No longer were incorporations speaking for the whole craft, but for only the employing section of it. It is true that there were still opportunities for some journeymen to move into the incorporation and to become employers, but these opportunities diminished rather than increased as the century went on. By the 1790s there were signs of collaboration between societies in different trades and an awareness that there was much in common in the changes that were taking place in different crafts. Improved communications, such as the opening of the Forth and Clyde Canal, allowed for collaboration between workers (and employers) in different towns. By 1810, not only had mutual support been extended, but there was enough collaboration to bring about in Glasgow a formal committee to campaign against the threatened introduction of the combination laws. From then on committees of trade societies were a regular feature of most of the Scottish cities, swinging into action when the need arose.

In stirring a political consciousness, the events of 1817 to 1820 were much more important than those of 1793. The hanging of Hardie, Baird and Wilson, all working men, gave martyrs to the radical movement and symbols for the future. But it also brought out the reality of the social conflict that existed in industrialising Scotland. There was limited middle-class involvement in the events of these years. The middle classes were firmly aligned with the forces of order, signing on in droves for the volunteer 'Sharpshooters' and most raucous in their denunciations of workers and their organisations. The language of the business community in these years is undoubtedly the language of class. At the same time, the harshness of the reprisals acted as a deterrent to workers' political action.

But it is in the experience of the workplace that a working-class identity is shaped in the 1820s. There was a growing sense that the economic system inevitably led to exploitation. There was a search for an ideology that would offer an alternative to the political economy espoused by a now dominant Scottish Whiggery. This search brought unprecedented levels of co-operation between groups of workers, despite the unevenness of industrialisation, as factory, home and workshop-based operations continued side by side. However, the slump of the late 1820s and the massive deterioration in the position of many groups of craft workers that followed 1825 helped forge a common sense of hostility to the economic structures that were producing such conditions. Something like a common working-class voice could be found in the short-lived unstamped press. It would be difficult not to see the language and the action of the trade unionists in the first half of the 1830s as reflecting class feeling and an awareness of class conflict. Scottish workers had experienced exploitation and had a sense of being exploited. They had fought battles over vital issues of independence, autonomy and authority against employers. They found the state and the law increasingly placed in the balance firmly on the side of the employers. At moments, it made them conscious of class. Class consciousness was to go under in the 1830s, but it is significant that Alexander Campbell was to remain a central and respected figure in Scottish trade unionism for four decades, coaxing, evangelising, organising, guiding and challenging workers to continue to search for co-operative alternatives to capitalism. The vision he offered, and to which many responded, was one which held that there was a way by which the advantages of the new forces of production could be more widely spread in a manner that would not destroy the independence of the tradesman and deprive working people of control over their own lives. It was a vision that never entirely succumbed, despite divisions on tactics, despite tensions between skilled and unskilled, between Irish and Scots. But it was a vision that was kept effectively curbed by the power and strategies of those in power by a mixture of propaganda and force. As Keith Burgess has written, there was a massive propaganda campaign to win the workers to seeing the world in the same way as the political economists: 'the ideology of economic liberalism began to colonize, albeit incompletely, the consciousness of the Scottish working class'. It effectively put across the view that the fault lay not in the capitalist system but in an unreformed part of it, the landed class. Employer and worker could combine to change that and all would be well. When the propaganda failed, which it did remarkably rarely, then force could be applied.[3] Sheriff Alison in 1838 was determined to use his legal power to ensure that unions would have little future in Scotland:

> I think that in fifty or a hundred years, when wealth is more generally diffused, and the enjoyments and artificial wants of society consequent upon wealth have taken root in the lower classes of society, we may then be prepared for liberal institutions, such as those connected with combinations, which possibly may be perfectly innocuous yet in London; but I fear that we are not arrived at that state yet.[4]

In large part he succeeded. For fifty years after, the way forward for Scottish trade unionism was slow, cautious, lacking in confidence and very unsuccessful at finding a defence against an aggressive capitalism.

Notes

Abbreviations used:

BLPES	:	British Library of Political and Economic Science
CU	:	Cooperative Union, Manchester
GL	:	Goldsmiths' Library, University of London
NLS	:	National Library of Scotland
OSA	:	*Old Statistical Account*
PP	:	*Parliamentary Papers*
SC	:	*Select Committee*
SP	:	*Court of Session Papers*
SRA	:	Strathclyde Regional Archives
SRO	:	Scottish Record Office Register House
WRH	:	West Register House, SRO

Unless otherwise indicated, place of publication is London.

Introduction

1. T. Dickson, *Capital and Class in Scotland*, (Edinburgh, 1982); J. D. Young, *The Rousing of the Scottish Working Class*, (1979).

2. K. J. Logue, *Popular Disturbances in Scotland 1780–1815*, (Edinburgh, 1979); S. G. E. Lythe, 'The Tayside Meal Mobs 1772–1773', *Scottish Historical Review*, XLVI, (1967).

3. A. Campbell, *The Lanarkshire Miners*, (Edinburgh, 1979).

4. R. J. Bezucha, *The Lyon Uprising of 1834*, (Cambridge, Mass., 1974); J. W. Scott, *The Glassmakers of Carmaux*, (Cambridge, Mass., 1974); W. H. Sewell, *Work and Revolution in France*, (Cambridge, 1980).

5. Sewell, *Work and Revolution*, p. 1.

6. John Rule, *The Experience of Labour in the Eighteenth Century*, (1980); Ion Prothero, *Artisans and Politics in Early Nineteenth Century London*, (1979).

7. C. R. Dobson, *Masters and Journeymen*, (1980).

8. R. Mitchison, 'Patriotism and national identity in eighteenth century Scotland', in *Nationalisty and the Pursuit of National Independence*, ed. T. W. Moody, (Belfast, 1978), p. 86.

9. T. B. Smith, 'Master and Servant', *Juridical Review*, (1958), p. 221; Alexander Grant, *Independence and Nationhood: Scotland 1306–1469*, (1984), pp. 66–7.

10. R. Mitchison, *History of Scotland*, (1970), p. 183.

11. Smith, 'Master and Servant', p. 222.

12. 'Slavery in Scotland', *Edinburgh Review*, Vol. 189, (January 1899), p. 135.

13. T. C. Smout, 'Lead-Mining in Scotland', in *Essays in Scottish Business History*, ed. P. Payne, (1967), p. 121.

14. Baron F. Duckham, *A History of the Scottish Coal Industry, Vol. I: 1700–1815*, (Newton Abbot, 1970), Chapter 9.

15. 'Slavery in Scotland', p. 123.

16. *Ibid.*, p. 124.
17. *Ibid.*, p. 132.
18. E. A. Horne, *The Conditions of Labour in Scotland in the Seventeenth Century*, (St. Andrews, 1907), p. 21.
19. *The Minutes of the Justices of the Peace for Lanarkshire 1707–23*, ed. C. A. Malcolm, (Scottish History Society, Edinburgh, 1931), p. xli.
20. Horne, *op. cit.*, p. 21.
21. Malcolm, *op. cit.*, p. xlii.
22. Erskine, *Institutes*, quoted in Duckham, p. 241.
23. Duckham, *op. cit.*, pp. 253–61; 'Slavery in Modern Scotland', p. 121; Horne, *op. cit.*, p. 11.
24. Rab Houston, 'Coal, class & culture: Labour relations in a Scottish mining community, 1650–1750', *Social History*, Vol. 8(1), (January, 1983), p. 6.
25. C. A. Whatley, 'From Servitude to Subjugation? Legal Records, Labour Relations and Colliers' Emancipation in the Eighteenth Century', paper delivered to Scottish Records Association, 26 Oct. 1985.
26. T. Johnston, *History of Working Classes in Scotland*, (Glasgow, 1920), p. 249.
27. T. B. Smith, 'Master and Servant', in *An Introduction to Scottish Legal History*, (Edinburgh, Stair Society, 1958), p. 137.
28. Malcolm, *Justices of Peace of Lanarkshire*, p. xli.
29. T. B. Smith, 'Master and Servant', in *An Introduction to Scottish Legal History*, Stair Society (Edinburgh, 1958), p. 135.
30. W. E. Minchinton (ed.), *Wage Regulation in Pre-Industrial England*, (Newton Abbot, 1972), pp. 192–3.
31. E. Heckscher, *Mercantilism*, Vol. I (1962), p. 311.
32. NLS, *At the Quarter Session of his Highnesse the Lord Protector before the Justices of the Peace for the Shire of Ayr the Sixth of August 1656*.
33. *Ayr Quarter Sessions*, 1657.
34. Malcolm, *Justices of Peace of Lanarkshire*, p. xli.
35. *Scotland and the Protectorate*, ed. C. H. Firth, (Scottish History Society, Edinburgh, 1899), pp. 405–6.
36. SRA. JP6/1. Minutes of JPs of Dumbartonshire 1 May 1744, 30 April 1759, 30 April 1760. I am grateful to Professor R. M. Mitchison for these references.
37. *Scotland and the Protectorate*, pp. 405–6.
38. *Ayr Quarter Sessions*, 1656.
39. Malcolm, *Justices of Peace of Lanarkshire*, p. 19.
40. D. Woodward, 'Wage Rates and Living Standards in Pre-Industrial England', *Past and Present*, 91, (1981), p. 30.
41. Malcolm, *Justices of Peace of Lanarkshire*, p. 195.
42. Houston, 'Coal, Class & Culture', p. 8.
43. *Ayr Quarter Sessions*, 1656.
44. E. Bain, *Merchant and Craft Guilds: A History of the Aberdeen Incorporated Trades of Aberdeen*, (Aberdeen, 1887), pp. 287–8.

Chapter 1

1. A. Durie, *The Scottish Linen Industry in the Eighteenth Century*, (Edinburgh, 1979), p. 10; R. H. Campbell, 'Anglo-Scottish Union of 1707 II. The Economic Consequences', *Economic History Review*, p. 301.

2. Quoted in Henry Hamilton, *An Economic History of Scotland in the Eighteenth Century*, (Oxford, 1963), p. 301.

3. J. Colville (ed.), *Letters of John Cockburn of Ormiston to his Gardner, 1727–44*, (Scottish History Society, Edinburgh, 1904), p. 30.

4. Hamilton, *Economic History of Scotland*, p. 307.

5. Durie, *Linen Industry*, p. 65.

6. M. Flinn *et al*, *Scottish Population History*, (Cambridge, 1977).

7. *Scotland and Scotsmen*, II, pp. 216–7; David Loch, *Essays on the Trade and Commerce, Manufactures and Fisheries of Scotland*, (Edinburgh, 1778), Vol. I, p. 236.

8. Flinn, *Scottish Population History*, p. 231.

9. R. Mitchison, *A History of Scotland*, (1970), pp. 346–7; Hamilton, *Economic History of Scotland*, pp. 319–23.

10. *Glasgow Mercury*, 8 August 1787.

11. *Scots Magazine*, LIII, (1791), pp. 562–3, cited in Hamilton, *Economic History of Scotland*, p. 333.

12. B. Lenman, *An Economic History of Modern Scotland* (1977); Gayer, Rostow and Schwartz, *The Growth and Fluctuation of the British Economy 1790–1850*, (2nd. ed., 1975), p. 25.

13. H. Hamilton, *The Industrial Revolution in Scotland*, (1966 ed.), p. 134.

14. T. Dickson (ed.), *Scottish Capitalism*, (1980), p. 139.

15. *Dundee and Dundonians Seventy Years Ago: Being Personal Reminiscences of an Old Dundonian*, (Dundee, 1892), p. 21.

16. T. Dickson, *Scottish Capitalism*, p. 185.

17. R. Price, *Labour in British Society*, (1986), p. 15.

Chapter 2

1. T. B. Smith, 'Master and Servant', in *Introduction to Scottish Legal History*, pp. 134–6.

2. *Basilikon Doron of James I*, ed. J. Craigie (1944), Vol. I, p. 93.

3. T. Johnston, *History of Working Classes*, p. 152.

4. R. Renwick, *Extracts from the Records of the Burgh of Glasgow*, Vol. V, 1718–*1738*, (Glasgow, 1909), pp. 254–5.

5. *Session Papers*, (henceforth *S.P.*), Vol. 4, No. 9, 5 July 1736.

6. W. Cramond, 'The Hammermen of Banff', *Transactions of the Banffshire Field Club*, (1902–3).

7. M. Wood, 'The Hammermen of the Canongate', *Book of the Old Edinburgh Club XIX*, (1933), p. 8.

8. W. H. Marwick, 'The Tailors of the Canongate', *Ibid.*, XXII, (1938), p. 99.

9. R. Chambers, *Domestic Annals of Scotland*, II, (Edinburgh, 1858), p. 41; Annette M. Smith, *The Three United Trades of Dundee: Masons, Wrights and Slaters*, (Dundee: Abertay Historical Society Publication No. 26, 1987), p. 16.

10. *Basilikon Doron*, p. 93.

11. Sir Patrick Lindesay, *Interest of Scotland Concerned with Regard to its Police in Imploying the Poor etc.*, (Edinburgh, 1733).

12. *SP*, Vol. 36, No. 51, 20 June 1749.

13. *SP*, Vol. 93, No. 20, 20 December 1767; Cramond, 'Hammermen of Banff'.

14. Johnston, *History*, pp. 135–6.

15. W. Campbell, *History of the Incorporation of Cordiners in Glasgow*, (Glasgow, 1893), p. 473.

16. *SP*, Vol. 83, No. 2, 5 August 1763.

17. *Incorporation of Bakers of Glasgow*, (Glasgow 1948), p. 75; H. Lumsden & P. Henderson Aitken, *History of the Hammermen of Glasgow*, (Paisley, 1912), p. 31.

18. H. Lumsden, *The Records of the Trades House of Glasgow, 1713–1777*, (Glasgow, 1934), 7 March 1732.

19. Lindesay, *Interest of Scotland*, pp. xxviii–xxix.

20. *Charter Writs and Public Documents of the Royal Burgh of Dundee*, (Dundee, 1880), 24 April 1734.

21. Renwick, *Extracts*, p. 216, 29 April 1725.

22. R. A. Leeson, *Travelling Brothers*, (1979) p. 71; Marwick, 'Canongate Tailors', p. 109.

23. *Incorporation of Bakers of Glasgow*, (1948), pp. 16–17.

24. GL. *Conditions of the Working Classes in Edinburgh and Leith*. (This is a bound collection of newspaper cuttings.)

25. A. Bain, *Merchant and Craft Guilds. A History of the Aberdeen Incorporated Trades*, (Aberdeen, 1887). p. 245.

26. *Ibid.*, p. 288.

27. W. Campbell, *History of the Incorporation of Cordiners in Glasgow*, (Glasgow, 1883), p. 301.

28. *OSA* VI, pp. 610–11; Marwick, 'Canongate Tailors', p. 111.

29. *Incorporation of Bakers of Glasgow*, p. 70.

30. *OSA* XVIII, p. 395.

31. *PP* 1810–11, II, *Committee on Handloom Weavers' Petitions*, evidence of James Hanley.

32. WRH. CS 230/E/1/15. *Petition of Journeymen Taylors of Edinburgh*, 8 July 1734.

33. GL. *Conditions of the Working Classes in Edinburgh and Leith*.

34. WRH. CS 230/C/1/15.

35. M. Wood, 'Edinburgh Poll Tax Returns', in *Book of the Old Edinburgh Club*, XXV, (1945).

36. *Morison's Dictionary of Decisions*, (1811), Appendix Part I. Corporation of Tailors v. Robert Forrester, Merchant, 26 January 1808.

37. WRH. CS 230/E/1/15. Minute to Taylors, 27 June 1734.

38. WRH. CS 233/T2/18.

39. £20 Scots in 1734. WRH. CS 230/E/1/15.

40. See below, p. 45.

41. WRH. CS 231/E/1/29.

42. John Rule, 'Artisans' Attitudes: Skilled Labour and Proletarianization in Europe and New England before 1848', paper to Fourth British–Dutch Social History Conference, Newcastle, 1984.

43. GL. *Conditions of Working Classes in Edinburgh*.

44. WRH. CS 231/E/1/29.

45. Ibid.

46. C. M. Burns, Industrial Labour and Radical Movements in Scotland in the 1790s, unpublished M.Sc. thesis, University of Strathclyde, (1971), p. 85.

47. WRH. CS 231/E/1/29.

48. *OSA* II, p. 196.

49. WRH. CS 231/E/1/29. Statement by witnesses, January 1798.

50. Ibid.

51. G. Frame (Sir James Steuart), *Considerations on the Interests of the County of Lanark in Scotland*, (Glasgow, 1769), p. 76, cited in Durie, *Linen Industry*, p. 76.

52. F. Braudel, *The Perspectives of the World: Civilization and Capitalism 15th–18th Century*, III, (1985), p. 372.

53. The information on the building trades is taken from GL. *Conditions of the Working Classes in Edinburgh.*

54. WRH. CS 231/E/1/25. Answer to Petitions of Master Cabinetmakers, 24 April 1788.

55. WRH. CS 231/E/1/25.; *S.P.*, Vol. 378, No. 60, 25 May 1797.

56. WRH. CS 271/57,435.

57. *SP*, Vol. 262, No. 34, 14 May 1811.

58. *Ibid.*

59. C. Gulvin, *The Scottish Hosiery and Knitwear Industry*. (Edinburgh, 1984).

60. H. Hamilton, *The Economic History of Eighteenth Century Scotland*, (1966 reprint), pp. 136–8.

61. A. J. Durie, *The Scottish Linen Industry in the Eighteenth Century*, (Edinburgh, 1979), p. 39; N. Murray, *The Scottish Handloom Weavers*, (Edinburgh, 1978), Chapter 2; John Fermie, *History of the Town and Parish of Dunfermline*, (Dunfermline 1815), pp. 51–8.

62. Murray, *Scottish Handloom Weavers*, p. 68.

63. Durie, *Scottish Linen Industry*, p. 60.

64. On the development of the putting-out system, see. R. Millward, 'The Emergence of Wage Labour in Early Modern England', *Explorations in Economic History*, Vol. 18 (1981), pp. 21–39; A. J. Durie, *Scottish Linen Industry*, pp. 59–60; H. Hamilton, *The Industrial Revolution in Scotland*, (1962), p. 161; S. Marglin, 'What do Bosses do?', in *The Division of Labour: the Labour Process and Class Struggle in Modern Capitalism*, (Brighton, 1970), p. 26.

65. N. Murray, *op. cit.*

66. *Ibid.*, pp. 40–2.

67. *SP*, Vol. 262, No. 34, 12 November 1811.

68. R. Mitchison, *Life in Scotland*, (1978), p. 78.

69. F. W. Galton, *Select Documents Illustrating the History of Trade Unionism: 1. The Tailoring Trade*, (1896), p. xxxv.

70. M. D. George, *London Life in the Eighteenth Century*, (1966 edition), pp. 166–7.

71. The comparison with figures in E. W. Gilboy, *Wages in Eighteenth Century England*, (Cambridge, Mass. 1934).

72. SRA. T-TH 2/8/1. Full Book'd Journeymen's Book of Glasgow Hammermen.

73. T. C. Smout, *A History of the Scottish People 1560–1830*, (1969), p. 176.

Chapter 3

1. *The Minutes of the Justices of the Peace for Lanarkshire, 1707–23*, ed. C. A. Malcolm (Scottish History Society, Edinburgh 1931), p. xli.

2. *Records of a Scottish Cloth Manufactory at New Mills, Haddingtonshire, 1681–1703*, (Scottish History Society, Edinburgh 1905), p. xlv.

3. *Register of the Privy Council*; 3rd. Ser. XLIV, quoted in T. Johnston, *op. cit.*, p. 149.

4. Rab Houston, 'Coal, Class and Culture'.

5. W. M. Reddy, 'The Textile Trade and the language of the Crowd at Rouen, 1752–1871', *Past and Present*. 74 (1977), pp. 62–89.

6. H. A. Turner, *Trade Union Growth, Structure and Policy*, (1962), p. 51; Smith, *The Three United Trades of Dundee*, p. 8.

7. Lindesay, *The Interest of Scotland*, p. 120.

8. *SP*, Vol. F, III, No. 2, 17 January 1728.

9. Helen Armet, *Extracts from the Records of the Burgh of Edinburgh*, (Edinburgh, 1967), 27 December 1704.

10. *SP*, Vol. F, III, No. 2, 12 January 1728; WRH. CS 234/M/4/36.

11. *SP*, Vol. 86, No. 2, 5 August 1763.

12. *SP*, Vol. 46, No. 50, 'Memorial for Samuel Mitchell, Shoemaker, 1761'.

13. GL. *Articles of the Journeymen Shoemakers of the City of Edinburgh*, (1778); WRH. CS 271/52,543.

14. *SP*, Vol. 29, No. 224, 24 July 1734.

15. WRH. CS 234/M/4/36.

16. *SP*, Vol. F, III, No. 2.

17. WRH. CS 234/M/4/36.

18. Ibid.

19. GL. *Articles of the Journeymen Shoemakers of the City of Edinburgh*, (1778).

20. *SP*, Vol. 444, No. 25, 1802.

21. GL. *Articles of Continuation of the Society of Journeymen Taylors in Glasgow*, (1775).

22. A. Bain, *Aberdeen Incorporated Trades*, (Aberdeen, 1887), p. 246.

23. WRH. CS 230/E/1/15, 8 July 1734.

24. Ibid.; *SP*, Vol. 29, No. 224.

25. *Ibid.*

26. WRH. CS 233/T2/18.

27. *SP*, Vol. 216, No. 11.

28. *Gentleman's Magazine*, XVIII, (1748), p. 427.

29. F. W. Galton, *The Tailoring Trade*, p. xxxv.

30. Lumsden, *Records of Trades House of Glasgow*, 2 Nov. 1748, SRA. T-TH1/1/5, 2 November 1748.

31. Renwick, *Extract from Records of Glasgow*, VI, 1 May 1750; Annette M. Smith, *The Three United Trades of Dundee*, p. 8.

32. Campbell, *Incorporation of Cordiners*, p. 474.

33. *Edinburgh Evening Courant*, 27 August 1754.

34. WRH. CS 238/A/1/81.

35. WRH. CS 96/1943. Minute Book of the Woolcombers' Society in Aberdeen begun 22 November 1755.

36. Ibid., 15 November 1762.

37. *Morison's Dictionary of Decisions*, (1811), M. 1961.

38. WRH. CS 233/T2/18. The imprisoned men were John Bathie, George Murray, Alexander McEwan, James Russell, William Bell and William Thompson.

39. H. Hamilton, *An Economic History of Scotland in the Eighteenth Century*, p. 346.

40. *Morrison*, M. 7682.

41. *SP*, Vol. 155, No. 21, 20 November 1770.

42. WRH. CS 233/T2/18.

43. Ibid.

44. *Edinburgh Evening Courant*, 15 July 1764.

45. Cutting from *Forfar Review* (Summer 1792) in Webb Trade Union Collection (BLPES) A/XIII/441.

46. *Edinburgh Evening Courant*, 23 July 1764.

47. *Forfar Review*, 1792. See note 45.

48. *Edinburgh Evening Courant*, 1 September 1764.

49. *Ibid.*, 29 April, 2 May 1767.

50. WRH. CS 233/T2/18.

51. Ibid.
52. *Edinburgh Evening Courant*, 16 May 1767.
53. Ibid., 18 May 1767; *Scots Magazine*, Vol. 29, June 1767, p. 326.
54. T. Johnston, *History of Working Class*, p. 378; Bain, *Aberdeen Incorporated Trades*, pp. 260–1.
55. *Black Kalendar of Aberdeen*, (Aberdeen, 1878), p. 93.
56. *Scots Magazine*, Vol. 30, December 1768, p. 688.
57. H. Hamilton, *Economic History of Scotland in Eighteenth Century*, p. 380.
58. *Scots Magazine*, Vol. 30, December 1768, p. 688.
59. *SP*, Vol. 155, No. 21.
60. *Ibid.*
61. WRH. CS 233/T2/18; *Scots Magazine*, Vol. 34, November 1777, p. 621.
62. *Morison*, M.7623; Robert Boyd, *The Office, Powers and Jurisdiction of His Majesty's Justices of the Peace and Commissioners of Supply*, (Edinburgh 1787), pp. 737–39.
63. *Ibid.* M.7670 and Appendix; Ann E. Whetstone, *Scottish County Government in the Eighteenth and Nineteenth Centuries*, (Edinburgh 1981), p. 49 is clearly wrong to suggest that JPs were not regulating craftsmen's wages.
64. *Scots Magazine*, Vol. 45, January 1783, p. 50.
65. *Ibid.*, Vol. 40, June 1778, pp. 329–31.
66. *Ibid.*
67. Adam Smith, *The Wealth of Nations*, (1887 ed.), p. 28.

Chapter 4

1. *OSA*, I (1791), p. 27.
2. *Ibid.*, VI (179), pp. 344–5.
3. *Ibid.*, Appendix.
4. M. W. Flinn, 'Trends in Real Wages, 1750–1850', *Economic History Review*, XXVII (3), 1974, p. 404.
5. M. Berg, *The Age of Manufacturers 1700–1820* (1985), pp. 235–246.
6. *Edinburgh Evening Courant*, 27 August 1754.
7. *SP*, Vol. 54, No. 9, 5 January 1761.
8. SRA. T-TH 1/5, Minutes of the Trades' House of Glasgow, 29 July 1760.
9. For the campaign by the Weavers' Incorporation to get restriction on numbers, see Ibid., 23 June 1752, 11 October 1753, 19 November 1754, 26 June 1761, 3 September 1761.
10. NLS. Acc. 4702. Fenwick Weavers, The Book of Records.
11. *Morison* 9564; see also *Faculty Decisions*, IV.
12. *SP*, Vol. 135, No. 9, 23 February 1768.
13. *Edinburgh Evening Courant*, 7 October 1767; *Burnett's Criminal Law*, p. 235; *Glasgow Journal*, 1–8 October 1767.
14. *SP*, Vol. 135, No. 9; *Glasgow Journal*, 3–10 December 1767; *Glasgow Weekly Chronicle*, 2–9 December 1767.
15. *Glasgow Journal*, 24 March 1768, quoted in J. D. Young, *Women in Popular Struggles*, (Edinburgh, 1985), pp. 62–3; *Scots Magazine*, XXX, December 1768, p. 668.
16. Fenwick Weavers, Book of Records, 9 November 1769.
17. *SP*, Vol. 93, No. 20; *SP*, Vol. 143, No. 19; *SP*, Vol. 164, No. 7; see also Minutes of the Trades House, 9 December 1756.
18. S. G. E. Lythe, 'Tayside Meal Mobs 1772–3', *Scottish Historical Review* XLVI (1), April 1967, p. 26.

19. A. B. Richmond, *Narrative of the Conditions of the Manufacturing Population*, (1824), p. 6. Archbishop Sharp had been assassinated by Covenanters in 1648 and Captain Porteous murdered by an Edinburgh mob in 1736.
20. W. Hector, *Selections from the Judicial Records of Renfrewshire*, (Paisley, 1878), p. 197.
21. *Burnett's Criminal Law*, pp. 236–7.
22. H. A. Turner, *Trade Union Growth, Structure & Policy*, p. 61.
23. *Scots Magazine*, XLVII, February 1785, pp. 70–2.
24. Renwick, *Extracts*, VIII (1913), 20 October 1786.
25. *Scots Magazine*, XLIX, July 1787, p. 359; *Glasgow Mercury*, 4–11 July, 25 July–1 August, 8–15 August 1787.
26. *Glasgow Mercury*, 4–11 July, 25 July–1 August 1787.
27. K. Logue, *Popular Disturbances in Scotland, 1780–1815*, (Edinburgh, 1979), p. 157.
28. *Scots Magazine*, XLIX, September 1767, pp. 465–6; *Glasgow Mercury*, 5 September 1787; A. Murray, *Scottish Handloom Weavers*, p. 185.
29. Renwick, *Extracts*, VIII, 27 September 1787; *Glasgow Mercury*, 10 October 1787.
30. *Scots Magazine*, XLX, 1788, pp. 360–1; *Glasgow Mercury*, 16, 30 April 1788.
31. *Scots Magazine*, XLIX, December 1787, p. 619; *Glasgow Mercury*, 19 September 1787.
32. NLS. Acc. 3943. Xerox of single sheet beginning 'We subscribers Journeymen Blacksmiths in Glasgow ... 22 September 1784'; H. Lumsden & P. Henderson Aitken, *History of the Hammermen of Glasgow*, p. 179.
33. *Glasgow Mercury*, 3, 24 October 1787.
34. Smith, *The Three United Trades of Dundee*, p. 8.
35. *SP*, Vol. 225, No. 19, 28 February 1804; S. C. Gillespie, *Scottish Typographical Association*, (Glasgow, 1953), p. 16.
36. *Glasgow Mercury*, 27 December 1786–3 January 1787.
37. *Ibid.*, 18–25 July 1787.
38. WRH. CS 231/E/1/25, 1787.
39. One of the few recorded disputes was a four or five-week strike in 1791 among Edinburgh shoemakers which pushed up rates from 20d. to 24d. for best shoes.
40. SRO. RH 2/4/63. Letter to H. Dundas, January 1792.
41. SRO. RH 2/4/64.
42. Ibid.
43. Logue, *Popular Disturbances*, pp. 11–12; *Scots Magazine*, XLIV, August 1792, p. 411.
44. Murray, *Scottish Handloom Weavers*, p. 209.
45. NLS. X. 223. d. 1(7). *Declaration of the Friends of the People*, 5 December 1792.
46. *Scots Magazine*, XLIV, December 1792, p. 569.
47. J. D. Brims, The Scottish Democratic Movement in the Age of the French Revolution, unpublished Ph.D. thesis, University of Edinburgh 1983, pp. 235–87.
48. *Scots Magazine*, XLIV, December 1792, p. 620.
49. SRO. RH 2/4/65.
50. SRO. RH 2/4/67.
51. Ibid.
52. C. M. Burns, Industrial Labour and Radical Movements in Scotland in the 1790s, unpublished M.Sc. thesis, University of Strathclyde, 1971, p. 134.
53. George Auldjo, Provost, to Lord Advocate, Aberdeen, 5 December 1792, printed in A. Aspinall, *Early English Trade Unions*, (1949), p. 17.
54. *Scots Magazine*, Vol. XLV, 1793, *passim.*
55. Renwick, *Extracts*, VIII, 10 June 1793.

56. SRO. RH 2/4/70/175–7.

57. For trial of Muir, see K. Logue, 'Thomas Muir', in *History is My Witness* (BBC publication), ed. G. Menzies (1976).

58. Hume, *Commentaries on the Law of Scotland Respecting Crimes*, (3rd edn. Edinburgh 1829), Vol. I, p. 556ff.

59. SRO. RH 2/4/73/272.

60. W. L. Mathieson, *The Awakening of Scotland*, (Glasgow, 1910), p. 135.

61. SRO. RH 2/4/73/265.

62. *State Trials*, eds. T. B. & T. J. Howell (1817), Vol. XXIII; *Second Report of the Committee of Secrecy of the House of Commons*, 12–13 May 1894.

63. Ibid.

64. WRH. CS 231/E/1/29.

65. Quoted in Johnston, *History of the Scottish Working Class*, p. 272.

66. Lamb Collection Dundee 39134, 9 July 1793, quoted in Burns, Industrial Labour and Radical Movements, p. 149.

67. H. Cockburn, *Memorials of His Time*, (Edinburgh, 1856), pp. 71–2.

68. WRH. CS 231/E/1/29, 1798.

69. Ibid.

70. *SP*, Vol. 416, No. 35, 4 February 1800.

71. Logue, *Popular Disturbances*, Chapter 3.

72. Burns, *op. cit.*, pp. 205–212; H. T. Dickinson, *British Radicalism and the French Revolution 1789-1815*, (Oxford, 1985), p. 50.

73. *Morison*, 9573; WRH. CS 271/61, 756, 1798; CS 231/E/1.2q., 1798.

74. Quoted in Johnston, *History of the Scottish Working Class*, p. 82. Dr. Chris Whatley of the University of Dundee has undertaken work that shows the extent of early colliers' combination. I am grateful to him for letting me see his unpublished material on this subject.

75. Alan Campbell, *The Lanarkshire Miners. A Social History of their Trade Unions 1775–1874*, (Edinburgh, 1979), p. 12. Except where indicated, I have relied on this work for this part on colliers.

76. R. H. Campbell, *Carron Company*, (Edinburgh 1961), pp. 67–70.

77. Campbell, *Lanarkshire Miners*, p. 16; SRO GD 26/5/369. Printed leaflet, Edinburgh, 27 December 1797. H. Hamilton, *Economic History of Eighteenth Century Scotland*, p. 373.

78. B. Duckham, *A History of Coal-mining in Scotland*, (Newton Abbot, 197), p. 307.

79. Campbell, *Lanarkshire Miners*, p. 17; *Observations on the Laws Relating to Colliers in Scotland* (Glasgow 1825).

80. E. Bain, *Aberdeen Incorporated Trades*, p. 261.

81. Hamilton, *Eighteenth Century Scotland*, p. 350.

82. CS 231/E. 1/29; *SP*, Vol. 266 No. 15, 26 June 1812, refers to this case.

83. *SP*, Vol. 414, No. 35, 6 February 1800; *SP*, Vol. 415, No. 14, 3 April 1800.

84. Logue *Popular Disturbances*, p. 25; *Autobiography of John Younger, Shoemaker, St. Boswells* (Kelso 1881), pp. 126–8.

85. WRH. CS 271/52173, 1800.

86. *SP*, Vol. 216, No. 11, 1801.

87. *SP*, Vol. 271, No. 8, 1801.

88. A list of the members of Muir's jury and of Skirving's jury can be found in NLS Ry IVe. 11(16) bound with a *Statistical Analysis of the Census of the City of Edinburgh*, 1851.

89. *SP*, Vol. 444, No. 23, 27 November 1802.

90. G.L., B853, *Condition of the Working Classes in Edinburgh and Leith*, III.

91. *SP*, Vol. 225, No. 19, 28 February 1805; WRH. CS 271/57,435; *Scottish Typographical Circular*, IV, June 1858.

92. *Glasgow Herald and Advertiser*, 11 February 1803, quoted in J. Neill, *Records & Reminiscences of Bonhill Parish*, (Dumbarton, 1912), p. 239.

93. Adam Ferguson, *An Essay on the History of Civil Society*, (1767), quoted in P. Stein, 'Law & Society in Eighteenth Century Scottish Thought', in *Essays on Scottish History in the Eighteenth Century*, ed. N. T. Phillipson & R. Mitchison, (Edinburgh, 1970), pp. 163–4.

94. P. Stein, 'The General Notions of Contract and Property in Eighteenth Century Thought', *Juridical Review*, 1963, p. 5.

Chapter 5

1. J. L. Gray, 'The Law of Combination in Scotland', *Economica*, VII, (1938), pp. 332–350.

2. *PP*, 1818, V. Appendix to *Third Report of Select Committee on Poor Laws*, lists 327 friendly societies, exclusive of Glasgow and Edinburgh; *PP*, 1831–32, XXVI, *Report of the Number of Friendly and Benefit Societies in Great Britain; Report on Friendly and Benefit Societies by a Committee of the Highland Society of Scotland*, (Edinburgh, 1824).

3. I am grateful to Professor J. Butt for drawing my attention to the number of societies that had property insured with the Sun Insurance Co. See, for example, Guildhall Library (GH) MS 11937/8, 26 November 1794; Ploughmen Friendly Society of Bainsford; GH MS 11937/18, Operative Masons' Society of St. John's College, Banff, 27 April 1797; GH 11937/31, Operative Masons of Kirkcaldy, 14 February 1800; GH 11937/33, Stabler Society of Edinburgh, 8 August 1800.

4. *Morison*, 9546; T. B. Smith, 'Master and Servant', in The Stair Society, *An Introduction to Scottish Legal History*, (Edinburgh, 1958), p. 140.

5. *SP*, Vol. 271, No. 8, 1801.

6. *Morison*, 9573; *Burnett's Criminal Law*, (1811), pp. 225–6.

7. *Edinburgh Evening Courant*, 10 August 1805, 7 November 1808; *Farmers' Magazine*, August 1806, cited in G. Houston, 'Labour Relations in Scottish Agriculture before 1870', *Agricultural History Review*, VI, (1958), pp. 27–41.

8. For the details of the papermakers' case, see G. Hutcheson, *Treatise on Offices of Justice of Peace*. (3rd edn. 1815), pp. 51–71.

9. *Burnett's Criminal Law*, pp. 227–35.

10. G. Hutcheson, *Treatise*, II, pp. 180–2.

11. *Burnett's Criminal Law*, p. 235.

12. R. Mitchison, 'The Creation of the Disablement Rule in the Scottish Poor Law', in *The Search for Wealth and Stability*, ed. T. C. Smout (1979), pp. 199–217.

13. *Glasgow Chronicle*, 10, 13 January 1810.

14. Hutcheson, *Treatise*, II, pp. 183–5.

15. Hume, *Commentaries*, Vol. I, p. 495, *Scots Magazine*, Vol. 73, 1811, p. 74.

16. See, for example, Govan Society in WRH. AD 14/13/8/9 declaration of George Donaldson, 23 Dec. 1812; Kilsyth Society, WRH. AD 14/13/31 precognition of John Young, 2 February 1813.

17. WRH. AD 14/13/8/1, printed sheet headed 'Unto the Honourable His Majesty's Justices of the Peace for Lanarkshire, the Petition of the undersigned Operative Weavers, 14 March 1812'.

18. Richmond, *Narrative*, pp. 8–9.

19. Hutcheson, *Treatise*, II, pp. 186–9: see also Vol. IV, Appendix I, No. LXIV.

20. WRH. AD 14/13/8/2, Active Committee Minutes, 15 November 1808.
21. *PP*, 1810–11. *Select Committee on the Petition of the Cotton Weavers* II.
22. J. L. & B. Hammond, *The Skilled Labourer*, (1979 edn.), pp. 56–62.
23. WRH. AD 14/14/8/2, Minutes, 25 June 1808.
24. Ibid., 9 July 1808.
25. Ibid., Active Committee Minutes, 17, 23 August 1808.
26. Ibid., 10 October 1808.
27. Ibid., 4 October, 12 November, 10 December 1808.
28. Ibid., 25 October 1808.
29. Ibid., 15 November 1808.
30. Ibid., General Committee Minutes, 18, February 1809.
31. See my 'Note on the Scottish Weavers' Association 1808–13', in *Scottish Labour History Society Journal*, No. 20 (1985), pp. 39–40.
32. WRH. AD 14/13/8/2, Minutes, 3 December 1808.
33. Ibid., General Committee Minutes, 18 February, 1809, 30 March 1810.
34. Ibid., 31 May 1809.
35. *PP*, 1824, V, p. 60. *Second Report of the Select Committee on Artisans and Machinery*, evidence of Alexander Richmond.
36. WRH. AD 14/13/8/2, General Committee Minutes, 30 September 1809.
37. Ibid., 3 February 1810.
38. WRH. AD 14/13/8/1. *Articles and Regulations for the General Association of Operative Weavers in Scotland, agreed upon by a Meeting of Delegates held at Glasgow, 24 June 1808*, (Glasgow 1812).
39. WRH. AD 14/13/8/2. Corresponding Committee Minute Book, 2 August 1809.
40. Ibid., Secretary's Account Book.
41. Ibid., Corresponding Minute Book, February 1810.
42. Ibid., 3 May 1810.
43. *Scottish Labour History Society Journal*, No. 20 (1985), pp. 39–40.
44. WRH. JC 33/12, General Committee Minutes, 6 October 1810.
45. WRH. AD 14/13/8/3, Printed pamphlet dated Edinburgh, 21 February 1811.
46. *Glasgow Herald*, 2 October 1810.
47. BLPES. Webb Trade Union Collection, A/XIII/435.
48. SRA. T-TH1./8, Minutes of Trades' House of Glasgow, 3 December 1810; Minute Book of the Association of Master Cotton Spinners, 22 October 1810.
49. WRH. AD 14/13/8/3, Pamphlet dated 21 February 1811.
50. Ibid.
51. BLPES. Webb Trade Union Collection, A/III/3; WRH. AD 14/13/8/3, James Dunn, London to Thomas Smith, 25 February 1811.
52. WRH. AD 14/13/8/1, *Articles and Regulations ... as amended*, 21 August 1811.
53. *PP*, 1810–11, *Select Committee on the Petition of Handloom Weavers*, II, 6, evidence of Thomas Smith, 7 June 1811.
54. *SP*, Vol. 266, No. 14.
55. *Faculty Decisions*, Vol. XVI, Fulton & others v. Mutrie & others, 21 June 1812.
56. Richmond *Narrative*, p. 23.
57. *Faculty Decisions*, Vol. XVI, Fulton v. Mutrie.
58. WRH. AD 14/13/8/4, printed sheet headed *Associated Weavers to Apprentices, Masters, Parents & Guardians of Children*, 16 July 1812.
59. *Glasgow Chronicle*, 21 November 1812.

60. A. Colquhoun to Lord Sidmouth, 9 November 1812, in Aspinall, *Early English Trade Unions*, letter 125.

61. *Glasgow Chronicle*, 21 November 1812.

62. Richmond, *Narrative*, p. 29.

63. WRH. AD 14/13/8/1.

64. *PP*, 1824, V, *Report of the Select Committee on Artisans & Machinery* p. 510; WRH. AD 14/13/8/5.

65. WRH. AD 14/13/8/5.

66. WRH. AD 14/13/8/5, *To the Operative Cotton Weavers of Renfrewshire*, 3 Dec. 1812; J. Gillespy, Secy. Carlisle, to James Johnston, 10 Dec. 1812. See also my 'Letters from Lancashire. 1811–12', in the *Bulletin of the Society for the Study of Labour History*, No. 44 (Spring 1982), pp. 15–18.

67. SRO. RH 2/4/99, Lord Sidmouth to J. J. Dillon, 28 December 1812.

68. Ibid., *Proclamation by the Sheriff of the County of Lanark, the Magistrates of Glasgow, & the Justices of the Peace for the Lower Ward of Lanarkshire*, 14 December 1812.

69. J. J. Dillon to Lord Sidmouth, 18 December 1812, in Aspinall, *Early English Trade Unions*, letter 133.

70. WRH. AD 14/13/8/5. Printed letter, 25 November 1812.

71. *PP*, 1824, V, *Second Report of S.C. on Artisans & Machinery*, evidence of A. Richmond, pp. 71–2.

72. SRO. RH 2/4/98, Copy of letter from Lord Advocate to Rt. Hon. Richard Ryder, 6 September 1811, enclosed in A. Colquhoun to Viscount Sidmouth, 4 July 1812.

73. SRO. RH 2/4/97, J. Dunlop to Lord Advocate, 3 February 1812.

74. SRO. RH 2/4/99, A. Colquhoun to Lord Sidmouth, 21 December 1812; M. Roe, 'Maurice Margarot: A Radical in Two Hemispheres 1792–1815', in *Bulletin of the Institute of Historical Research*, XXXI, (1958), p. 68.

75. *Ibid.*, J. J. Dillon to Viscount Sidmouth, 31 December 1812.

76. *PP*, 1824, V, *Second Report of S.C. on Artisans & Machinery*, p. 62, evidence of Alexander Richmond.

77. A. Colquhoun to Viscount Sidmouth, 17 January 1813, in Aspinall, *Early English Trade Unions*, letter 137.

78. Kirkman Finlay to Viscount Sidmouth, 5 February 1813 in *Ibid.*, letter 141.

79. A. Colquhoun to Viscount Sidmouth, 13, 14, 16, 20 March 1813, in *Ibid.*, letters 142–4.

80. Gray, 'Law of Combination', p. 342.

81. *Reformers' Gazette*, (Glasgow), 30 July 1838, 'History of the Weavers' Strike by John Wilson, their Secretary'.

82. Quoted in Hamilton, *Economic History of Eighteenth Century Scotland*, p. 344.

83. Hutcheson, *Treatise*, (3rd. edn.), p. 80.

84. *PP*, 1837–38, VIII, *First Report of the Select Committee on Combination of Workmen*, Q.2621. My interpretation of the law of combination and of the events of 1812–13 differs substantially from that of W. W. Straka in 'The Law of Combination in Scotland Reconsidered', *Scottish Historical Review*, LXIV (2), October 1985, pp. 128–142.

85. *PP*, 1803–4, V, *Report from Committee on Calico Printers' Petitions*, pp. 16–18.

86. *PP*, 1806, III, *Report from Committee on the Minutes of Evidence respecting Calico Printers*, p. 4.

87. WRH. AD 14/14/16, *Calico Printers' Bond*, 15 December 1810.

88. John Neill, *Records and Reminiscences of Bonhill Parish*, (Dumbarton, 1912), p. 240.

89. *Faculty Decisions*, Vol. XVI, Appendix II, McAllister & others v. Procurator Fiscal of

Lanarkshire, 22 June 1812. This was later quashed when it was found that the Sheriff-substitute had passed sentence without the accused being present.

90. WRH. AD 14/14/16, Illegal Combination of Calico Printers, Dumbarton.

91. *PP*, 1836, XXXIV, *Report of the State of the Irish Poor in Great Britain*, p. 133.

92. Z. N. Brassay, The Cotton Spinners in Glasgow and the West of Scotland *c.* 1790–1840: A Study in Early Industrial Relations, unpublished M.Litt. thesis, University of Strathclyde, 1974, pp. 32–3.

93. SRA. Minute Book of the Association of Master Cotton Spinners, 1810–11. The Glasgow employers were also in touch with the Paisley Master Spinners who were facing similar problems.

Chapter 6

1. T. R. Gourvish, 'The Cost of Living in Glasgow in the Early Nineteenth Century', *Economic History Review*, XXV (1), February 1972, pp. 65–80; M. W. Flinn, 'Trends in Real Wages 1750–1850', *Economic History Review*, XXVII (3), 1974, pp. 395–413; P. H. Lindbent and J. G. Williamson, 'English Workers' Living Standards during the Industrial Revolution: A New Look', *Ibid.*, XXXVI, (1), 1983, p. 1–25; R. A. Cage, 'The Standard of Living Debate: Glasgow 1800–1850', *Journal of Economic History* XLIII (March 1983), pp. 175–82. For a useful discussion of the difficulties of drawing conclusions from the 'Standard of Living Debate', see R. A. Cage, *The Working Class in Glasgow 1750–1914* (1987), pp. i–xix.

2. Richmond, *Narrative*, p. 57.

3. See the introduction to the *Articles of the Lodge of Journeymen Masons, Edinburgh*, (1827) WRH. FS 1/17/91.

4. *Scots Magazine*, Vol. LXXVIII, 1816, p. 633.

5. Renwick, *Extracts*, X, 27 June, 19 November 1816, 23 January 1817.

6. Cockburn, *Memorials*, pp. 306–7.

7. *Ibid.*, p. 309.

8. *Scots Magazine*, Vol. LXXVIII, 1816, p. 873.

9. Richmond, *Narrative*, p. 53.

10. C. M. Burns, Industrial Labour and Radical Movements, pp. 205–212.

11. SRO. RH 2/4/98. Lord Advocate to Rt. Hon. Richard Ryder, 6 Sept. 1811, enclosed in letter of A. Colquhoun to Viscount Sidmouth, 4 July 1911.

12. WRH. AD 14/13/8/4.

13. R. Mitchison, 'The Creation of the Disablement Rule', *loc. cit.*; for Chalmers, see S. J. Brown, *Thomas Chalmers and the Godly Commonwealth*, (Oxford, 1982), Chapter 3.

14. Cockburn, *Memorials*, p. 270; R. A. Cage, *The Scottish Poor Law, 1745–1845*, (Edinburgh 1981).

15. J. Paterson, *Autobiographical Reminiscences*, (Glasgow, 1871), p. 64.

16. W. M. Roach, Radical Reform Movements in Scotland from 1815 to 1822, unpublished Ph.D. thesis, University of Glasgow, 1970; NLS. Melville Papers Ms. 1054 f. 154. A. Maconnachie to Viscount Melville, 15 November 1817.

17. *Glasgow Chronicle*, 14 August 1817.

18. Richmond, *Narrative*, p. 54.

19. Dundee Central Library. Lamb Collection 195 (27), *A Letter on the Subject of Parliamentary Reform addressed to the Members of the Nine Trades of Dundee and to Tradesmen in General by William Thomas Baxter, 23 November 1816*; SRO, RH 2/4, 112. A. Maconochie to Sidmouth, 24 December 1816.

20. Roach, *op. cit.*, p. 52; see also W. M. Roach, 'Alexander Richmond and the Radical Reform Movements in Glasgow 1816–17', *Scottish Historical Review*, Vol. 51, (1972), pp. 1–19.
21. WRH. AD 14/17/8, Declaration of persons accused to treason, 1817.
22. Ibid., Declaration of John Buchanan.
23. Ibid., Declaration of John Paton.
24. Richmond, *Narrative*, p. 61.
25. *Glasgow Chronicle*, 27 February 1817, cited in Roach, *op. cit.*, p. 97.
26. Richmond, *Narrative*, p. 86.
27. *Scots Magazine*, Vol. 79, 1817, p. 235.
28. *Ibid.*
29. *Scots Magazine*, Vol. 79, 1817, p. 577.
30. P. Berresford Ellis & S. Mac A'Ghobhainn, *The Scottish Insurrection of 1820*, (1970), p. 111; SRO, RH 2/4, 116, 117.
31. Roach, *op. cit.*, pp. 56–65.
32. WRH. AD 14/16/21.
33. BLPES, Webb Collection E/A/XXX/241–5. Extracts from Minute Books of the Glasgow Typographical Society. Strathclyde University Archives, T-GTS 1/1/1. Glasgow Typographical Society Minutes, first volume.
34. W. H. Fraser, 'The Glasgow Cotton Spinners 1837', in *Scottish Themes*, ed. J. Butt & J. T. Ward (1976).
35. A. Swinton, *Report of the Trial of Thomas Hunter etc. Operative Cotton Spinners in Glasgow*, (Edinburgh, 1838), p. 74.
36. WRH. AD 14/17/10.
37. Campbell, *Lanarkshire Miners*, p. 58.
38. WRH. AD 14/18/38.
39. Ibid.
40. Ibid.
41. Campbell, *Lanarkshire Miners*, p. 57.
42. Hume, *Commentaries*, I, p. 496.
43. WRH. AD 14/18/112, Colliers Tranent.
44. *Glasgow Chronicle*, 14 August 1817.
45. NLS. Melville Papers, MS 2054 ff. 172–3. John Hope to Viscount Melville, 10 August 1819 and Melville's reply.
46. *Ayr Advertiser*, 12 August 1819, quoted in Roach, *Radical Reform Movements*, p. 152.
47. James Paterson, *Autobiographical Reminiscences*, (Glasgow, 1871), p. 67.
48. *Ibid.*, p. 64.
49. *The Radical Revolt: A Description of the Glasgow Rising in 1820* (Glasgow, n.d.).
50. WRH. AD 14/19/298; *Glasgow Chronicle*, 14 Sept. 1819.
51. *Scots Magazine*, N.S., Vol V, Sept. 1819, pp. 274–5.
52. NLS. MS 2973, C. H. Hutcheson, Ms. Diary 1820–1848.
53. WRH. AD 14/19/10.
54. Roach *op. cit.*, p. 313.
55. NLS. MS. 2773, C. H. Hutcheson, Ms. Diary 1820–1848.
56. SRA. Monteith Correspondence, 23 February 1820.
57. Richmond, *Narrative*, pp. 183–4; *Scots Magazine*, N.S., VI, March 1820, pp. 280–1. Most of the radical reformers were into reformed eating. The *Black Dwarf* recommended herbal tea and herbal tobacco. P. Hollis, *The Pauper Press*, (Oxford, 1970), pp. 255–6.
58. Ellis & Mac A'Ghobhainn, *Scottish Insurrection*, pp. 138–9; Roach, *op. cit.*

59. SRA. Monteith Correspondence. Letter from Col. Norcott, 20 March 1820.

60. Ibid. Letter from Thomas Sharp, Manchester, 12 March 1820; Letter from H. Hobhouse, 22 March 1820.

61. *Glasgow Herald*, 3 April 1820; see also Hutcheson, Ms. Diary, p. 44; T. Dickson, *Capitalism and Class in Scotland* (Edinburgh, 1982), p. 40.

62. Ellis & Mac A'Ghobhainn, *Scottish Insurrection*, pp. 158–164.

63. SRA. Monteith Correspondence. Letter from Oliver Jamieson, Paisley, 3 April 1820.

64. Ibid.

65. Ellis & Mac A'Ghobhainn, *Scottish Insurrection*, pp. 166–178.

66. *Ibid.*, pp. 179–190. Numbers had dropped to about twenty-five by the time they approached the city; *A True Narrative of the Radical Rising in Strathaven ... by John Stevenson, One of the Party*, (Glasgow 1835).

67. *Ibid.*, David Gilmour. *Paisley Weavers and Other Days*, (Edinburgh 1898), p. 121.

68. *Statement of the Proprietors of Cotton Works in Glasgow and the Vicinity*, (Glasgow, 1825).

69. *Scots Magazine*, N.S. VIII, July 1820, pp. 77ff; August 1820, pp. 166ff.

70. Ellis & Mac A'Ghobhainn, *Scottish Insurrection*, pp. 25–80.

71. Roach, *op. cit.*, pp. 273–4; *Scots Magazine*, N.S. VII, August 1820, p. 176.

72. *Scots Magazine*, N.S. VII, August 1820, pp. 174–5.

73. *Ibid.*, VIII, June 1821, p. 580; Renwick, *Extracts*, X, 3 May 1821.

Chapter 7

1. *PP*, 1834, X, Q. 183. *Report from the Select Committee on Hand-Loom Weavers' Petitions*, evidence of John Kingan.

2. NLS. L.C. Folio 73 (61), (63), Glasgow Broadsheets, 1823; WRH. AD 14/23/104. Precognitions.

3. WRH. AD 14/23/241; SRA. TD 734. Volume of memoranda on criminal cases.

4. NLS. L.C. Folio 73. Glasgow Broadsheets.

5. WRH. AD 14/23/241. Letter from G. W. Sidmond, Procurator Fiscal and Crown Agent, 22 August 1823.

6. WRH. AD 14/23/239. NLS. L.C. Folio 73 (17), Glasgow Broadsheets.

7. BLPES. Webb Trade Union Collection E/A/XXXIV.

8. Brassay, *The Cotton Spinners in Glasgow*, p. 56.

9. *PP*, 1824, V, *Fifth Report of S.C. on Artisans and Machinery*, p. 477, evidence of Henry Houldsworth.

10. *Ibid.* The differing accounts of this dispute are to be found in *Observations by the Operative Cotton Spinners*, (Glasgow, 1824); *Statement of the Proprietors of the Cotton Mills in Glasgow*, (Glasgow, 1828); *Narrative of the Late Occurrences in the Cotton Mills of Glasgow*, (Glasgow, 1828).

11. Memorial of the Master Cotton Spinners of Glasgow and Neighbourhood to Robert Peel, April 1825, Aspinall, *Early English Trade Unions*, letter 414.

12. NLS. L.C. 73 (78), Glasgow Broadsheets.

13. *PP*, 1825, VI, *Report of the Select Committee on the Combination Laws*, evidence of Sheriff Depute of Lanarkshire, p. 327.

14. WRH. AD 14/24/258.

15. *PP*, 1825, IV, *Report of the Select Committee on the Combination Laws*, evidence of W. R. Robinson, p. 329.

16. R. G. Kirby & A. E. Musson, *The Voice of the People*, p. 30; Richard Price, 'Structures

of Subordination in nineteenth century British Industry', in *The Power of the Past: Essays for Eric Hobsbawm*, ed. P. Thane, G. Crossick, R. Floud, (Cambridge, 1984).

17. *Ibid.*, p. 31.

18. N. Murray, *The Scottish Handloom Weavers*, p. 191; the Articles of the General Association are given as Appendix 16 of the *Report of the Select Committee on the Combination Laws, PP*, 1825, IV.

19. *PP*, 1825, VI, *Report of the S.C. on the Combination Laws*, Appendix 16, p. 52. Articles of the General Association of Weavers in Scotland.

20. Murray, *Scottish Handloom Weavers*, pp. 192–3. WRH. AD 14/25/258.

21. Murray, *Scottish Handloom Weavers*, pp. 193–4.

22. *Ibid.*, p. 194.

23. SRO. RH 2/4/157/1. Letter from John Wilson, 27 March 1829; RH 2/4/157/32. Petition for Weavers of Lanarkshire to Peel, May 1829; RH 2/4/157/11. Petition to Peel from Paisley.

24. *PP*, 1825, V. *Report of the Select Committee on Artisans and Machinery, Fifth Report*, p. 364. WRH. AD 14/16/50.

25. Ibid., p. 363.

26. C. Gulvin, *The Scottish Hosiery and Knitwear Industry 1680–1980*. (1984), pp. 49–51.

27. D. Chapman, 'The Combination of Hecklers in the East of Scotland 1822 to 1827', *Scottish Historical Review*, Vol. 27 (1948), pp. 156–64.

28. *PP*, 1825, IV, *Report of the S.C. on Combination Laws*, p. 65, evidence of George Taylor.

29. *Ibid.*, p. 99.

30. NLS. *An Address to the Colliers of Ayrshire at the Formation of the Colliers' Association in 1824* (Kilmarnock 1824, reprinted for Ayrshire Miners' Union, n.d.).

31. *Ibid.*

32. Campbell, *Lanarkshire Miners*, p. 64. This and Dr. Campbell's paper, 'The Scots Colliers' Strikes of 1824–26: The Years of Freedom and Independence?', are the main source of this section on the miners except where indicated.

33. *PP*, 1825, IV, *Report of the S.C. on Combination Laws*, p. 643, Appendix 17 of this Report consists of the Rules of the Ayrshire Colliers' Association; 'Articles and Regulations of the Operative Colliers of Lanark, Dumbarton and Renfrewshire, 1824' are printed in *Observation on the Laws Relating to the Colliers of Scotland*, (Glasgow, 1825).

34. *PP*, 1825, IV, p. 643.

35. SRO. RH 2/4/145/192, Depositions of Susan George and Arthur George.

36. *PP*, 1825, IV, p. 636.

37. SRO. RH 2/4/144/317, 262; RH 2/4/145/185; RH 2/4/156/437, Precognitions.

38. SRO. RH 2/4/144/262. Precognition of Alex Sneddon, 9 April 1825.

39. SRO. RH 2/4/155; RH 2/4/156. 437. Sheriff Depute of Stirlingshire to Lord Advocate, 26 April 1825; SRO RH 2/4/145/221, Deposition of James Wilson, 6 April 1825; RH 2/4/147/133. Sheriff Depute of Stirlingshire to Secretary of State, 4 June 1825.

40. *Glasgow Herald*, 15 August 1825, quoted in Campbell, 'The Scots Colliers' Strike', p. 14.

41. SRO. RH 2/4/147/416, MacDonald, Depute Sheriff of Renfrewshire, 6 Oct. 1825.

42. Campbell, *Lanarkshire Miners*, p. 71.

43. *Glasgow Herald*, 15 May 1826.

44. WRH. AD 14/28/139.

45. *Glasgow Herald*, 31 Oct. 1825, cited in Campbell, 'Scots Colliers' Strikes', p. 15; see also *PP*, 1839, XLII, *Reports of the Assistant Handloom Weavers' Commissioners*, p. 16.

46. Unless otherwise stated, most of the Edinburgh material in this section comes from G.L., *Conditions of the Working Classes of Edinburgh and Leith.*

47. James Cruikshank, *Sketch of the Incorporation of Masons; and the Lodge of Glasgow St. John*, (Glasgow, 1879), pp. 76–7. For a discussion of general contracting, see R. Price, *Masters' Unions and Men*, (Cambridge 1980), pp. 22–34.

48. BLPES. Webb Trade Union Collection, E/A/XIII/436. Ibid., A/XXII/38; NLS. Bookbinders' Minutes, 11, 22 July 1829.

49. *Pioneer*, No. 20, 18 January 1834.

50. Alexander Somerville, *Autobiography of a Working Man*, pp. 58–9, 108.

51. G.L., *Conditions of the Working Classes in Edinburgh*; see also *Autobiographical Reminiscences of David Johnston an Octogenarian Scotchman*, (Chicago 1885), p. 31.

52. BLPES. Webb Trade Union Collection, E/A/XXX/223.

53. Ibid.

54. NLS. PDL 50/1 (5). *Statement of the Causes which led to the present Difference between the Master and Journeymen Bookbinders of Edinburgh*, (Edinburgh, 1825). Mitchell Library. Glasgow Bookbinders' Minutes, 26 May 1825.

55. NLS. Microfilm. Edinburgh Bookbinders' Minutes, 1825.

56. NLS. Glasgow Bookbinders' Minutes, 19 October 1825.

57. NLS. *Articles of Journeymen Bookbinders' Union Society of Glasgow*, 23 March 1831.

58. *Report of Highland Society*.

59. *Scots Magazine*, N.S., XVII, Dec. 1825, pp. 753–7.

60. R. Price, 'Structures of Subordination in British Industry', in P. Thane *et al*, *The Power of the Past*, p. 126. The attempted murder of a cotton spinner by John Kean in 1825 brought the first public use of the cat o' nine tails as punishment and encouraged the Lord Advocate to try to extend Lord Ellenborough's Act, bringing in the death penalty for attempted murder in Scotland. NLS. LC. Folio 73 (78). The Glasgow Chamber of Commerce petitioned Sir Robert Peel, the Home Secretary, for this. British Museum, Add. Mss., 40,339 f.231, Petition of Glasgow Chamber of Commerce 19 May 1825, but the Act was not finally passed until 1830.

61. BLPES. Webb Trade Union Collection, A/III, *Glasgow Chronicle*, 23 October 1824.

62. *Glasgow Chronicle*, 12 October, 18 November 1824.

63. *Scots Magazine*, N.S., XVIII, Nov. 1825, pp. 628–9.

64. The references to this Mechanics' Union are to be found in NLS. Minutes of Edinburgh Society of Journeymen Bookbinders, 3 Oct. 1825, 8 Sept. 1825, 2 May 1826, 15 Dec. 1826, 1 Feb. 1827, 29 March 1827, 3 August 1827. See also James Campbell, *A Century of Trade Unionism*, (n.d. Edinburgh).

65. Kirby & Musson, *The Voice of the People*, pp. 40–1.

66. For example, the Edinburgh Operative Painters' Society appealed to the Bookbinders, NLS Minutes of Edinburgh Society of Journeymen Bookbinders, 11, 22 July 1829.

Chapter 8

1. GL. *Conditions of the Working Classes of Edinburgh and Leith.*
2. *Ibid.*
3. *Ibid.*
4. A. Tyrrell, 'Political economy, Whiggism and the education of working-class adults in Scotland 1817–40', *Scottish Historical Review*, XLVIII, (1969), p. 151.
5. *Ibid.*, p. 155.

6. N. W. Thompson, *The People's Science. The Popular Political Economy of Exploitation and Crisis 1816–1834*, (Cambridge, 1984), p. 60.

7. For Owen's ideas, see J. Butt (ed.), *Robert Owen: Prince of Cotton Spinners*, (Newton Abbot, 1971).

8. For details of the Orbiston Community I have relied largely on Ian Donnachie's essay in Butt, *Robert Owen*; see also *Scots Magazine*, N.S. XVII (October 1825), p. 498 and XVIII (May 1826), p. 623; CU, Manchester, Owen Collection 348, A. J. Hamilton, 5 December 1830.

9. CU. Owen Collection 1A, William Wilson, Edinburgh, 15 November 1822.

10. Hamilton of Dalzell Collection, Motherwell Public Library, *Articles of Agreement of Orbiston Company, March 18, 1825*, Preamble.

11. Butt, *Robert Owen*, pp. 135–67.

12. Motherwell Public Library, Hamilton of Dalzell Collection, Advertisement headed *Orbiston October 1826*.

13. Donnachie, *loc. cit.*, pp. 154–9.

14. *Scots Magazine*, N.S. XVIII, May 1826, p. 623.

15. Some details of Campbell's life at this period are to be found in a series of letters in the *Glasgow Sentinel*, published between 5 July and 30 August 1862.

16. CU. Owen Collection 85, Alexander Campbell, Hamilton Jail, 3 October 1828.

17. *Glasgow Sentinel*, 30 August 1862.

18. W. Maxwell, *A History of Scottish Co-operation*, (1910).

19. M. W. Thompson, *People's Science*, pp. 144–6.

20. A. Campbell to Littleton, MP for Staffordshire, 26 January 1831, quoted in Maxwell, *Scottish Cooperation*, p. 59.

21. *Herald to the Trades' Advocate*, No. 26, 19 March 1831.

22. CU. Owen Collection 607, L. Pitkeithly, 3 December 1833.

23. *Glasgow Evening Post*, 6 April 1833, quoted in F. A. Montgomery, Glasgow Radicalism 1830–1850, unpublished Ph.D. thesis, University of Glasgow 1974, p. 131.

24. CU. Owen Collection 782, Alexander Campbell, Glasgow, 21 March 1836.

25. Ibid., 768, Alexander Campbell, 30 January 1836.

26. Ibid., 999, John McIntyre, Edinburgh, 16 March 1838; Ibid., 1024, George Fleming, Birmingham, 27 June 1838; *PP*. 1839 XLII, *Reports from the Assistant Handloom Weavers' Commissioners*, p. 35; J. F. C. Harrison, *Robert Owen and the Owenites in Britain and America: The Quest for the New Moral World* (1969), pp. 222, 251.

27. Maxwell, *Scottish Cooperation*, p. 66.

28. *Glasgow Argus*, 14 August 1834.

29. *Herald to the Trades Advocate*, 25 September 1830.

30. *Ibid.*, 30 October 1830.

31. *Ibid.*, 19 March 1831.

32. Dennis Chapman, 'The New Shipwright Building Company of Dundee, 1826 to 1831', *Economic History Review*, Ser. 1, X, (1940).

33. *Herald to the Trades Advocate*, 19 March 1831.

34. *Ibid.*, 28 May 1831.

35. *Aristocratic Spirit of the British People* (pamphlet successor to *Herald to the Trades Advocate*).

36. *Glasgow Sentinel*, 9 August 1862; *Herald to the Trades Advocate*, No. 28, 2 April 1831.

37. *Herald to the Trades Advocate*, No. 1, 25 September 1830.

38. John Cameron, *Calico Printing in Campsie*, (Kirkintilloch 1891), p. 15.

39. *Herald to the Trades Advocate*, 12 March 1831.

40. *Glasgow Sentinel*, 16 August 1862.

41. SRO. RH 2/4/161. Sheriff of Lanark to the Home Secretary, 18 May 1831.

42. For the argument that this was the main characteristic of the Glasgow working class in these years, see F. A. Montgomery, Glasgow Radicalism.

43. *Scots Times*, 8 January 1831, speech by Joseph Miller, cotton spinners; F. A. Montgomery, 'Glasgow and the Struggle for Parliamentary Reform, 1830–1832', *Scottish Historical Review*, LXI (2), October 1982, pp. 130–145.

44. W. M. Millar (ed.), *An Account of the Edinburgh Reform Jubilee, celebrated 10 August 1832*, (Edinburgh, 1832).

45. *Ibid.*

46. *The Trades Examiner: a Political and Literary Review*, No. 1, 17 November 1832; No. 2, 1 December 1832.

47. *Glasgow Saturday Post*, 4 August, 15 September 1832; Montgomery, Glasgow Radicalism, pp. 109–111.

48. *Glasgow Free Press*, 15 February 1834; Johnston, *History of Scottish Working Class*, p. 328.

49. *Glasgow Free Press*, 4 December 1833; *The Pioneer*, No. 20, 18 January 1834.

50. *Glasgow Free Press*, 19 February 1834; BLPES, Webb Trade Union Collection, E/A/XIII/425ff. English Masons' Fortnightly Return April 1837.

51. *Glasgow Free Press*, 8 May 1833.

52. BLPES, Webb Trade Union Collection, E/A/XI/232ff. Notes from minute books of United Joiners of Glasgow. Alexander Campbell was the first secretary.

53. Ibid., A/XI/242ff.

54. NLS. Acc. 5436. Minutes of the Edinburgh Branch of the Scottish National Union of Cabinetmakers, 1833–37; Ian MacDougall, 'The Edinburgh Branch of the Scottish National Union of Cabinet and Chairmakers, 1833–37', in *Book of the Old Edinburgh Club*, XXXIII (1), 1969.

55. *Glasgow Argus*, 22 February 1833; *The Pioneer*, No. 26, 1 March 1834; NLS. Aberdeen Female Operative Union, *Detailed Report of the Proceedings of the Operatives at Broadford Mill*, (Aberdeen, 1834).

56. Alexander Thomson, *Random Notes and Random Recollections of Drydock, or Kelvindale all now Known by the more modern name of Maryhill, 1750–1894*, (Glasgow 1895), pp. 16–7; Cameron, *Calico Printing*, pp. 25–6.

57. *Ibid.*, p. 26.

58. *Glasgow Free Press*, 5, 8 February 1834; SRO. RH 2/4, 164 Francis Jeffrey to Lord Melbourne, 5 February 1834.

59. SRO. RH 2/4/164, Jeffrey to Lord Melbourne, 5 February 1834.

60. *Glasgow Argus*, 3 July 1834; Andrew Thomson, *Random Notes*, p. 24.

61. *Glasgow Free Press*, 15, 19, 26 February, 5, 12, 15, 26 March 1834.

62. SRO. RH 2/4/164/483, Duke of Montrose to Lord Melbourne, 24 March 1834.

63. *Glasgow Free Press*, 12 November 1834.

64. Cameron, *Calico Printing*, p. 31.

65. Campbell, *Lanarkshire Miners*, pp. 77–9; WRH. AD 14/32/429; AD 14/31/302; *Glasgow Courier*, 12 June 1832, quoted in Johnston, *History of Scottish Working Class*, p. 331; *Trial of William Brown, James Henderson and Hugh Brown, Colliers before the High Court of Justiciary, Edinburgh 13 November 1832*, (Edinburgh 1832).

66. *Glasgow Free Press*, 27 July, 3, 21 August 1833.

67. *Ibid.*, 25 September 1833.

68. *Ibid.*, 15 January, 19 February 1834; SRO, John Greig, Edinburgh to Lord Advocate, 16 March 1838.

69. *Glasgow Free Press*, 9 March, 6 April 1833.

70. Murray, *Scottish Handloom Weavers*, p. 196.

71. *PP*, 1834, X, *Report of the Select Committee on Handloom Weavers' Petitions*, Q.727; *Glasgow Herald*, 19 January 1834. For a useful discussion of the issue, see M. Berg, *The Machinery Question and the Making of Political Economy, 1815–48*, (1980), pp. 235–49.

72. Paul Richards, 'The State and Early Industrial Capitalism: The Case of the Handloom Weavers', *Past and Present*, No. 83, 1979, pp. 106–7; *Weavers' Journal*, 31 October, 31 December 1835.

73. *Glasgow Argus*, 24 July 1834.

74. SRO. RH 2/4/158, John Stewart and Daniel Macaulay to Sir Robert Peel, 20 February 1830.

75. *Herald to the Trades Advocate*, 16 October, 13, 27 November 1830.

76. Montgomery, Glasgow Radicalism, pp. 235–245.

77. J. T. Ward, *The Factory Movement*, (1962), p. 75; see also his 'The Factory Reform Movement in Scotland', *Scottish Historical Review*, XLI (1962), pp. 100–123; W. Cobbett, *Tour in Scotland*, (1833), pp. 190–4.

78. G. Menzies (ed.), *History is My Witness*, p. 75; *Letters to the Rt. Hon. Lord Ashley on the Cotton Factory System and the Ten Hours Factory Bill by Kirkman Finlay, Esq.*, (Glasgow 1833).

79. *PP*, 1833, II, 263. *Factory Commission Report*; BLPES, Webb Trade Union Collection, E/A/XXXIV.

80. *Weavers' Journal*, May 1836; *PP*, 1837–38 VIII. *First Report of the Select Committee on Combinations of Workmen*, evidence of Angus Campbell, Q.989–992.

81. *Glasgow Argus*, 3 July 1834; F. A. Montgomery, 'The unstamped press: the contribution of Glasgow, 1831–36', *Scottish Historical Review*, LIX 81980), pp. 154–70.

82. *Herald to the Trades Advocate*, 14 May 1831.

83. *The Pioneer*, No. 26, 1 March 1834.

84. *The Tradesman*, 12 April 1834.

85. Johnston, *History of the Scottish Working Class*, p. 385.

86. *Glasgow Courier*, 22 April 1834; *Glasgow Argus*, 21 April 1834.

87. *Ibid.* W. H. Oliver, Organisations and Ideas Behind the Efforts to Achieve a General Union of the Working Classes in England in the Early 1830s unpublished D.Phil. thesis, Oxford University 1954, p. 228.

88. *Argus*, 22 February 1833; *The Pioneer*, No. 26, 1 March 1834.

89. *Glasgow Free Press*, 25 September 1833, quoting *The Liberator*.

90. *Edinburgh Evening Courant*, 21 April 1834; MacDougall, 'Edinburgh Cabinetmakers', p. 23.

91. *Scotsman*, 6, 10 September 1834.

92. NLS. Aberdeen Female Operative Union, *Detailed Report of the Proceedings of the Operatives at Broadford Mill*, (Aberdeen, 1834); *Ibid.*, *Third Report ... containing remarks on the improper interference of the clergy, correspondence, etc.*, (Aberdeen, 1834).

93. *Dundee Advertiser*, 13 June 1834, quoted in Houston, 'Labour Relations in Scottish Agriculture', pp. 36–7.

94. *Glasgow Argus*, 15 September 1834.

Chapter 9

1. *Glasgow Courier*, 3, 24, 26 March 1836.
2. Kirby & Musson, *The Voice of the People*, pp. 85–92.
3. *PP*, 1837–38, VIII. *First Report of Select Committee on Combinations of Workmen*, Qs. 267–8, evidence of J. Houldsworth.
4. SRO. AD 14/39, Declaration by William Houldsworth, 10 March 1838.
5. SRO. AD 14/39, George Salmond to D. Cleghorn, 29 August 1837; *SC on Combinations*, Q. 715, evidence of Angus Campbell.
6. *Factory Enquiry Commission 1833, First Report*, 126; *Second Report*, 39.
7. 'Practical Working of Trades' Unions', *Blackwood's Edinburgh Magazine*, XLIII, (March 1838), p. 288.
8. *SC on Combinations*, Qs, 1087, 1094, evidence of James McNish.
9. *Ibid.*
10. The strike and its background are discussed in W. H. Fraser, 'The Glasgow Cotton Spinners, 1837', in *Scottish Themes*, ed. J. Butt & J. T. Ward, (Edinburgh 1976).
11. *Monthly Liberator*, III, 9 June 1838.
12. Fraser, 'Glasgow Cotton Spinners', p. 90; *SC on Combinations*, Qs. 1255–61, evidence of James McNish; *Ibid.*, Q. 789, evidence of Angus Campbell.
13. *Ibid.*, Q. 335, evidence of J. Houldsworth; *Ibid.*, Q. 452, evidence of Charles Todd.
14. *Ibid.*, Qs. 1692–1709, evidence of Andrew Gemmill.
15. A. Swinton, *Report of the Trial of Thomas Hunter, Peter Hacket, Richard McNeil, James Gibb & William McLean, Operative Cotton Spinners in Glasgow* . . ., (Edinburgh, 1838); *Scots Times*, 10, 17 June, 5 July 1837.
16. *The Northern Liberator*, 13 January 1838.
17. For the arrest and trial, see W. H. Fraser, 'The Glasgow Cotton Spinners', in *History is my Witness*, ed. G. Menzies (BBC, 1976), pp. 67–91.
18. A. Alison, *Some Accounts of my Life and Writings: An Autobiography*, edited by Lady Alison (Edinburgh, 1883), p. 374.
19. *Ibid.*, pp. 373–6.
20. *Ibid.*, p. 300.
21. BLPES, Webb Trade Union Collection E/A/XIII/425ff, *English Masons' Fortnightly Return*, April 1837; *Glasgow Courier*, March 1837.
22. *Scots Times*, 3 December 1836.
23. Alison, *Autobiography*, p. 300.
24. NLS. Ms. 833, Minutes of the Edinburgh Lodge of Friendly Society of Operative Carpenters and Joiners, February, March, May 1837; NLS. Ac. 5436(2), Minutes of Edinburgh Cabinetmakers' Society May–August, 1837.
25. SRO. GD 1/42/2/21. *Memorial for the Proprietors of Capledrae Colliery in the County of Fife, 1837*; Campbell, *Lanarkshire Miners*, pp. 80–3.
26. A. MacGeorge, *The Bairds of Gartsherrie*, (Glasgow 1875), pp. 67–8.
27. Alison, *Autobiography*, p. 390; *PP*, 1839, XLII. Report from *Assistant Handloom Weavers' Commission*, p. 530.
28. Swinton, *Report of the Trial*, p. 2.
29. SRO. Memo: Glasgow Cotton Spinners, 8 February 1838; Precognition of Robert Christie, 12 February 1838.
30. Swinton, *Report of the Trial, passim*; 'Practical Working of Trades' Unions', pp. 294–5; *PP*, 1837–38 VIII, *Report of the Select Committee on Combinations of Workmen*, pp. 302–3.

31. Swinton, *Report of the Trial.*

32. *PP*, 1839 XLII, *Reports from the Assistant Handloom Weavers' Commissioners*, p. 51; *Northern Star*, 2 September 1843.

33. *SC on Combinations*, Qs. 1986–7, evidence of A. Alison.

34. J. Dunlop, *Artificial Drinking Usages in North Britain* (Greenock, 1836).

35. S. Pollard, 'The Ethics of the Sheffield Outrages', *Transactions of the Hunter Archaeological Society*, VII (3), 1953–54.

36. *SC on Combinations*, Qs. 1533, evidence of John McCaffer; *Ibid.*, Q. 1181, evidence of James McNish.

37. SRO. Declaration of James Todd, 11 August 1837, 23 May 1838; see also *SC on Combinations*, Qs. 2825, evidence of A. Gemmill; *Monthly Liberator*, No. 3, 9 June 1838.

38. *Ibid.*

39. R. Harrison (ed.), *Independent Collier, The Coal Miner as Archetypal Proletarian Reconsidered* (1978).

40. For some discussion of those developments, see W. Lazonick, 'Industrial relations and technical change: the case of the self-acting mule', *Cambridge Journal of Economics*, 1979 (3), pp. 231–62.

41. John Foster, *Class Struggle and the Industrial Revolution: Early Industrial Capitalism in Three English Towns*, (1974), p. 150.

42. *New Liberator*, 6 January 1838; *Glasgow Argus*, 30 November 1837, 25 January 1838.

43. *Northern Star*, 6 January 1838.

44. 'Practical Working of Trades' Unions', p. 301.

45. *SC on Combinations*, Q. 2825, evidence of Gemmill.

46. SRO. Summons by Andrew Thomson, Victualler, Bridgeton against the members of the Association of Operative Cotton Spinners of Glasgow and Neighbourhood, 25 April, 1838; George Salmond to the Lord Advocate, 7 May 1838; *Glasgow Argus*, 10 May 1838; Bill Chamber Process, Second Division, 26 June 1838, William Shanks and others v. Andrew Thomson.

47. *Glasgow Argus*, 7 May 1838.

48. Johnston, *History of Scottish Working Class*, p. 248.

Chapter 10

1. For this, see R. Mitchison, 'Patriotism and National Identity in Eighteenth Century Scotland', in *Nationality and the Pursuit of National Independence*, ed. T. W. Moody, (Belfast, 1978).

2. I. G. C. Hutchison, *A Political History of Scotland 1832–1924: Parties Elections and Issues*, (Edinburgh, 1986), esp. Chapter 2.

3. In T. Dickson, (ed.), *Scottish Capitalism*, p. 205.

4. Quoted in J. D. Young, *The Rousing of the Scottish Working Class*, (1979), p. 87.

Select Bibliography

A Note on Primary Sources

The indispensable guide to primary source material on Scottish Labour History is Ian MacDougall's *Catalogue of Some Labour Records in Scotland*, (Scottish Labour History Society, 1978) and there seems little point in replicating the relevant references in that. There are probably still cases involving trade societies to be identified in the unextracted processes of the Court of Session held in West Register House. Among the most useful 'finds' in these were some of the minutes and other records of the Woolcombers' Society in Aberdeen between 1755 and 1762, as well as many of the tailors' cases. More information about labour relations in the eighteenth century can be garnered from the printed Court of Session Papers, the most complete set of which is to be found in the Signet Library in Edinburgh.

Kenneth J. Logue, in *Popular Disturbances in Scotland, 1780–1815*, pp. 218–221, has a useful guide to the criminal records which I used. In the Lord Advocate's Department's Papers in West Register House are records and information on the Weavers' Combination 1808–13, the Calico Printers 1809–14, the Glasgow Shoemakers and Hawick Stocking Makers 1816, the Ayrshire Colliers 1817, and the Glasgow Cotton Spinners, as well as on various riots and disturbances. The main sources for political radicalism are the Home Office Papers, Scotland, held on photostats in the Scottish Record Office. Other manuscript material used is cited in the notes.

A number of Parliamentary Papers have extensive material on Scottish labour in the early nineteenth century. These include:

PP 1803–4 V, *Report and Minutes of Evidence of the Committee on Petitions of Calico Printers*
PP 1810–11 II, *Report of the Select Committee on the Petitions of the Cotton Weavers*
PP 1824 V, *Reports of the Select Committee on Artizans and Machinery*
PP 1825 IV, *Reports of the Select Committee on the Combination Laws*
PP 1834 X, *Report of the Select Committee on Handloom Weavers' Petitions*
PP 1835 XIII, *Report from the Select Committee on Handloom Weavers' Petitions*
PP 1837–38 VIII, *Reports of the Select Committee on Combinations of Workmen*
PP 1839 XLII, *Report from the Assistant Handloom Weavers' Commissioners: South of Scotland*

Newspapers and Periodicals

Edinburgh Advertiser
Edinburgh Evening Courant
Gentlemen's Magazine
Glasgow Argus
Glasgow Courier
Glasgow Herald
Glasgow Journal
Glasgow Saturday Post

Glasgow Mercury
Herald to the Trades Advocate
The Liberator
The Pioneer
Scots Magazine
Scots Times
The Scotsman
The Trades Examiner (Edinburgh)
Weavers' Journal

Secondary Works

Alison, A., *Some Accounts of My Life and Writings: An Autobiography edited by Lady Alison* (Edinburgh 1883)
Armet, Helen, *Extracts from the Records of the Burgh of Edinburgh* (Edinburgh 1967)
Aspinall, A., *Early English Trade Unions* (1949)
Bain, E., *Merchant and Craft Guilds: A History of the Aberdeen Incorporated Trades* (Aberdeen 1887)
Berg, Maxine, *The Machinery Question and the Making of Political Economy, 1815–1848* (1980)
Butt, John (ed.), *Robert Owen, Prince of Cotton Spinners* (Newton Abbot 1971)
Cage, R. A., *The Working Class in Glasgow, 1750–1914* (1987)
Campbell, A., *The Lanarkshire Miners: A Social History of their Trade Unions 1775–1874* (Edinburgh 1979)
Campbell, R. H., *Carron Company* (Edinburgh 1961)
Campbell, R. H., *Scotland since 1707, The Rise of an Industrial Society* (Oxford 1975) (second edition, Edinburgh)
Campbell, W., *History of the Incorporation of Cordiners in Glasgow* (Glasgow 1893)
Colville, J. (ed.), *Letters of John Cockburn of Ormiston to his Gardener, 1727–44* (Edinburgh, Scottish History Society 1894)
Cruikshank, J., *Sketch of the Incorporation of Masons; and the Lodge of Glasgow St John* (Glasgow 1879)
Dickson, T. (ed.), *Capital and Class in Scotland* (Edinburgh 1982)
Dickson, T. (ed.), *Scottish Capitalism* (1980)
Dodson, C. R., *Masters and Journeymen: a Prehistory of Industrial Relations, 1717–1800* (1980)
Duckham, B. F., *A History of the Scottish Coal Industry, Vol. I: 1700–1815* (Newton Abbot 1967)
Durie, A., *The Scottish Linen Industry in the Eighteenth Century* (Edinburgh 1979)
Ellis, P. Berresford & Mac A'Ghobhainn, S., *The Scottish Insurrection of 1820* (1970)
Firth, C. H. (ed.), *Scotland and the Protectorate* (Edinburgh, Scottish History Society 1899)
Flinn, M. W. *et al*, *Scottish Population History* (Cambridge 1977)
Galton, F. W., *Select Documents Illustrating the History of Trade Unionism, I: The Tailoring Trade* (1896)
Gillespie, S. C., *Scottish Typographical History* (Glasgow 1953)
Gilmour, D., *Paisley Weavers and Other Days* (Edinburgh 1898)
Gulvin, C., *The Scottish Hosiery and Knitwear Industry* (Edinburgh 1984)
Hamilton, H., *An Economic History of Scotland in the Eighteenth Century* (Oxford 1963)

Harrison, J. F. C., *Robert Owen and the Owenites in Britain and America: The Quest for a New Moral World* (1969)
Harrison, R. (ed.), *Independent Collier. The Coal Miner as Archetypal Proletarian Reconsidered* (1978)
Hector, W., *Selections from the Judicial Records of Renfrewshire* (Paisley 1878)
Horne, E. A., *The Conditions of Labour in Scotland in the Seventeenth Century* (St Andrews 1907)
Johnston, D., *Autobiographical Reminiscences of David Johnston, an Octogenarian Scotchman* (Chicago 1885)
Johnston, Thomas, *A History of the Working Classes in Scotland* (Glasgow 1920)
Kirby, R. G. & Musson, A. E., *The Voice of the People. John Doherty, 1798–1854. Trade unionist, radical and factory reformer* (Manchester 1975)
Leeson, R. A., *Travelling Brothers, the six centuries' road from craft fellowship to trade unionism* (1979)
Lenman, Burce, *An Economic History of Modern Scotland* (1977)
Logue, K. J., *Popular Disturbances in Scotland, 1780–1815* (Edinburgh 1979)
Lumsden, H. & Henderson Aitken, P., *History of the Hammermen of Glasgow* (Paisley 1912)
Lumsden, H., *Records of the Trades House of Glasgow, 1713–1777* (Glasgow 1934)
MacGeorge, A., *The Bairds of Gartsherrie* (Glasgow 1875)
Malcolm, C. A., *The Minutes of the Justices of the Peace of Lanarkshire, 1707–1723* (Edinburgh, Scottish History Society 1931)
Marwick, W. H., *A Short History of Labour in Scotland* (1967)
Mathieson, W. L., *The Awakening of Scotland* (Glasgow 1910)
Maxwell, W., *A History of Scottish Co-operation* (1910)
Meikle, H. W., *Scotland and the French Revolution* (Glasgow 1912)
Menzies, Gordon (ed.), *History is My Witness* (1976)
Mitchison, Rosalind, *A History of Scotland* (1970)
Mitchison, Rosalind, *Life in Scotland* (1978)
Mitchison, Rosalind, *Lordship and Patronage: Scotland, 1603–1745* (1983)
Murray, Norman, *The Scottish Handloom Weavers* (Edinburgh 1978)
Neill, J., *Records and Reminiscences of Bonhill Parish* (Dumbarton 1912)
Paterson, J., *Autobiographical Reminiscences* (Glasgow 1871)
Prothero, I., *Artisans and Politics in Early Nineteenth Century London* (1979)
Renwick, R., *Extracts from the Records of the Burgh of Glasgow* (Glasgow 1909)
Richmond, A. B., *Narrative of the Condition of the Manufacturing Population* (1824)
Rule, John, *The Experience of Labour in Eighteenth Century Industry* (1980)
Smith, Annette M., *The Three United Trades of Dundee: Masons, Wrights and Slaters* (Dundee: Abertay Historical Society 1987)
Smout, T. C., *A History of the Scottish People, 1560–1830*
Thompson, N. W., *The People's Science: the Popular Political Economy of Exploitation and Crisis, 1816-1834* (Cambridge 1984)
Thomson, A., *Random Notes and Random Recollections of Drydock or Kelvindale all now known by the more modern name of Maryhill, 1750–1894* (Glasgow 1895)
Ward, J. T., *The Factory Movement* (1962)
Whetstone, A. E., *Scottish County Government in the Eighteenth and Nineteenth Centuries* (Edinburgh 1981)
Young, J. D., *The Rousing of the Scottish Working Class* (1979)
Younger, J., *Autobiography of John Younger, Shoemaker, St. Boswells* (Kelso 1891)

Articles and Essays

(Alison, A.), 'Practical Working of Trades Unions', *Blackwoods Edinburgh Magazine* XLIII (March 1838)

Alison, A., 'Trade Unions and Strikes', *Edinburgh Review* LXVII (April 1838)

(Anon.), 'Slavery in Scotland', *Edinburgh Review* 189 (January 1899)

Cage, R. A., 'The Standard of Living Debate in Glasgow, 1800–1850', *Journal of Economic History* XLIII (March 1983)

Chapman, D., 'The Combination of Hecklers in the East of Scotland, 1822 to 1827', *Scottish Historical Review* XXVII (1948)

Chapman, D., 'The New Shipwright Building Co. of Dundee, 1826 to 1831', *Economic History Review* Ser. 1 X (1940)

Cramond, W., 'The Hammermen of Banff', *Transactions of the Banffshire Field Club, 1902–3*

Fraser, W. Hamish, 'Glasgow Cotton Spinners, 1837', in *Scottish Themes*, edited by J. Butt and J. T. Ward (Edinburgh 1978)

Fraser, W. Hamish, 'Letters from Lancashire, 1811–12', *Bulletin of the Society for the Study of Labour History* 44 (Spring 1982)

Fraser, W. Hamish, 'Note on the Scottish Weavers' Association, 1808–13', *Journal of the Scottish Labour History Society* 20 (1985)

Gourvish, T. R., 'The Cost of Living in Glasgow in early Nineteenth Century', *Economic History Review* XXV (1) (February 1972)

Gray, J. L., 'The Law of Combination in Scotland', *Economica* VII (1938)

Houston, G., 'Labour Relations in Scottish Agriculture before 1870', *Agricultural History Review* VI (1958)

Houston, Rab, 'Coal, class and culture: Labour relations in a Scottish mining community 1650–1750', *Social History* VIII (January 1983)

Lythe, S. G. E., 'The Tayside Meal Mobs, 1772–1773', *Scottish Historical Review* XLVI (April 1967)

Marwick, W. H., 'Tailors of the Canongate', *Book of the Old Edinburgh Club* XIX (1933)

Mitchison, Rosalind, 'The Creation of the Disablement Rule in the Scottish Poor Law', in *The Search for Wealth and Stability*, edited by T. C. Smout (1979)

Mitchison, Rosalind, 'Patriotism and National Identity in Eighteenth Century Scotland', in *Nationality and the Pursuit of National Independence*, edited by T. W. Moody (Belfast 1978)

Montgomery, F. A., 'Glasgow and the Struggle for Parliamentary Reform, 1830–32', *Scottish Historical Review* LXI (October 1982)

Montgomery, F. A., 'The Unstamped Press: the Contribution of Glasgow', *Scottish Historical Review* LIX (April 1980)

MacDougall, Ian, 'The Edinburgh Branch of the Scottish National Union of Cabinet and Chairmakers, 1833–37', *Book of the Old Edinburgh Club* XXIII (1969)

Richards, Paul, 'The State and Early Industrial Capitalism: The Case of the Handloom Weavers', *Past and Present* 83 (1979)

Roach, W. M., 'Alexander Richmond and the Radical Reform Movement in Glasgow 1816–17', *Scottish Historical Review* LI (1972)

Smith, T. B., 'Master and Servant', in *An Introduction to Scottish Legal History* (Edinburgh, Stair Society 1958)

Smith, T. B., 'Master and Servant', *Juridical Review* (1958)

Smout, T. C., 'Lead mining in Scotland', in *Essays in Scottish Business History*, edited by P. Payne (1967)

Straka, W. W., 'The Law of Combination in Scotland Reconsidered', *Scottish Historical Review* LXIV (October 1985)
Ward, J. T., 'The Factory Movement in Scotland', *Scottish Historical Review* XLI (1962)
Whatley, C. A., 'From Servitude to Subjugation? Legal Records, Labour Relations and Colliers 'Emancipation' in the Eighteenth Century', *Scottish Records Association, Conference Report* No. 5 (March 1986)
Wood, M., 'Edinburgh Poll Tax Returns', *Book of the Old Edinburgh Club* XXV (1945)
Wood, M., 'The Hammermen of the Canongate', *Book of the Old Edinburgh Club* XIX (1933)

Theses

Brassay, Z. N., The Cotton Spinners in Glasgow and the West of Scotland c.1790–1840: a Study in Early Industrial Relations, M.Litt., University of Strathclyde 1974.
Brims, J. D., The Scottish Democratic Movement in the Age of the French Revolution, Ph.D., University of Edinburgh 1983
Burns, C. M., Industrial Labour and Radical Movements in Scotland in the 1790s, M.Sc., University of Strathclyde 1971
Montgomery, F. A., Glasgow Radicalism 1830–1850, Ph.D., University of Glasgow 1974
Roach, W. M., Radical Reform Movements in Scotland from 1815 to 1822, Ph.D., University of Glasgow 1970

Index

Aberdeen, 9–10, 31, 34, 37, 43, 46, 51, 65, 67, 74, 87, 97, 131, 141–2, 149
Acts of Parliament, regulating rates of pay and hours of work in burghs (1424) 26, 1605, 1606, (1607) 4; by JPs (1617) 6, 53; appointing commissioners to erect manufactories (1641) 4, 5; abolition of heritable jurisdictions (1747) 6, forbidding Weavers' Incorporations charging entry money (1751) 59; Colliers' Emancipation Act (1775) 72–4; Corn Law (1791) 70; Militia Act (1797) 70–1; Colliers' Emancipation Act (1799) 73–4; Combination Laws (1799, 1800) 81–2, 84, 89, 119, 128; Arbitration Act (1802) 85; Bank Act (1819) 124; Six Acts (1819) 109; Combination Laws (1824–25) 114, 119, 121, 123, 127–8, 161, 169
Agricultural Improvement, 11
Agricultural Labourers, 149 (see also ploughmen and farm servants)
Airdrie, 123, 145, 156
Alison, Archibald, Sheriff of Lanarkshire, 154–6, 161–2, 170
America, United States of, 13, 15–6, 105, 151–2
Anderston, 34, 116, 143–4
Angus, 13, 32
Apprenticeship, 9, 18, 22–3, 26, 47, 59, 87, 90, 92, 96–7, 105, 119, 124, 126–7, 131, 137, 142–4, 152, 161, 163, 167
Armadale, Lord, 83
Arnot, Peter, shoemaker, 72, 82
Arthur, Alexander, cotton mill manager, 154, 157
Artisans, see Tradesmen
Assessment of Wages, see Wage Regulation
Auchtermuchty, 57
Australia, 112, 115
Ayr, 5, 84, 109, 111, 122, 136
Ayr Bank, 13, 61
Ayrshire, 7, 8, 32, 59, 84, 86–7, 106–8, 121–2, 145

Baird, John, radical, 111–2, 169
Baird, William & Co, Gartsherrie, 16, 156
Bakers, 23, 49, 63, 125–6, 140
Balfour, James of Pilrigg, 52
Banff, 131
Bannatyne, Lord, 91
Barbers, 21, 46
Barony Kirk, 104
Barr *v* Carr, 59
Barrhead, 86
Barrowmen, 7, 8, 51
Basilikon Doron, 17, 19
Belfast, 119, 154
Benbow, William, 148
Black Dwarf, 108
Blacksmiths, 34, 63, 90, 111, 128, 131, 138, 144
Bleaching, 31
Bolton, 86, 90
Bonnymuir, 110, 115
Bookbinders, 29, 30, 31, 111, 126–7
Boyle, Lord, 91, 96, 158
Brassfounders, 34
Braxfield, Lord, 68–9
Brayshaw, Joseph, radical, 109
Brechin, 61
Breweries, 11
Bricklayers, 141, 156
Bridgeton, 108, 111, 154
Brotherhoods, 6
Brushworkers, 34, 148
Buchanan, James and Archibald, cotton masters, 14
Building, 13–6, 27, 50, 53, 57, 114, 124, 130–1, 140
Burghs, 9, 17, 18, 20, 21, 55
Burnett, John, writer on law, 84, 96

Cabinetmakers, 21, 28–9, 54, 64, 89, 90, 103, 111, 128, 131, 141, 156
Calico Printers, 96–7, 128, 142–3, 148
Calton, 20–1, 62, 72, 86, 101, 103–4, 116
Camlachie, 62, 103
Campbell, Alan, 1, 73, 160, 170
Campbell, Alexander, 134–6, 140, 146–8, 155
Carlile, Richard, 108–9
Carlisle, 88, 119, 121
Carpenters and Joiners, 28, 34, 90, 124, 128, 131, 141, 147, 156
Carron Company, 12–14, 73, 110, 123
Cartwright, Major John, 95, 101, 108
Carvers and Gilders, 34, 128
Catrine, 13, 57, 114
Chadwick, Edwin, 159
Chalmers, Thomas, 102
Charitable Boxes, 41–2, 70, 81, 100, 164
Chartists, 140, 159, 161, 168

Church of Scotland, 24
Clerk, Sir John, 8
Clockmakers, 34
Coachmakers, 34
Coalmining, 14, 15, 57, 72–4, 106, 114, 123 (see also Miners)
Cobbett, William, 103–5, 108, 146, 150
Cockburn, Archibald, 52
Cockburn, Henry, 70, 84, 104, 108
Cockburn of Ormiston, 11
Colliers, see Miners
Combination, 81, 83, 89, 93, 95, 103, 106–7, 115, 119, 126, 162, 165 (see also Societies)
Compositors, see Printers
Confectioners, 34
Cooperation, Cooperative Societies, 85, 134–5, 142, 145, 150, 167
Coopers, 43
Coppersmiths, 34
Cordiners, see Shoemakers
Corn Laws, 15, 61–2, 65, 68, 139
Cotton, 13–15, 32, 91; manufacturers 17; spinning mills 57, 110–1, 129–30, 132–3, 146, 159, 161
Cotton spinners, 85, 90, 97, 103, 105–6, 110, 116–8, 128–30, 146–8, 151–9, 160–1, 166
Court of Session, 2, 5, 18, 21, 30, 42–4, 48–9, 53, 55–6, 59, 60, 64–5, 72, 74–9, 81, 91–2, 127
Craftsmen, see Tradesmen
Cullen, Lord, 18, 23
Cupar, 17
Cutlers, 34

Dale, David, of New Lanark, 132
Dalgleish, Robert, calico printer, 138
Deanston, 13, 57, 86, 94, 114
Dempster, George, MP, 61
Denny, 97
Derbyshire, 93
Desuetude, 4
Dingwall, Alexander, stocking manufacturer, 46–8
Discharge Certificate, 64, 74, 89
Dixon, William, coalmaster, 107, 123, 156
Document, 97, 116, 150
Doherty, John, 137, 146, 151
Drinking, 117–8, 125, 142, 159
Dumfriesshire, 57, 66, 121
Dunbartonshire, 7, 68, 79, 111–2, 122, 128
Dundas, Henry, 1st Viscount Melville, 52, 65, 67
Dundas, Robert, 2nd Viscount Melville, 69, 108
Dundee, 10, 20, 32, 37, 40, 46, 63, 65–9, 71, 74, 103, 121, 137, 141, 146, 148–9
Dunfermline, 32, 66, 87
Dunlop, Colin, coalmaster, 123, 138
Dunlop, James, cotton manufacturer, 14, 26, 94, 106, 117–8, 153
Duns, 26
Duntocher, 112, 152–3
Dyers, 34

Edinburgh, 11, 12, 18, 24, 29, 34, 37–8, 40–1, 43–4, 49, 51, 57, 61–3, 68–9, 72, 77, 79, 80, 88, 90, 93, 101–2, 104, 121, 131, 135–6, 141, 157, 166; New Town 13–15, 27; population 14, 123; Canongate 18, 19, 40–1, 53, 124; JPs 8, 10, 78; Tailors' Incorporation 21, 23–4, 75; cabinetmakers 29; wrights 29, 70; bookbinders 31, 126–7, 129; printers 35, 78, 126–7; tailors 41–3, 45, 48, 55–6, 82, 125, 164, 166; papermakers 82; colliers 106, 121–2; plasterers 124; bakers 125–6; School of Arts 132; Trades' Union 139
Edinburgh Review, 132
Eglinton, Earl of, 5
Embezzlement of yarn, 33, 119
Emigration, 13, 117, 159
Employers, 3, 23, 26, 39, 47, 50, 51, 55, 63, 64, 71–3, 88–9, 98, 106–7, 111, 114, 116–8, 120, 123, 125, 127, 129, 131, 140–2, 144–6, 150, 152–5, 164
Engineers, 144
England, 4, 7, 9, 11, 12, 15, 19, 35, 46–7, 57, 67, 79, 82, 84, 86, 94, 141, 165

Falkirk, 110–1, 122, 141
Farm Servants, see Agricultural Labourers and Ploughmen
Fenwick weavers, 59, 60–1
Ferguson, Adam, 79
Fife, 13, 14, 16, 32, 87, 123, 156
Finlay, Kirkman, 95, 104, 146
Fishermen, 4
Fletcher of Saltoun, Alexander, 5
Forth & Clyde Canal, 13, 14, 169
Framework knitters, 120
France, 13–15, 59, 67, 76, 101, 155
French Revolution, 65–71, 155
Friendly Societies, 55, 76, 85, 98, 100, 105, 123, 127, 141
Friends of the People, 65–6, 68

Galashiels, 31
Galloway, 5
Gartsherrie Iron Works, 16, 156
Gemmill, Andrew, lawyer, 143, 154, 162
Gerrald, Joseph, radical, 69, 101
Glasgow, 6, 11, 14, 15, 17, 19, 31–4, 38, 43, 57, 63, 66, 68–9, 81, 84, 95, 108–110, 115, 117, 124–5, 135–7, 140, 143, 145, 159, 166; population 10, 14, 123; hammermen 20, 35; tailors 20, 21, 24, 43; cordiners 22; bakers 23;

shoemakers 26, 70–1, 74, 84, 105; cabinetmakers 29; weavers 59, 61, 86, 87, 90, 92, 100, 102, 107; Chamber of Commerce 62, 132; wrights 74; stonemasons 89, 140–1; calico printers 97; cotton spinners 98, 105, 106, 110, 118–9, 128, 130, 152–5, 159, 166; Typographical Society 105, 126; Town Council 17, 108; radicals 110–1; printers 126; bookbinders 127; associated trades 128–9; Mechanics' Institute 132; Cooperative bazaar 135; bricklayers 141; powerloom weavers 146; Association for Protection of Labour 147

Glasgow Chronicle, 128
Glasgow Herald, 109–111
Glasgow Mercury, 13
Gorbals, 20
Govan, 86, 135
Grand National Consolidated Trades Union, 148
Grangemouth, 68
Granger, James, weaver, 62, 95
Guilds, 17, 19, 40, 41 (see also Incorporations)
Gunsmiths, 34

Hackett, Peter, cotton spinner, 146, 155–6, 158
Hamilton, 26, 101
Hamilton, A. J. of Dalzell, 133
Hammermen, 163
Hampden Clubs, 95, 101, 103
Handloom weaving, see Weavers
Hardie, Andrew, radical, 109, 111–2, 169
Hawick, 120
Herald to the Trades Advocate, 136–9, 140, 146–7
Hermand, Lord, 77, 83
High Court of Justiciary, 62, 82, 116, 128, 143, 157
Highlands, 15, 167, 168
Highland Society, 127
Hobsbawm, E. J., 46
Hodgkin, Thomas, 138
Holidays, 34, 156
Horner, Leonard, 132
Houldsworth, Henry, cotton manufacturer, 177–8, 128, 144, 151, 160
Hours of Work, 30, 34, 37, 38, 46, 50–1, 63–4, 74, 85, 150
House of Call, 3, 45, 52, 63, 75–6, 164–5
Hull, 71
Hume, Joseph, MP, 129, 138
Hume's *Commentaries*, 84
Hunt, Henry, 108, 150
Hunter, Thomas, cotton spinner, 155–6, 158
Huskisson, William, MP, 128
Hutcheson, Gilbert, writer on law, 84, 96

Immigrant workers, 5, 27, 31, 51
Incorporations, 17–19, 21–2, 38, 43, 46, 51–2, 54, 58–9, 81, 89; weavers 18; Banff Hammermen 18; Canongate Tailors 19; Glasgow Hammermen 20, 35; Dundee Weavers 20; Glasgow Bakers 21; Cordiners 26; Glasgow Weavers 32, 59, 86; Edinburgh Tailors 40, 42, 44, 49, 52, 63; Aberdeen Wrights 43; Glasgow Wrights 46; Brechin Weavers 6
Ireland, 15, 79, 82
Irish, 16, 94, 97, 117, 122–3, 155, 167–8, 170
Iron works, 14, 57, 106, 123, 156, 164

Jacobite Rebellion, 12
Jeffrey, Francis, Whig lawyer, 83–4, 95, 104, 128
Joiners, see Carpenters
Journeymen, 3, 19, 20–7, 30–1, 35, 38–9, 40, 42–3, 45, 48, 50–1, 53, 64, 71, 76, 89, 105, 125, 164
Justices of the Peace, 6–10, 44, 49, 52–3, 60, 64–5, 70, 72–4, 76–9, 82–4, 91–3, 96–8, 108, 120, 137

Kilmarnock, 31, 87, 97, 108, 122
Kilsyth, 145
Kincardine, 46
King's Freemen, 21
Kirkcaldy, 37
Kirkintilloch, 67–8

Labourers, 7, 15, 36, 69, 108, 123, 149, 151, 156
Laissez-faire, 102, 165
Lanarkshire, 7, 8, 74, 86–7, 136, 139, 151, 156, 160; cotton mills 14; iron ore 16; weavers 32, 58, 95; wages 37; sheriffs 68, 89, 91–2, 113, 116, 128; miners 74, 106, 119, 122, 143–4
Lancashire, 16, 35, 85, 90, 93, 124, 130, 140, 142, 146, 151–3
Larkhall, 135
Lasswade, 8, 82
Lathsplitters, 28, 34, 131
Leadhills, 4
Leith, 5, 43, 76, 141
Lennoxtown, 135
Liberator, 140, 150, 155
Lindesay, Sir Patrick, 9, 19, 20, 40
Linen, 7, 11–3, 15–6, 31–3, 46, 57, 61
Linlithgow, 92, 97
Liverpool, 141, 148
London, 10, 11, 26, 31, 35, 44, 50, 52, 103, 124, 127, 133, 148, 159
London Corresponding Society, 95
Lothians, 32, 73–4, 82, 106, 109, 123, 156
Loyal Reformers' Gazette, 138–9
Luddism, 93–4

McAulay, Daniel, powerloom weaver, 136, 138–9, 146
McCulloch, JP, 132
McGowan, Patrick, cotton spinner, 146–7, 151
MacDuff, Patrick, master tailor, 42–3
MacIntyre, John, weaver, 86–7
McKenzie, Peter, publisher, 138
McKimmie, William, weaver, 95
MacLeod, Gilbert, publisher, 109, 115
Manchester, 86, 108, 110, 119, 129, 141, 148, 154
Manufacturers, 59, 61–2, 91, 119
Margarot, Maurice, radical, 65, 95, 101
Maxwell, Sir John, 145–6
Maxwell, Sir William, 66
Mealmaker, George, radical, 68, 71
Mechanics' Institution, 129
Militia, 21, 94
Millar, John, 72, 80
Miners, 1, 4, 6, 8, 39, 40, 72–4, 106, 121, 122, 127–8, 130, 143–4, 155, 156, 160, 168
Monteith, Henry, cotton master, 110
Montrose, 32, 93
Mudie, George, Owenite, 133
Muir, Thomas, of Huntershill, 67–8, 76, 98
Muslin, 58, 62
Musselburgh, 31

National Association of United Trades, 135, 137
Netherlands, 9, 12, 13
Newcastle, 72, 154
New Lanark, 13, 57, 117, 132–3
Newmills, 39
Nish, James, cotton spinner, 136, 146
Nottinghamshire, 93

Ormiston Community, 132–4
Owen, Robert, 132–4, 136
Owenites, 133, 135–7, 141, 150

Paine, Thomas, 66, 68, 71, 108–9
Painters, 29, 131
Paisley, 12, 14, 16, 27, 32–4, 38, 46, 58–9, 60–1, 66, 69, 71, 81, 86, 88, 103, 108, 110–111, 126, 135–6, 145
Palmer, Thomas Fishe, radical, 68–9
Papermakers, 82, 84
Parliament of Scotland, 24, 62
Parliamentary Reform, 101, 103, 105, 107, 112, 114, 138–9, 146, 150
Paternalism, 102
Peel, Sir Robert, 128, 146
Perth, 26, 31, 65, 67, 69, 82, 86–8, 90, 97, 149
Perthshire, 13, 32, 86, 131
Peterloo, 108–9
Piecework, 25–6, 75
Pitkeithly, Laurence, Owenite, 135
Pitt, William, 14
Plasterers, 28, 34, 124
Ploughmen, 82
Plumbers, 28, 34, 131
Political economy, 132
Poll Tax, 24
Poor Relief, 84, 101–2, 107, 133
Porteous, Captain, 65
Port Glasgow, 21
Powerlooms, 90, 94, 101, 114–6, 145, 148, 155
Prices, 11, 14–15, 17, 35, 57–8, 61, 64, 69, 73, 76–8, 85, 87, 93, 100, 107, 109, 152
Printers, 29, 30, 34–6, 63, 78, 105, 126–7, 155

Quarrymen, 156
Queensferry, 20, 41

Radicals, 69, 76, 99, 101, 103–4, 107–12, 114, 132, 150, 155, 158, 164
Redding, 122–3
Reform Bill, see Parliamentary Reform
Religion, 108–9
Renfrewshire, 5, 14, 32, 58, 92, 95, 97, 103, 113, 122, 128, 136, 145, 154
Richmond, Alexander, weaver, 92, 95, 100, 103–4, 107, 139
Riots, 1, 12–14, 17, 57, 62–5, 67, 86, 93, 100–1, 108, 110, 112, 115, 125, 139, 143–4, 149
Rochdale, 86
Rope and Twine Spinners, 128–9
Ross-shire, 110

Saddlers, 34–5
Saltcoats, 41
Salters, 4, 39
Sawyers, 28, 77, 125, 128
Scots Magazine, 14
Scotsman, 133, 149
Self-actors, 154
Serfdom, 72–4
Sheffield, 159
Shipwrights, 37, 43, 76, 137
Shoemakers, 3, 7, 9, 17, 25–7, 36, 41, 43, 51, 69, 70, 82, 105, 111, 127
Sidmouth, Lord, 92, 94–5, 104, 112
Silk, 12–13
Silversmiths, 34
Sinclair, Sir John, 57, 96
Skilled Labour, 4, 5, 17, 21, 27, 45, 50, 53, 55, 106, 131–2, 144, 149, 155, 160
Skills, lack of, 9, 14, 15
Slaters, 28, 36, 111, 138, 141
Smith, Adam, 7, 12, 54; *Wealth of Nations* 53, 72, 79, 80, 98
Smith, John, cotton spinner, 155, 157
Smith, Thomas, cotton spinner, 86–8, 102
Smout, T. C., 1, 38, 163

Societies, 3, 39, 45, 54, 71, 76, 78, 88 (see also Combination)
Sommerville, Andrew, 125
Spence, Thomas, 103, 109
Spirit of the Union, 109, 115
Stair, Viscount, 5
Statistical Account of Scotland, 22, 57
Staymakers, 52
Stewart, Alexander, master shoemaker, 26, 70
Stirling, 23, 31, 69, 88, 111, 143
Stocking makers, 32, 93, 120, 128
Stockport, 86, 108
Strathaven, 110
Strikes, 2, 12, 39, 43, 48–9, 63, 73, 86, 107, 112, 116–7, 129, 137; Aberdeen shoemakers (1668) 9; Edinburgh tailors (1734) 43; Glasgow hammermen (1748) 46; Paisley weavers (1754) 58; Aberdeen woolcombers (1759) 47; Edinburgh masons and wrights (1764) 50; Edinburgh tailors (1767) 51; Glasgow weavers (1767) 60; Edinburgh masons (1778) 53–4; Glasgow weavers (1787) 62; Glasgow bakers (1787) 63; Aberdeen sailors (1792) 67; Edinburgh shoemakers (1798) 71; Aberdeen tailors (1797) 74–5; Lanarkshire weavers (1812) 1, 92–3, 103; Glasgow boot and shoemakers (1816) 105; Glasgow miners (1817) 106; Glasgow powerloom weavers (1823) 115; cotton spinners (1823) 117; Hawick stockingmakers (1817–22) 120–1; colliers (1823) 121; colliers (1825) 123; Edinburgh masons (1824) 124; Edinburgh tailors (1823) 125; Edinburgh bookbinders (1825) 127, 129; bakers (1834) 140; masons (1834) 141; calico printers (1834) 142–3; Lanarkshire miners (1832) 143–4; engineers (1834) 144; Glasgow slaters (1834) 147–8; labourers (1836) 151; Glasgow spinners (1836–7) 152–5; Glasgow masons (1837) 156; Lanarkshire colliers (1837) 156
Sunday School, 63
Sweated Labour, 125

Tailoring, 23, 26, 45, 49, 52
Tailors, 1, 3, 7, 9, 19, 20, 23–5, 34–6, 40–2, 44, 49, 51–2, 55–6, 63, 74–5, 82, 90, 111, 125, 128, 131
Tait, John, 136, 138, 140, 150, 155
Tanners, 34
Taxation, 100, 103, 109, 138, 145
Taylor, Dr John, Chartist, 140, 155, 161
Textiles, 16, 85, 114, 116 (see also cotton, linen, silk, wool)
Thistlewood, Arthur, 109
Thompson, E. P., 67, 79, 149, 168
Thompson, William, writer, 138
Thomson, William, co-operator, 136, 145
Tinsmiths, 34
Tobacco spinners, 29, 128
Tolpuddle Martyrs, 104, 148–9, 161
Trade Boards, 145–6
Trades Committee, Glasgow (1811) 90; Glasgow (1824) 128; Edinburgh (1825) 129; Glasgow United Trades Committee (1830) 136–9; Edinburgh Trades' Union (1831) 139; United Trades of Aberdeen (1834) 142, 149; United Trades of Glasgow (1834) 146, 148; Edinburgh (1833) 149; Glasgow Trades' Delegates (1837) 155, 161, 169
Trades House, 20, 46, 59, 89, 101
Tradesmen, 16, 17, 23, 35, 38, 41, 63, 65–7, 72, 79, 98–9, 100, 129, 130, 131–2, 163
Tradeston, 86, 97, 101, 116
Tramping, 22
Tranent, 71, 107
Treason trials, 111, 112, 114
Turner, James, of Thrushgrove, 101
Turners, 137

Unemployment, 6, 13, 15, 70, 100, 104, 108, 117, 127, 134, 141, 164
Union Canal, 122
Union Societies, 109
Unions, see Societies
United Scotsmen, 71, 101
Universal Trading Company of Paisley, 59, 81
Upholsterers, 28
Unstamped press, 169

Vagrants, 4

Wages, 1, 6–8, 14–5, 23, 25, 27, 30–1, 34–7, 39, 41, 44, 49, 50, 53–5, 57–9, 62–3, 68–9, 70, 73, 77, 80, 82–3, 90–2, 100, 106–7, 109, 111, 119, 120, 124–7, 129, 140, 142, 150–2, 154, 164
Wage Regulation, 7, 64–5, 72, 74–7, 80–1, 83, 85, 91–2, 96, 98–9, 145, 147, 165
Watt, Robert, radical, 69
Weavers, 7, 9, 13, 15, 17, 29, 31–4, 38, 44, 58, 60, 68, 85–8, 90, 92, 95, 100, 102–5, 107–8, 113–5, 120, 123, 128, 142, 145–7, 155, 166
West Indies, 13
Whitbread, Samuel, MP, 87
Wigan, 86
Wigmakers, 21
Wilson, James, of Strathaven, radical, 110–12, 169
Wilson, John Fauldhouse, miners' leader, 106–7, 121, 128
Wireworkers, 34
Women workers, 58, 60–1, 115, 141–2, 148–9
Wool, 9, 11, 31, 46
Woolcombers, 47, 48, 51
Wrights, 7, 9, 19, 28, 29, 35–6, 40, 43–4, 50, 54, 63, 70, 74

Yorkshire, 108